Herodotus in the Anthropocene

Herodotus in the Anthropocene

JOEL ALDEN SCHLOSSER

The University of Chicago Press

Chicago and London

The University of Chicago Press, Chicago 60637
The University of Chicago Press, Ltd., London
© 2020 by The University of Chicago
Published 2020

29 28 27 26 25 24 23 22 21 20   1 2 3 4 5

ISBN-13: 978-0-226-70470-8 (cloth)
ISBN-13: 978-0-226-70484-5 (paper)
ISBN-13: 978-0-226-70498-2 (e-book)
DOI: https://doi.org/10.7208/chicago/9780226704982.001.0001

Library of Congress Cataloging-in-Publication Data

Names: Schlosser, Joel Alden, author.
Title: Herodotus in the anthropocene / Joel Alden Schlosser.
Description: Chicago : The University of Chicago Press, 2020. |
    Includes bibliographical references and index.
Identifiers: LCCN 2019042711 | ISBN 9780226704708 (cloth) |
    ISBN 9780226704845 (paperback) | ISBN 9780226704982 (e-book)
Subjects: LCSH: Herodotus. History. | Human ecology—Early works to 1800. |
    History, Ancient—Early works to 1800. | Political science—Early works to 1800.
Classification: LCC DE86.S35 2020 | DDC 304.2—dc23
LC record available at https://lccn.loc.gov/2019042711

To J. Peter Euben

History, in contradistinction to nature, is full of events; here the miracle of accident and infinite improbability occurs so frequently that it seems strange to speak of miracles at all. But the reason for this frequency is merely that historical processes are created and constantly interrupted by human initiative, by the *initium* man is insofar as he is an acting being. Hence it is not in the least superstitious, it is even a counsel of realism, to look for the unforeseeable and unpredictable, to be prepared for and to expect "miracles" in the political realm. And the more heavily the scales are weighted in favor of disaster, the more miraculous will the deed done in freedom appear; for it is disaster, not salvation, which always happens automatically and therefore must always appear to be irresistible.

HANNAH ARENDT, "What Is Freedom?"

Perhaps . . . the solution to the crisis of reason, as Montesquieu suggested, is not in simplification but in complexity. But how does complexity itself avoid appearing as a simple solution? Perhaps it has to do with treating complexity as signifying diverse claims and life forms so that marks of a solution are not simplicity or elegance or reduction, as we have been taught, but the creation of conditions which encourage complexities that live by different laws and defy Cartesian solutions.

SHELDON WOLIN, "Montesquieu and *Publius*"

Contents

INTRODUCTION

Kemal Ali operated a successful well-digging business for farmers in north-ern Syria until the water table began to drop in the winter of 2006–7. With a sustained and intensive drought, Ali went from digging 60 or 70 meters to 500 meters. "The water kept dropping and dropping." Business disappeared and Ali could not find work. As social unrest rose, Ali was almost killed in crossfire. He now uses a wheelchair and has fled Syria to a refugee camp on the Greek island of Lesvos.[1]

"The start of the revolution was water and land," declares Mustafa Abdul Hamid, a thirty-year-old farmer from Azaz, near Aleppo.[2] This simple ex-planation contains the welter of causes offered by climate scientists, political ecologists, political scientists, journalists, and others. Water and land are the sites and substances of complex human and nonhuman interaction across space and time. Contending explanations for the conflict in Syria also illu-minate partial truths, all of which are contained in Hamid's beguiling, poetic phrase.

According to many climate scientists, the precarious situation of migrants like Ali has its roots in climate change. The Fertile Crescent is drying out. Re-cent research has shown that the birthplace of agriculture some 12,000 years ago might cease to support human life entirely by the end of the century.[3] As the region's droughts become more frequent and more severe for the fore-seeable future, migrations will continue.[4] According to the United Nations High Commission on Refugees, one person every second has been displaced by a disaster, with an average of 22.5 million people displaced by climate- or weather-related events since 2008.[5] The Intergovernmental Panel on Climate Change notes that severe social effects could follow from the resulting re-source scarcities.[6]

Political ecologists offer different explanations for Ali's story.[7] They point to a lack of clear evidence that drought-related migration contributed to the onset of civil war in Syria. Before the war began, an agrarian crisis struck the governorate of Hasakah in northeastern Syria. The central causes of this crisis were extreme water resource degradation, deepening rural poverty, and specific features of Syria's political situation such as its agrarian and rentier model of state building and development. Hasakah's status as an ethnically contested borderland and frontier zone also played an important role. On this argument, politics and conflict are central to environmental scarcities and insecurities.[8]

Political scientists put heavier emphasis on political factions when trying to explain the broader questions prompted by Ali's story. The Islamic State ("ISIS") plays an important role here.[9] The inability of Western powers to support Arab Spring activists in Syria led in part to ISIS's rise.[10] When ISIS took power over large swaths of Syria, adaptation to the changing climate became much more difficult.[11] Ali's home village lay only a short distance from Kobane on the Turkish border, which ISIS had wrecked. He headed to Damascus, Syria's capital, to seek safety and work. On his way there, his vehicle was struck by a rocket. He awoke in a Damascus hospital, paralyzed from the waist down.

Other political scientists emphasize how Syrian president Bashar al-Assad's neoliberal autocracy produced conditions for the conflict.[12] Neoliberal autocracies do not simply rely on coercive power to force obedience. Instead, to organize desire and quell dissent, they use the promise of affluence gained by economic liberalization as well as fears of sectarian disorder that might disturb enjoyment of the fruits of this affluence. In Syria, according to Lisa Wedeen, al-Assad's neoliberal autocracy connected fantasies of upward mobility and status quo stability to preserve its authoritarian rule.[13] This strategy prevented the 2011 uprising's success and, along with the al-Assad regime's cultivation of militant activists (as part of the strategy of fomenting fear of instability), helped to destabilize the region.

Ali's story is not just a story of Syria but a story replayed across the world. "The greatest single impact of climate change could be on human migration with millions of people displaced by shoreline erosion, coastal flooding, and agricultural disruption."[14] Weather extremes such as heat waves, floods, and severe storms form one tangible aspect of the problem. Extreme events will breed other challenges such as global food crises and mass migrations.[15] The responses of political regimes to these events and the resulting instability and conflict will create new problems and dilemmas. All these potentialities imply, implicitly or explicitly, a more basic question raised by the story of Kemal Ali and so many millions like him: can human beings flourish on earth without destroying the very basis of such flourishing?

Thinking the Anthropocene

In the last few decades, scholars have begun to describe the complex set of problems arising from dynamic interactions among climate, politics, and human flourishing under the heading of "the Anthropocene." At the most literal level, the Anthropocene as a concept captures a new climatic period in which humanity as a whole has initiated global change.[16] Paul Crutzen and Eugene Stoermer were the first to publicize broadly this momentous geological event, marking the year 1800 CE as the moment when methane and CO_2 brewed by the gargantuan machines of the Industrial Revolution began to influence the earth's climate.[17] The advent of the Anthropocene shifts previous understandings of the relationship between human beings and the earth. The earth no longer simply constrains human activity through its given limits and boundaries; human beings now affect the system itself in fundamental ways.[18]

Beyond denoting a new geological era, the Anthropocene encompasses a broader set of questions and issues figured by stories like Kemal Ali's. As Jedediah Purdy writes, "the Anthropocene is, in important ways, a slogan for the age of climate change."[19] No longer does "nature" stand outside and apart from human activity. Human activity has set in motion processes that endanger continued human life. The droughts and heat waves and dropping water table that prompted Ali to flee to Lesvos cannot be explained simply as "natural phenomena." The *name* of the Anthropocene highlights how human beings have played a role.[20] The Anthropocene is a human-made epoch that in Frankenstein fashion appears destined to destroy its maker.[21]

Human beings hold responsibility, but the frame of the Anthropocene also calls attention to the importance of nonhumans for flourishing on earth. The imagined divide between nature and culture appears as the fiction it always has been. Human beings cannot wall themselves off from the storms raging around them. Scholars of the Anthropocene have introduced the language of "actants" to describe these nonhumans, which include not only land and water but worms, electricity, matsutake mushrooms, wolves, jaguars, and rubber trees (among myriad others).[22] "Actants," according to Bruno Latour, can be human or nonhuman or a combination of both. They are things that "act or to which activity is granted by others."[23] Human beings themselves are "biocultural creatures," composites of human and nonhuman interaction.[24] Other scholars refer to actants as "things": things with power, things with fragility, things that human beings in the Anthropocene now need to realize have always shared the stage of history.[25]

Including nonhumans requires new forms of inquiry. The usual search for causes must be radically expanded in at least two ways. First, situations such as Ali's now involve land, water, and genetically modified crops as well as autocrats, sectarian divides, and border disputes. The domain of what you consider relevant for explaining any given phenomenon must increase enormously. Political scientists need to think about mosquitoes and climate scientists need to consider grassroots organizing.[26] Second, causation itself needs rethinking. The concept of causality requires complication to include multiple and overlapping causes. Human beings hold some responsibility but not all of it; nonhuman actants must also be included. The typical isolation of causes from effects no longer obtains when everything appears in dynamic interaction.[27]

The Anthropocene calls attention to the manifold actants that human beings have too long ignored or overlooked; this introduces new levels of complexity requiring new qualities and intensities of observation. Not only do you need to cast broader nets; you need to do so with eyes and ears wide open for what you previously missed. As the editors of *Arts of Living on a Damaged Planet* write, "we need to relearn multiple forms of curiosity," forms that attune themselves to "multispecies entanglement, complexity, and the shimmer all around us."[28] The Anthropocene requires the development of new arts of attention directed at the edges of perception.

The dynamic complexity of the world human beings inhabit also challenges conventional political institutions and the forms of knowledge on which they rely.[29] Old approaches to resource management that subordinated "nature" to human beings are inadequate for dealing with all the things, human and nonhuman, involved in earthly life. The world's dynamic complexity, moreover, defies administrative centralization.[30] Thus, the Anthropocene requires imaginative responses to address the new reality—which is really quite old— that it names. Political theorists in the Anthropocene have responded to these questions with new norms and political institutions capable of doing justice to this reality.[31]

The entanglement of human and nonhuman and the dynamic complexity this involves have led many political theorists in the Anthropocene to expand the traditional sites of politics beyond formal laws and institutions. How do you govern Forest, France, India, Indigenous Peoples, Atmosphere, and Oceans? Bruno Latour has invoked the ancient Greek word for "custom, culture, and law," *nomos*, to describe forms of governance not restricted to the "government" you might imagine enshrined in white marble Greek Revival edifices. *Nomos* names the patterns or orders of collective life including both humans and nonhumans. A *nomos* may be a practice of radical curiosity. It may also be a law granting equal standing to dolphins and the United States Navy. Taken together, new *nomoi* (plural of *nomos*) of the earth could help to organize what Latour and others have called a "parliament of things":[32] a convening of all actants involved in the earth to deliberate and decide how, in Josiah Ober's words, to "go on together."[33] *Nomos* thus describes "a general theory of relations,"[34] a vision of how to organize political responses and the capacity to learn and develop creative responses to the challenges of the Anthropocene.[35]

The need for the participation and involvement of all kinds of actants has led writers inquiring into the Anthropocene to reconsider the forms with which they communicate their inquiries.[36] The abstractions and concepts predominant in analytical inquiries lack the ability to connect and evoke and enliven the imagination as stories do.[37] As Rebecca Solnit writes, "every conflict is in part a battle over the story we tell, or who tells and who is heard."[38] Stories can shape readers and listeners into engaged participants.[39] They can cultivate the arts of attention and desire necessary for inquiry into the dynamic complexity of the Anthropocene.[40] "Human-interest" stories like Ali's can generate concern not just for him but for the dropping water table, the orange life jackets and deflated rafts heaped on the shores of Lesvos, the Syrian fields cratered by barrel bombs. Poetry has new importance in the Anthropocene.[41] As William Ophuls puts it, "a world begins when a metaphor is born."[42]

The thinkers of the Anthropocene stem from a variety of academic disciplines yet share a commitment to broadening *what* might be considered relevant for the political and ecological challenges of the twenty-first century as well as *how* these considerations might be crafted and circulated. Flourishing on earth requires attention not only to the matter of politics—what actants, human and nonhuman—but also to the form of politics, to how it is conducted. It's at the intersection of the *what* and the *how* that the center of this book, Herodotus, can contribute to thinking and acting well in the Anthropocene. Turning to writings composed in the shadow of the Fertile Crescent 2,500 years ago, *Herodotus in the Anthropocene* develops a vision of earthly flourishing that can inspire and inform action in the twenty-first century.

Herodotus in the Anthropocene

Herodotus lived long before the Anthropocene, from roughly 484 until 414 BCE; he is known as the author of what is called the *Histories*.[43] This epic work chronicles the interactions between the Greek city-states (*poleis*) and their powerful neighbors in the Near East, interactions that culminated in the Persian invasions of Greece in 490 and 480 BCE. Herodotus delves far into the past to explain this conflict, following the Persians' rise to mastery over a multiethnic and multicontinental empire. Herodotus himself was born on the edge of this empire, along the eastern coast of the Mediterranean in what is now Turkey. While few details of his life remain, the *Histories* testifies to his visits to the Black Sea region and Scythia, Phoenicia, Palestine, and especially Egypt, where he sailed up the Nile to Elephantine. It's possible that he also traveled to Babylon. He shows great familiarity with the Greek world and, later in his life, became a citizen of Thurii, a Panhellenic colony in southern Italy.

Distant in time, Herodotus and the *Histories* are nonetheless deeply relevant to the Anthropocene. Herodotus's *Histories* illuminates an essential paradox in the present epoch: just at the moment when human beings appear to have more influence than ever over the fate of the planet, humans also must assert collective agency to have any hope of avoiding the worst. In this way, the conditions of the Anthropocene resemble the conditions of antiquity from which Herodotus wrote: at the heart of the *Histories* stands a concern with the complex interactions of human and nonhuman forces—of political leaders and ordinary groups of people, on the one hand, and oceans, rivers, and ineffable, perhaps divine forces, on the other. Human beings number among the shining heroes across the *Histories* but they alone do not determine the events Herodotus chronicles. Unlike accounts offered by his contemporaries, Herodotus's explanation of the origins of the Persian Wars introduces a multitude of causes, some human and others nonhuman. Viewed from the twenty-first century, Herodotus's *Histories* thus anticipates the dynamic and complex reality to which the Anthropocene calls attention.

While chronicling this reality, Herodotus places human action at the center of his story. The dynamic complexity of reality demands specific political responses. Political regimes with responsive leaders, active populaces, and the ability to adapt in the face of surprises fare much better than those with rigid structures, isolated leaders, and unbending cultures. No single regime form will always prove adequate, but the type of regime—monarchy, oligarchy, democracy, or other—must support practices of deliberation and equal participation that allow for inclusive and reflective debate about the best course of action. These practices aim toward equilibria of human and nonhuman forces. Forms of political rule that insulate themselves from self-criticism or only follow the guidance of so-called experts will fail to achieve equilibrium, no matter how great or how glorious. Indeed, greatness itself is more likely to end in disaster than the lowly and ordinary. Herodotus's *Histories* thus points to what Murray Bookchin called "a prudent rescaling of man's hubris," so needful in the Anthropocene.[44]

Herodotus also widens the frame of political inquiry. The scope of the *Histories* illustrates how focusing on a single political community is too limiting. The *polis*, the traditional locus of all politics in ancient Greek political thought, exists only in relation to other *poleis*; all human communities, moreover, participate in nonhuman communities. This blurring of boundaries among *poleis* as well as humans and nonhumans means that the political order cannot separate itself from a broader cosmic order. Nor can "nature" be cordoned off from "culture" without ignoring powerful forces constitutive of political life. The modern ruse hidden by the very word "environment," with its promise that everything nonhuman merely surrounds the political community, is dangerous if not deadly. Politics must confront everything together because everything is potentially political.

These approaches to complexity and politics point to how Herodotus expands the very concept of the political. Politics must concern itself with more than formal laws and institutions. Anticipating Latour, Herodotus employs the term *nomoi* to describe the customs, cultures, and laws of the communities he chronicles. Yet unlike Latour, Herodotus emphasizes how human beings hold responsibility for creating and sustaining these *nomoi*.[45] According to Herodotus, *nomoi* consist of collective activities; their strength depends upon their repeated practice across time. *Nomoi* do not oppose some external "nature" but rather arise through responsive interaction among humans and nonhumans. Deliberative and inclusive *nomoi* are best equipped to adjust and respond to shifting situations. Without regular collective practice, *nomoi* can suffer corruption and deterioration by human as well as nonhuman forces.

When human and nonhuman communities sustain a nomistic equilibrium that allows for abundant and diverse life-forms, they experience earthly flourishing: vital development of the manifold complexity of all the earth's constituent participants, human and nonhuman, animal and mineral and otherwise. Earthly flourishing names the vibrant conditions of life that Herodotus celebrates and that his inquiry seeks to support. Human prosperity is necessary but not sufficient for this flourishing. Although Herodotus praises deliberative and inclusive political practices, these cannot guarantee success; rather, they create conditions for negotiating the inevitable shifts and fluctuations entailed by living in a world marked by dynamic complexity. Human beings can pursue freedom through practices of equality; freedom names the human component of flourishing that Herodotus puts in an earthly, planetary context. Herodotus's *Histories* displays the rise and fall of earthly flourishing and how human beings too often fail to organize themselves and their communities to respond to challenges in adequate fashion.[46] To readers in the Anthropocene, the *Histories* offers a vision of what collectives might pursue, with appropriate humility and wonder, instead of the self-destructive patterns of late modernity.

Herodotean Inquiry

As theorists of the Anthropocene have only recently realized, thinking about politics cannot remain only within the human sphere, because not everything political is human. Herodotus's *Histories* models an approach to inquiry that supports such an expansive political vision. Acknowledging the multiple forces that form and shape political life decenters the human. Herodotus insists that human beings cannot control or even comprehend all the actors and forces relevant for politics. Despite its name, the reality of the Anthropocene suggests as much: humans may have played fundamental roles but they are not the only actors onstage.[47] Yet this situation introduces a problem: political thinking proceeds from a human perspective, and practices of deliberation and inclusion still require speech and action.[48] In addition to proposing earthly flourishing as a goal and the kinds of political practices that might contribute to it, Herodotus's *Histories* demonstrates a form of inquiry that respects and responds to the dynamic complexity, nonhuman as well as human, that it explores. This inquiry serves human agents tasked with creating and sustaining *nomoi* needful for earthly flourishing. By balancing an appreciation for the nonhuman but focusing on what human beings can do (especially as collectives), Herodotean inquiry is well suited for the challenges raised by including nonhumans in deliberations about the future of the Anthropocene.

With his work, Herodotus declares in the opening sentence of the *Histories*, he presents a demonstration (*apodeixis*) of his inquiry (*historia*). *Historia*, the root of "history," is translated as "inquiry." This is the method of approach Herodotus takes in the *Histories*. This inquiry concerns why the Persian Wars started: what caused this world-spanning conflict and who is responsible? To explain the causes of the Persian Wars, Herodotus inquires. He examines competing explanations; investigates the cultures, customs, and laws of the political communities involved; and assesses the stories told about the conflict. His inquiry does not limit itself to human actors, moreover; he discusses terrains, rivers, animals, oceans, and even the divine. An enormous variety of things—actors, agents, forces, and others—are relevant to explaining the conflict Herodotus takes as his starting point.

Inquiry supports all the history offered in his *Histories*. Unlike his rival historian Thucydides, moreover, Herodotus not only writes up the results of his inquiry but also offers reflections about how his inquiry proceeds. In Adam Parry's formulation, Thucydides is reluctant to speak for himself; Herodotus, in contrast, is "objective about his relation to history."[49] In other words, Herodotus describes *how* he came to his results and not just *what* resulted from his inquiry. In the course of the *Histories*, Herodotus reports the journeys and itineraries he pursued; the people he met whose stories he now recounts; the unreached places about which he can only speculate. In this way, the stories of the *Histories* tell not only about their subject (the Persian Wars) but also about the activity of the historian (the inquiry that discovers these histories in the first place). Herodotus interweaves these two tasks—the *what* and the *how*—across the *Histories*, instructing his readers not just about *what* happened in the historical event that forms his subject but also showing his readers *how* to inquire more generally.

Two facets of Herodotean inquiry are especially relevant for politics in the Anthropocene. First, by describing how he conducts his inquiry, Herodotus also notes its limitations. The human inquirer is limited by time and space. She can travel only so far. So, too, the stories she hears from fellow travelers or priests or historians have limited authority. The *Histories* highlights the limited influence human beings wield in the dynamic complexity of the cosmos; similarly, the *Histories* shows how the inquiring historian can know only what she experiences, be it firsthand through sight or hearing or secondhand through the stories of others. Herodotus's inquiry thus emphasizes the need to examine the rough-textured surface of reality while also revealing how inquiry can never achieve a global perspective. The way of knowing characteristic of Herodotean inquiry both instills humility in the inquirer and underscores the relational encounters—the sensing of, seeing, and listening to others, both human and nonhuman—that undergird all knowing.

Second, Herodotus offers wonder as integral to inquiry in a complex and dynamic world of human and nonhuman things. In the course of his inquiry, Herodotus confronts many things, forces, and events that cannot be explained. Indeed, even when offered an explanation that seems reasonable, Herodotus still looks beyond the domain that others have considered sufficient for explaining a given phenomenon. When Herodotus cannot properly explain or categorize something, he responds with wonder. Anticipating calls in the Anthropocene for curiosity and attention, wonder names an attitude of astonishment and curiosity that leaves the fundamental strangeness of the encountered thing intact. In this way, wonder allows the unknown or unintelligible to remain while still maintaining a relationship to it. When Herodotus wonders at something—a marvelous piece of architecture or an animal or a *nomos*—Herodotus allows it to speak, giving it a place in the *Histories*, without foreclosing continued revelation or reducing it to a single message.

Herodotean inquiry serves the pursuit of earthly flourishing by revealing the dynamic complexity of the world of things involved in political life and instructing humans on how best to respond to these things. Nonhuman things cannot speak directly for themselves, but Herodotean inquiry equips inquirers with humility and wonder about the nonhuman while also gathering these many things into the text of the *Histories*. In this way, Herodotus constructs a model assembly in the form of the *Histories*, a metaphorical collective which includes nonhuman things without determining, once and for all, their meaning and significance. To this assembly, Herodotus calls his human readers as students, judges, and actors. A fundamental principle of inclusion marks Herodotean inquiry: this encourages as many voices as possible to be put into play, stories to be placed alongside one another, and wondrous things to speak without being spoken for. By putting all these things into play, the *Histories* indicates how political bodies might form and best deliberate about the paths toward earthly flourishing.

Reading Herodotus

The dynamic complexity that Herodotus conveys through the *Histories* is also evident in the text of the *Histories* itself. Reading this text presents distinctive challenges, challenges that lead readers into dilemmas of interpretation and judgment relevant to dealing with the complexity of the Anthropocene. In a way, the *Histories* resembles the world itself: multiplex, sometimes contradictory, polyphonous. The *Histories* combines diverse sources, ranging from epigraphical observations by the narrator to secondhand rumors retold with qualifications; it draws on oral traditions only some of which remain extant; it develops entirely new narrative strategies; it owes debts to a scientific discourse that it also engages critically; it attempts to portray many different "others" with whom the author had limited or no contact; and it emerges at a moment of powerful political ideology, both Athenian and Hellenic. How you read the *Histories* thus depends a great deal on what elements you emphasize, be it the narratological or the ideological or the philological (or something else).

Yet this world is whole. As an article of faith, I begin by maintaining the coherence of the *Histories* as a unified text. A century ago, Felix Jacoby insisted on separate ethnographic and historical interests that represented stages in Herodotus's career—first a fascination with the various cultures around the

Mediterranean and then a retelling of the specific events that formed the Persian Wars. Nature and culture were severed from one another. Yet since this argument surfaced, interpreters have illuminated the strength and density of the connective tissue between these two apparent "parts."[50] Reading Herodotus requires making sense of the relationships between the ethnographic and the historical aspects of the narrative, as well as the many digressions and observations and non sequiturs alongside them. What appeared to Jacoby as distinct sections are ordered in time as well as theme. The *what* and the *how* of Herodotus's *Histories* emerge together and cannot be separated.

The *what* and the *how* of the *Histories* also usefully confront readers with the problem of truthfulness. How do you know whether to trust Herodotus? How can you distinguish the good story from the true one? Accusations that Herodotus was a bad historian date from nearly the time of publication of the *Histories*, beginning possibly with Thucydides and Ctesias of Cnidus, who "everywhere in his narrative opposes Herodotus and calls him a liar and a fabulist."[51] Plutarch brings these charges in his long essay *On the Malice of Herodotus* when he accuses Herodotus of mischaracterizing many of his subjects, especially the Greek ones. Detlev Fehling has updated this argument by contending that the majority of Herodotus's sources are fictitious.[52] According to Fehling, when the narrator of the *Histories* describes having heard or seen something, this is made up—it's a rhetoric of evidence rather than an adducing of actual examples. You may read Herodotus as coherent on his own terms, yet Fehling claims that such coherence has no correspondence to the actual historical world.

On my argument, these critics ignore the complexity of the world Herodotus attempts to describe and the subtle judgments his *Histories* elicits and develops. For Herodotus, truth and reality consist in multiple overlapping and often-contradictory interpretations; good judgment involves comprehending this complexity and charting a careful course through it. This is a problem in Herodotus's text much as it remains a problem in the Anthropocene.[53] Rather than being the founder of what W. S. Pritchett calls "the liar school" of history, Herodotus introduces the problem of speaking truthfully about a world of dynamic complexity. The charge of fictionalizing sources proceeds from an anachronistic idea of what historical truth should look like.[54] When at the beginning of the *Histories* Herodotus introduces competing accounts of the cause of the wars between the Greeks and the Persians, this section makes sense only when you assume that Herodotus takes seriously each of these stories; much like this introduction's opening story of Kemal Ali, each illuminates some aspect of the more complicated story that Herodotus proceeds to unfold. Herodotus introduces each account as if it had some merit. While he offers his interpretation of the data, he also allows the reader to judge by including those pieces of evidence with which he disagrees. As Robert Fowler has put it, Herodotus *discovers* the problem of sources.[55]

The inquiry of the *Histories* thus sets up readers to continue what the *Histories* begins—namely, an inquiry into the causes of political phenomena and the dynamic complexity of reality. Herodotus shows the limitations and shortcomings of his inquiry along the way, calling his readers' attention to the process and construction of inquiry and thus its potential flaws. Allowing for disagreement within the text sets the stage for disagreement outside it: readers must decide for themselves which account to credit and for what reasons. The interpretation of evidence is as particular and contingent as any other interpretation. Indeed, the *Histories* shows again and again how human beings interpret data to accord with stories they already believe. Herodotus improves upon this practice by offering means of falsifying his claims: statues or landmarks that can be visited again; measurements and comparisons that you can make for yourself. He also foregrounds the stories as stories, prompting readers to question why some evidence seems more salient or compelling than others.

Herodotus not only collected information but sought to illuminate the meaning of this information through stories. Herodotus marshals these stories for his own purposes, using well-known stories to serve the larger aims and projects of the *Histories*. Although early interpreters saw only the pure transmission of oral stories in Herodotus's text, the narrative layering of these stories is evident throughout the *Histories*. Examination of the role of stories and storytelling in the *Histories* shows how setting aside accusations of incoherence or lying sets the stage for a painstaking and difficult work of interpretation.

How you read these stories depends on assumptions about what stories are meant to do. That is, stories might simply serve the larger narrative—leading some readers to complain of Herodotus's "digressive" tendency, for example, when a story does not appear to contribute directly to the narrative—or stories might be meant to settle scores with contemporaries who "got it wrong" in Herodotus's judgment. Storytellers in Herodotus's lifetime partook in a tradition of "memorialists" or "remembrancers." These storytellers provided accounts both official and unofficial that joined the public record.[56] Herodotus may repeat previously preserved accounts or tweak them for his own purposes. Regardless of Herodotus's intention, the *Histories* participates in a broader politics of memory, supporting some stories while undercutting others. Because what is remembered has a form of power, the *Histories* itself is a political deed. The *Histories* performs acts of public memorial, remembering stories in ways that constitute the memory of its audience and provide the basis for further inquiry.

The text of the *Histories* thus embodies a series of tensions: coherent yet polyvocal, traditional yet innovative, scientific yet performative. Because of this, the *Histories* contains an amplitude that few texts in the tradition of political thought approach.[57] That is, it instructs about both the *what* of politics (what is political and why) and the *how* of political theory (how to understand, interpret, and communicate political phenomena). This amplitude challenges the often-narrow approach to theorizing politics. Yet it also poses challenges for a reader in pursuit of parsimony and exactitude. The world revealed by the *Histories* does not afford simple explanation. But this is also a kind of thinking and writing needful in the Anthropocene, a time when the costs of simplified explanations have become clear and the dynamic complexity of the world is undeniable (if also threatened).

Plan of the Book

While respecting the difficulties of reading the *Histories*, the following chapters elaborate the claims about both the *what* of Herodotus's understanding of politics and the *how* of the approach of the inquiry developed across the *Histories*. The chapters roughly follow the narrative arc of the *Histories*—from the origins of the Persian Wars through to their conclusion—while tacking between these two core insights from reading Herodotus in the Anthropocene, with chapters 1, 3, and 5 elaborating the *what* and chapters 2 and 4 the *how*. I frame all these chapters with broad considerations about why Herodotus speaks to the Anthropocene in particular; once I have developed the specifics of both Herodotus's *what* and *how*, I return to the intersection of Herodotus and the Anthropocene more directly in the conclusion.

Chapters 1, 3, and 5 elaborate the *what* of politics in Herodotus's *Histories* by examining the dynamic complexity of political things (chapter 1), *nomoi* as responsive interactions among humans and nonhumans (chapter 3), and the political regimes most conducive to earthly flourishing (chapter 5). These chapters also track the most famous moments in the narrative of Herodotus's explanation of the Persian Wars, from the accounts of Croesus, Cyrus, and the rise of the Persian Empire (chapter 1) to the Persian Empire's deterioration under Cambyses (chapter 3) and to the triumph of the Panhellenic alliance over the invading Persians (chapter 5).

Chapter 1, "The Nature of Things," canvasses the multitude of forces involved in political life within the *Histories*. "Politics" includes human and nonhuman agents and influences. Herodotus's implicit account of historical causation illuminates the diversity of things, both human and nonhuman, that play vital roles in the formation of political communities. This expansive understanding of political things also has implications for the organization of political institutions. Across the *Histories*, Herodotus shows how singular rulers—what the Greeks called tyrants and what you and I might call autocrats or despots—fail to appreciate and respond to the complexity of political life. Tyrants seek control and mastery, when the nature of things resists such grasping. The nature of things demands political institutions more capable of attention and responsiveness; it also creates an opening for the kind of complex and ample counsel that Herodotus models in the *Histories*.

Chapter 3, "The Practice of *Nomos*," focuses on how *nomoi* form the center of Herodotus's political theory. "Custom," "culture," and "law" are all translations of the Greek term *nomos*, but I show how *practice*—the active constitution and reconstitution of *nomoi*—unites these possible translations. *Nomoi* are what people do. *Nomoi* vary among political communities, but they also provide a consistent lens for understanding the substance of collective life across diverse communities. Herodotus's emphasis on the practice of *nomoi* avoids the "nature/culture" dichotomy espoused by many of his contemporaries, such as the Sophists Protagoras and Antiphon. *Nomoi* are neither determined nor arbitrary. *Nomoi* participate in the dynamic complexity of the world of things. They also have durability across time without losing openness to revision and change. *Nomoi* are the substance of political agency, the material of politics for all political communities, and the basis for an equilibrium inclusive of both humans and nonhumans.

Chapter 5, "Freedom and Earthly Flourishing," connects Herodotus's theory of *nomoi* to the broader politics of freedom in the *Histories*. Political communities can sustain freedom when they have practices and institutions to constitute *nomoi* on equal terms. In other words, freedom comes when *nomoi* emerge from the willing practices of participants in the political community. To illustrate the realization of freedom, Herodotus points to specific practices in the Athens of his day, but he also notes moments of freedom around the Mediterranean world. Across diverse political communities, freedom demands active popular power, the people's shaping of the conditions of collective life. Yet because nonhumans are always involved in this shaping, the human ability to sustain the conditions of freedom is limited. Freedom itself is not sufficient for earthly flourishing; *nomoi* must adapt to the nonhuman things that constitute the political community.

Into my examination of the *what* of Herodotus's understanding of politics in chapters 1, 3, and 5, I interweave an account of the *how* of Herodotean inquiry. Again, these chapters seek to hew closely to the course of the *Histories*.

Chapters 2 and 4 examine Herodotus's two longest digressions, on Egypt and Scythia, both of which are prompted by Cambyses's fateful expeditions as the Persian Empire surges toward conflict with the Hellenic world. These excursions into foreign lands provide Herodotus with occasions to elaborate on how he maps a knowable world—that is, how his writing captures and conveys a sense of the world such that it can be the subject of knowledge. Put in simpler and more tangible terms, in these chapters Herodotus prompts readers to reflect on the usefulness and the limitations of the mental maps created by inquiry, which can serve to highlight salient features of a given terrain but also promise, falsely, a complete or finished knowledge of the places they describe. Herodotus shows how no map can fully contain the dynamic complexity of the world it purports to illuminate. Instead of maps, Herodotus provides stories rooted in specific encounters between the inquiring historian and a given person or place. Stories, moreover, require interpretation and application by the reader, involving the reader in precisely the kinds of practical judgments necessary in a dynamic and complex world.

In chapter 2, "The Known World," I show how Herodotus *locates* his inquiry in his own travels and movement through the world he describes. Unlike tyrants, who use inquiry to control the world, Herodotus's inquiry unsettles stable categories. Herodotus has been accused of operating with binary categories of Greek self and barbarian other. On this argument, Herodotus's assumptions about reality—in particular his inherited structures of understanding—undermine his promise of remembering both sides equally. In contrast, I show how Herodotus's itineraries of inquiry provide frequent foils to the assumptions about the world he inherited. Herodotus's insistent reflection on the particularity he and others encounter through their inquiries distinguishes him from the Hippocratic writers, whose empiricism was limited by assumptions about the structure of reality and whose inquiries lacked explicit connection to space and time. The tension between these conventional understandings and Herodotus's itinerant empiricism appears strikingly in Herodotus's treatment of the Scythians. These mostly nomadic peoples in the areas north and west of the Black Sea unsettled conventional assumptions about the shape of the world. Herodotus's treatment of the Scythians' wild frontiers shows the limitations and provisional nature of the inquirer's stories about the inhabited world (*oikeomenê*) and how much its being known depends on the movements of the inquirer.

Chapter 4, "Narrating Inquiry," examines the *how* of Herodotus's mode of communicating the results of his inquiry: namely, storytelling. Stories function in a variety of ways across the *Histories*. I focus on how they serve to evoke particular responses from their readers. Plutarch's outrage at the

Histories underscores these stories' evocative power; his reading also illuminates the moral complexity and process of judgment into which Herodotus
leads his readers. The stories of the *Histories* elicit further inquiry even while
advancing provocative arguments critical of the dominant thinking of their
day.

The conclusion ties together the separate strands of chapters 1, 3, and 5, on
the one hand, and chapters 2 and 4, on the other. The *what* of the *Histories'*
insights into politics cannot be separated from the *how* of its inquiry: the provisional and processual inquiry that underlies the *Histories* is precisely what
allows the dynamic complexity of the world to remain alive in the minds and
actions of political actors. This understanding supports the responsiveness
and flexibility of their *nomoi* and whatever freedom they might achieve. The
active, adaptive, and collective politics that Herodotus offers to the Anthropocene requires open-ended, narrative, and situated forms of inquiry.

★

By reading Herodotus in the Anthropocene, I acknowledge that my context
of reading shapes the interpretations I offer; the horizon of understanding in
the twenty-first century from which I write is profoundly defined by the complex challenges figured by the Anthropocene. This starting point entails two
important qualifications. First, at times I write that Herodotus or his *Histories* "anticipates" some of these challenges; I mean this not in the most literal
sense of clairvoyance about the state of the world twenty-five hundred years
later but rather in a more figurative way. These ancient texts take into consideration problems analogous (although not identical) to today's. The history
of political thought does not serve as a resource so much as a partner in thinking; in the end you must think for yourself, but you can do so better (and with
more pleasure!) when accompanied by the imaginative and provocative presence of someone like Herodotus. The distance between the world of Herodotus and today's—the vast differences in technology, culture, and knowledge
about the world and its inhabitants—can allow for defamiliarization and perspective that contemporary interlocutors cannot. In this way, Herodotus in
the Anthropocene is what Margaret Leslie calls a "useful anachronism."[58] The
language of "anticipates" points to the underlying wager of the book: that the
Anthropocene requires new forms of political thinking, not all of which are
readily available in the modern terms bequeathed to it; that ancient political
thought, in particular the thinking of Herodotus, can prove generative for the
twenty-first century, not by providing answers but by offering useful concepts
with which to think through some of the dilemmas and problems prompted

by the Anthropocene; and that, most important, the concept of earthly flourishing, with which I gather together Herodotus's thoughts on the world's dynamic complexity, cultural practice within this complexity, and the collective power necessary for freedom, can seed fruitful thinking about how to go on together as earthbound collectives in the twenty-first century.

The other important qualification entailed by my starting point concerns my particular perspective. As Kathryn Yusoff has pointed out, much of the writing on the Anthropocene proceeds from a claim about what "we" must do, yet this "we" is never explained or justified.[59] Often "we" excludes many of those most affected by the centuries of exploitation and domination that have culminated in the present climate crisis. The Anthropocene involves all of "us," yet those most affected already are rarely participants in the conversation about "our" future. In other words, responses to the Anthropocene use the "we" unthinkingly: "we" must deal with the situation the Anthropocene describes; "we" are the *anthropoi* who have fomented the Anthropocene; but who "we" are and how "we" can act remain gapingly, profoundly open.

Herodotus does not employ the first-person plural pronoun in his writing. As I show in the following chapters, he writes from his singular perspective; at the same time, however, Herodotus seeks to relate and connect his perspective to others. His perspective grows by listening to the stories of others, investigating their claims for himself, and reflecting on the logic of circulating myths and legends. What knowledge Herodotus presents in the *Histories* comes qualified by his own limitations as an inquirer, humbled by the complexity of the world and chastened by his own fallible judgment. Herodotus speaks to how a "we" might form through collective action and the stories that can shape it. In *Herodotus in the Anthropocene*, I try to emulate Herodotus's own care about his claims and their ability to speak for an "us." With one exception, I don't employ the first-person plural either. Although I believe the ideas, stories, and arguments have broad appeal, I don't claim to speak for such an "us." Like Herodotus, I instead hope to call a collective into being.

These two qualifications connect with one another in an important way. The challenges of the Anthropocene, as many commentators have noted, require a collective response; individual behavior cannot shift the entrenched interests and structures born of what Andreas Malm calls "fossil capitalism." Yet this collective remains elusive: powerful social movements like 350.org or the groups that Naomi Klein names "Blockadia" have arisen in the past decades, yet their power has not yet resulted in decisive action.[60] "Living in denial"— not actively but rather passively denying the mounting catastrophe—remains the norm in wealthy countries.[61] By contrast, Herodotus's *Histories* presents stories of cooperative success and flourishing achieved through collective power. The *Histories* chronicles the cooperative efforts of the earliest democracy, ancient Athens, and the moment of Panhellenic cooperation that united against the threat of Persian invasion. From many singular communities, a collective "we" was born. By emphasizing how cooperation can create new and powerful responses to overwhelming problems, Herodotus does not yet anticipate the responses occasioned by the Anthropocene's dilemmas. But I hope the *Histories* proves prophetic.

1

The Nature of Things

Humans have become geological agents very recently in human history. In that sense,
we can say that it is only very recently that the distinction between human and natural
histories—much of which had been preserved even in environmental histories that saw
the two entities in interaction—has begun to collapse. For it is no longer a question
simply of man having an interactive relation with nature. This humans have always had,
or at least that is how man has been imagined in a large part of what is generally called
the Western tradition. Now it is being claimed that humans are a force of nature in the
geological sense. A fundamental assumption of Western (and now universal) political
thought has come undone in this crisis.

DIPESH CHAKRABARTY, "The Climate of History"[1]

I will cover minor and major human settlements equally, because most of those which
were important in the past have diminished in significance by now, and those which
were great in my own time were small in times past. I will mention both equally because
I know that human happiness never remains long in the same place.

HERODOTUS, *Histories* 1.5[2]

Thinking about politics begins with naming what counts as political. The
word "political" stems from the ancient Greek word for political community,
polis; *ta politika* describes the things pertaining or related to the *polis*. Yet
within this definition also lurks a dangerous occlusion: "politics" is not just a
matter of the *polis*. For one, there is no *polis* taken by itself: no *polis* abstracted
from relationships to other political communities, not to mention the material conditions that form and inform the *polis*—the land, climate, topography,
position in relation to trade routes—what thinkers of the Anthropocene call
actants. For another, there are political communities organized in non-*polis*
forms: empires, alliances, dispersed tribes or ethnicities, splintered colonies.
In such a world, how do you begin to name what counts as political?

Herodotus offers an expansive and, on my argument, *accurate* approach
to describing the nature of political things. Here I mean "accurate" in its root
sense of "toward care" (*ad cura*). Donald Lateiner notes Herodotus's careful attention in contrast to Thucydides's approach: "When he speaks of cor-
rectness, he offers not Thucydides' *akribeia*, 'precision,' a word not found in
this text, but *atrekeiê*, an account without purposeful distortion or deflec-
tion."[3] As will become evident in what follows, Herodotus brings his readers
toward caring for the diverse multiplicity of things involved in political life.

"Accuracy" in this sense is the opposite of the flagrant grasping for knowledge characteristic of tyrants. It goes without saying that Herodotean accuracy differs from twenty-first-century standards of "rigor."[4]

For Herodotus "nature" simply describes everything not within the control of human beings, including human nature itself.[5] Herodotus considers a diverse multiplicity of things as relevant for forming, sustaining, and understanding political communities: rivers and oceans, true stories and fictions, oracles and the gods, camels and horses (and many other animals), climate and the arrangement of the land's physical features—to name only a few. Political thinking cannot partition political things from nonpolitical things; every political community exists in a web of interdependent and dynamic relationships with many other things, some known and many unknown.

While affirming the importance and imbrication of human and nonhuman things, however, Herodotus also writes from a human perspective. The *Histories* expresses a dual concern named in its introductory sections: to prevent human deeds from fading with time and to remember the many wonders of the epoch they chronicle. The *Histories* inquires into the ultimate responsibility (*aitios*) for the conflict between the Greeks and the Persians. Yet in addition to examining this responsibility, the *Histories* speaks of much more than human beings and their affairs. The human auditors of the *Histories* must encounter and consider many nonhuman phenomena, all of which have political significance.

The *aitios* of the conflict means the *cause* as well as the *responsibility*.[6] Herodotus's implicit account of causation contains the specific ingredients of political life. The most obvious causes, such as human greed (*pleonexia*) or fear of the rising power of another—those that, since Thucydides, have become staples of political explanation—have their place. Yet Herodotus illuminates the often-conflicting motivations within human actors, complicating human-centered explanation, while also populating the realm of causes with many nonhumans: the natural world, chance, the gods, and divine principles of reciprocity or revenge. Any attempt to explain the domain of politics must include these forces and agents within its theory.

The expansive approach to political things evident in the *Histories* has consequences for understanding political life in the Anthropocene. The narrowed domain of politics anticipates the modern state, which, in James C. Scott's words, sought "to make a society legible." "Seeing like a state" organizes the natural world to parallel the gridding, recording, and monitoring of the population. "Scientific forestry and agriculture and the layouts of plantations, collective farms, ujamaa villages, and strategic hamlets" made "the terrain, its products, and its workforce more legible—and hence manipulable—from above and from the center."[7] With Herodotus, by contrast, politics is much more complicated. Once you acknowledge the political community as part of an expansive constellation of other communities, all of which are populated with human and nonhuman things, this project of legibility and the manipulation it promotes come into question. Herodotus's understanding of the nature of things thus shifts what it means to organize and maintain a political community.

Within the *Histories* runs a powerful critique of tyranny—autocratic or despotic rule—in its many forms. Tyrants deserve opprobrium not just for their cruelty and violence but also because they tend to fail. Tyrants attempt to generalize and categorize for the sake of control; they simplify and do violence to the complex and never fully ascertainable order of the world.[8] This critique extends beyond tyrants: all forms of political rule that fail to understand the political with sufficient capaciousness and openness will deteriorate if not destroy themselves. The approach to politics characteristic of the modern state precludes the kind of capacious seeing necessary for flourishing in the Anthropocene. You need to attend to minor and major human settlements equally, because most of those significant in the past have diminished and those great now were small hitherto.[9]

Dipesh Chakrabarty's thesis on the climate of history asserts that the loss of an "outside" to human actions cuts to the very foundations of Western political thought. Yet the *Histories* propounded such a view nearly twenty-five hundred years ago. Today theorists seek entirely new organizations to respond to this dynamic complexity, but Herodotus shows the possible benefits of an ancient approach rooted in humility and responsiveness rather than new political technologies. Narrowly conceived political rule, the antecedent of seeing like a state, is limited by its own tendencies to generalize and simplify. In contrast, the *Histories* shows how successful politics requires a sense of wonder as well as humility. To give and to receive wonder demands patience and restraint. Key scenes in book 1 of the *Histories* illuminate the distinction between wonder and other approaches to knowledge; these differences highlight the practice of the inquirer, modeled by Herodotus in his role as narrator, as an alternative to the claims of knowledge upon which conventional political rule depends. The *Histories* thus points to political practices informed by an understanding of the dynamic complexity of things that can work within rather than against this complexity's wonderful multiplicity.[10]

The Proem

The introductory and programmatic beginning of the *Histories* (known as the Proem) introduces a twofold concern, a human perspective on the causes of the wars as well as an expansive interpretation of political things including and going beyond the human.[11]

> Here are presented the results of the enquiry carried out by Herodotus of Halicarnassus. The purpose is to prevent the traces of human events from being erased by time, and to preserve the fame of the important and remarkable achievements produced by both Greeks and non-Greeks; among the matters covered is, in particular, the cause of the hostilities between Greeks and non-Greeks.[12]

The opening sentence contains the combination of scientific discourse (presenting research, *historiēs apodexis*) and a poetic Homeric influence, of preventing human events from fading with time, becoming *aklea* or losing their heroic fame. These two influences appear again in the following invocation of "great and wonderful deeds" (*erga megala te kai thōmasta*) that Herodotus will prevent from going unsung—another clear echo of Homer—contrasted with the "cause" (*aitiēn*) that led the Greeks and barbarians to make war on one another.

Before Herodotus begins his inquiry he recounts two other explanations of the cause of the wars. The Persians and Phoenicians explain the conflict between the Greeks and the barbarians by pointing to the abduction of Io. Persian authorities claim the Phoenicians caused the dispute when they took Io, the daughter of a Greek king, to Egypt. This led to score settling: the Greeks abducted a Phoenician king's daughter and then the daughter of the king of Colchis. All this provoked Alexandros (also known as Paris) to take Helen from the Greeks, which prompted the Greeks to make war on the Persians. From that time, the Persians have considered the Greeks their enemies. Herodotus comments:

> These are the stories told by the Persians and the Phoenicians. I myself have no intention of affirming that these events occurred thus or otherwise. But I do know who was the first man to begin unjust acts against the Greeks. (1.5)

The Persians and the Phoenicians say these things about who is responsible. Herodotus refuses to affirm these stories and instead positions his narrative as much more expansive in its ken. Although the opening of the *Histories* speaks of *aitia* here a more modest claim is advanced: Herodotus can identify the first man to perform unjust acts against the Greeks; the solution to the problem of *aitia* is postponed, its demand for clear responsibility unmet. Against the desire to attribute a singular cause or type of cause—the abduction of Io or the stealing of women more generally—Herodotus opens up explanation to all things however great or small:

I will cover minor and major human settlements equally, because most of
those which were important in the past have diminished in significance by
now, and those which were great in my own time were small in times past.
I will mention both equally because I know that human happiness [*tên an-
thrôpêiên . . . eudaimoniên . . .*] never remains long in the same place. (1.5)

The accounts of the Persians and the Phoenicians consider cause (*aitia*) too
narrowly. They think of cause in terms of affixing responsibility, the juridical
sense in which the term arose.[13] Yet searching for responsible agents tends to
lead to the most obvious sources—it becomes too easy to reach for the singular salient explanation rather than surveying the many possible causes.[14]
Herodotus responds to these desires for parsimony of explanation with complication. Because of reality's dynamic complexity, the inquirer must examine
what seems minor as well as what seems great; the present condition of things
does not mean they have always lacked influence over the course of history.
You need to look for what you consider irrelevant or digressive, to sing of wonders whose relevance may be doubtful.

Human events (*genomena ex anthrōpon*) concern Herodotus, yet the expansive sense of cause (*aitia*) extends his explanation to events and actors beyond the human. The invocation of "human settlements" (*astea*) foreshadows
this: Herodotus will speak of political communities and not merely individuals or particular cities. The *astus* (singular of *astea*) has a history, a geography,
a place in a lively and dynamic cosmos.[15] By speaking of "human happiness"
(*eudaimonia*), Herodotus increases this sense of looking for causes in a world
of vital things. *Eudaimonia* carries the sense of fate (*daimon*), a concept rich
with meanings and stories. The fates of human beings never remain long in
one place. Rather, humans are battered and blown by forces outside their control or influence. The Proem thus opens to a world of things encircling and
penetrating the human events it promises to chronicle. Told from a human
perspective, the *Histories* will survey a multitude of human and nonhuman
things.[16]

Responsibility and Causation

As if to emphasize its points about the flux of human fortunes as well as the
many influential factors beyond human control that intervene in this flux, the
first word after the Proem is "Croesus."[17] Croesus is the man who first committed unjust acts against the Greeks. Neither Greek nor Persian, the figure
of Croesus also suggests the expansive kind of explanation that the *Histories*
undertakes: he wrongs the Greeks yet does not receive immediate response

from them; instead, Croesus sets in motion a series of actions and reactions that occupy the whole of the *Histories* and provide characters and stories far exceeding those offered by the Persians and the Phoenicians.

"Croesus" also locates the twofold concern of the *Histories*. The story of Croesus is told from his perspective and thus brings readers to encounter the world of things in the company of the readers' fellow human beings. (In narratological terms, Croesus "focalizes" the initial explanation, providing the viewpoint through which readers experience the events described.)[18] Yet the story of Croesus also discloses worlds of forces and agents beyond the human: the gods, principles of reciprocity and vengeance, environment and natural powers, and chance. Herodotus's account of multiple causation is outlined through the story of Croesus.

Thucydides famously explained the conflict between the Athenians and the Spartans as arising from Spartan fears of the rising power of the Athenians.[19] This materialist explanation has had vast influence since Thucydides.[20] Herodotus also offers material reasons for Croesus's aggression against the Greeks: Herodotus implies that Croesus attacks and subjugates for the sake of wealth; Croesus offers justifications from case to case, rustling up a flimsy pretext as necessary (1.26).

Yet unlike Thucydides, Herodotus goes beyond a material explanation of the conflict.[21] The figure of Croesus introduces a tangle of psychological motivations as well as nonhuman forces, all of which have some claim to being *aitios* to the wars between the Greeks and the Persians. Croesus may hold moral responsibility—Herodotus does name him first—but Herodotus's treatment shows how Croesus would not have been Croesus without a multitude of contributing factors.[22]

To begin with, Croesus's motivations are not simple. While he pursues wealth, he also seeks recognition for his happiness (*eudaimonia*). After crafting the laws of Athens, Solon visits Croesus in Sardis, where Croesus inquires about the happiest (most eudaimon) of men. Solon's response—first Tellus, who died beautifully after a long and full life, and then Cleobis and Biton, who fell asleep never to awaken after having towed their mother in an oxcart to a festival—infuriates Croesus. When Croesus pushes the question, insisting that Solon must recognize Croesus's own wealth as a sign of success, Solon warns him against trusting in his present condition. But Croesus cannot hear Solon: he dismisses Solon because Solon displeases him (1.32).[23]

Solon's words, however, introduce a note of doubt into Croesus's calculations. Croesus now must seek to convince himself of what at first seemed natural. Politics contains much more than diffident parties fearful of being subordinated to one another—and the solitary, poor, nasty, brutish, and short life that ensues. Croesus tests the oracles around the Mediterranean to find the "true gift of prophesy" (1.47). Now Croesus's action proceeds on the basis of *elpis*, hope or expectation, grounded on reports from the oracles.[24] Croesus also propitiates Delphi, the oracle that passes Croesus's tests, yet his own expectations lead him to misinterpret Delphi's response to his question about whether or not Croesus should go to war. Croesus is "secure now in firm conviction" but he has heard what he wants to hear; his "confidence" (*elpis*, 1.56) stems from convincing himself rather than from truth or knowledge.

Herodotus not only introduces complex psychology into Croesus's mixed motives but also emplots other actors alongside the figure of Croesus. Croesus's actions play a role in completing the arc of historical narrative set in motion by fate and the gods; he is not the sole controller of his deeds. After introducing Croesus, the narrative skips back five generations to when the rulership of the Lydian Empire first passed into Croesus's family, the dynasty named the Mermnads. How the Mermnads took the throne forms the upshot of the story of Gyges. Impelled by uncontrollable eros, Candaules, the last king before the Mermnads, invites Gyges to see his naked wife. Gyges protests that this would violate customs against seeing another man's wife naked, but Candaules insists. Although Candaules assures Gyges that he would not be seen, Candaules's wife glimpses Gyges as he bolts from the room after the fateful viewing. She then confronts Gyges later and presents him with a stark dilemma: kill Candaules or be killed himself. Gyges opts to save his own life and he assassinates the king and marries his wife.

This story alone contains a welter of psychological motivations, all of which help to explain the ascendancy of the Mermnads and thus Croesus as the first to aggress against the Greeks.[25] The story also introduces the importance of the gods: Gyges's taking of the throne appears illegitimate to the Lydians until Delphi approves it (1.13).[26] Gyges in turn gives back to Delphi, establishing the principle of "give-and-take" between human and divine that structures much of the historical narrative in the *Histories*.[27] Yet when the priestess of Delphi confirms Gyges's power, she adds a crucial qualification: after five generations, she declares, the Heraclids would be revenged upon Gyges's line. Croesus is this fifth generation. His fate—and thus the character of his aggression toward the Greeks—is shaped by events and motivations hundreds of years before his kingship.[28]

The fall of Croesus has its own structure of multiple causation and complication. Again Croesus acts on a conviction (*elpis*, 1.71) that proves fallible. Herodotus describes Croesus's many motivations, each of which contains a partial explanation for the fateful conquest:

The main reasons for Croesus' invasion of Cappadocia, in addition to the fact that his desire for land led him to want to increase his share of territory, were his faith in the oracle and his wish to punish Cyrus for what had happened to Astyages. (1.73)

Alongside Croesus's lust (*hemeros*, which echoes Candaules's *erôs*) and his doubt-assuaging confidence (here *pistis*, "belief"), you can place his longing for vengeance (*tisis*).[29] All these things lead Croesus into Cappadocia and the contest with Cyrus that ends Croesus's reign over the Lydians.

Nonhumans also influence the course of events. The Lydians' horses balk and flee when they see the Persian camels approach. The terrain of the conflict also deceives the Lydians into believing in their safety, a deception that the Persians overcome through close observation: the acropolis of Sardis lay unguarded at a single point because of a precipitous rise that no one imagined could be scaled. Hyroeades, one of Cyrus's men, however, had watched a helmet roll from the summit and then a Lydian descend to retrieve it. "Up the cliff he went and other Persians quickly began to follow in his wake" (1.84).

The falling of the helmet might also be ascribed to luck. Indeed, luck (*tuchê*) slips into the cracks of the Croesus narrative to split open explanations focused on his character or the political machinations of aggressive (or fearful) rulers. In their encounter Solon reminds Croesus of the role of luck: "Human life is nothing if not subject to the vagaries of chance [*sumphorê*]" (1.32). The narrative demonstrates the intimacy of luck and fate as nonhuman forces beyond control. Is it luck or fate that Candaules's wife catches Gyges in her chamber? Is it luck or fate that makes Croesus the fifth generation after Gyges? Croesus leaves behind material testaments to the inevitability of luck and fate: the votive offerings scattered around the Mediterranean, all attempts to placate the gods, could not save Croesus from the pyre.[30]

The Limits of Understanding

The story of Croesus figures a broader theme across the *Histories* and a theme with significance for beginning to comprehend the distinctiveness of the *Histories'* approach to politics. The pattern of overreach based on false confidence about the tyrant's ability to comprehend the situation appears in the story of Gyges. Candaules believes he can violate the Lydian *nomoi* against seeing the king's wife naked; he convinces Gyges to view his wife despite these *nomoi* and thus coerces illicit action. Candaules holds that his cleverness and power will allow him to get away with his misdeed, yet while the episode is entirely "plotted," Candaules cannot foresee every contingency. He is caught.

He imagines himself master of his fate but he cannot control a bedroom. This episode illuminates a pattern of overreaching ruler, failure, and punishment. The pattern runs throughout the *Histories*. The diverse multitude of things exceeds human comprehension; plans that presume to control this world will inevitably fail.

The Cyrus story has a similar structure to the Croesus story, which amplifies this pattern. Cyrus is the ruler of the Persians who defeats Croesus; after Herodotus's narrative describes their encounter, it loops back to describe how Cyrus became king (1.95). Cyrus ascends to power against the intentions and activities of the Persian king at the time of his birth. Cyrus's grandfather, Astyages, dreams that his daughter Mandane has given birth to a vine encompassing all of Asia. Astyages consults his dream interpreters and they tell him that this dream means that his daughter's offspring would rule in his place. When Cyrus is born, Astyages summons his relative Harpagus to dispose of the child. Harpagus promises that he will kill the child but he cannot bring himself to do it. Instead, he gives the child to a shepherd; rather than kill the child, the shepherd substitutes his own recently stillborn son for the designated victim, delivering the corpse swaddled in royal garments. The child is raised as the son of the shepherd until he is discovered as Cyrus through his kingly behavior: Cyrus lords it over other children and has one of them whipped when the child does not obey him. When the whipped child reports this to his father, the father brings Cyrus to the king's palace for punishment. There the truth about his parentage is revealed.

Cyrus's rise to power may seem inevitable, but Herodotus does not tell such a simple story. Cyrus gives the order to whip the child but his discovery as the grandson of Astyages turns on chance: that the shepherd saves him as a baby; that the scheme comes off because the shepherd's wife has birthed a stillborn child that can substitute for the necessary corpse; that Cyrus happens to have whipped the son of a nobleman who then complains to Astyages. At each decisive turn in the story, the sequence could have gone otherwise. Cyrus's role in the conflict between the Persians and the Greeks turns as much on chance as on his character and choices.

Cyrus rises to power and the pattern of his fall traces yet again the pattern first illustrated by Croesus. His success and self-confidence lead Cyrus across a river too far. When the Gnydes River drowns one of Cyrus's sacred white horses—who, "wild with overconfidence," plunges into the river only to be swept underwater and away to its death—Cyrus reacts with fury. He swears that he will enfeeble the torrent and abandons his expedition to Babylon. Cyrus then divides his army in two, marks out on both banks of the waterway a hundred and eighty trenches, each drawn straight and radiating out in every direction, and has his men begin to dig channels to drain the offending river. This operation takes the whole of the summer; only the following spring can Cyrus resume the march on Babylon. The overconfidence of Cyrus's sacred white horse foreshadows Cyrus's own fate—to drown in his own blood, as Queen Tomyris, leader of Cyrus's final foes, the Massagetae, threatens and then enacts following Cyrus's defeat. The punishment of the river's arrogance suggests the hubristic belief underlying the tyrant's claim to power. Herodotus marks this overconfidence as an error in the judgment of the ruler when he describes Cyrus's motives:

> Manifold and weighty were the factors which stirred in him this yearning, and served to goad him on: chief was the seemingly supernatural circumstance of his birth, and secondly the remarkable good fortune that had always been the complement of his campaigns. Certainly, no nation that had found itself the object of Cyrus' ambitions had ever been able to devise a means of escaping him. (1.204)

Similar to the case of Croesus, part of the problem lies in how success occludes the prospect of future failure. Rulers tend to believe that the future will reenact the past. Being born to a calling of greatness has further detrimental effects. Even more than Croesus, who found himself a king, Cyrus must take the reins of rule. Although his success depends on the Persians who choose to follow him, Cyrus believes primarily in himself.[31]

You might see this problem as one afflicting only tyrants, but even the brief mention of other forms of rule in book 1 suggests otherwise.[32] The Athenian democracy is easily fooled by the schemes to regain the tyranny by Pisistratus, an aspiring ruler (1.60). Its affliction is not one of power, as it was for Croesus and Cyrus, but of a desire for power—for the end of factional strife and the restoration of glory that Pisistratus promises. This susceptibility of people to flee from conflict into tyranny is also one way to read the story of Deioces, the earliest of the Persian despots (1.96). Deioces designed to become a tyrant and accomplished his wish through clever means. Already a person of standing in his village, he began to practice justice more wholeheartedly, to make an example of his own justice even when this was a time of considerable lawlessness among the Medes. This conduct earned him the praise of his fellow citizens; he became known as the only one among them who would reliably deliver fair judgments. People heard about Deioces and went to him for judgments. Eventually he became the only one to whom Medes turned.

When Deioces realizes that everyone is coming to him, he begins to refuse to hear new cases (1.97). Without him, theft and lawlessness return to the villages—even, Herodotus notes, on a larger scale. The Medes meet and consider how to proceed. (Herodotus comments: "I suspect that Deioces' supporters played a major role in this debate.") The people find only one response to the rampant anarchy: "We must appoint a king."[33] Deioces, of course, is the first and only choice. And quickly, he becomes not just a judge but a tyrant: he first has a fortress built for himself and then conducts all business through messengers. He becomes a "harsh champion of justice" (1.100) and rules for fifty-three years.

The description of how the Lacedaemonians came by their good laws (*eunomia*) might suggest an alternative reading to the emphasis on the over-reaching of political rulers. Unlike the Athenians, the Lacedaemonians experience the good fortune of having Lycurgus as a lawgiver. Lycurgus is recognized by the Delphic oracle as worthy of great esteem and also successful in his efforts to improve the constitution immeasurably (1.65–66). But the Lacedaemonians also suffer from arrogance that accompanies their success, believing themselves destined to subjugate the neighboring Arcadians. The Delphic oracle speaks indirectly in response, but the Lacedaemonians refuse to recognize the ambiguity of its response. They hear what they wish to hear and set off to attack Tegea, a settlement in Arcadia. They take chains with them, believing that they would reduce the people of Tegea to slavery. However, they lose the engagement and they find themselves wearing the chains they brought, measuring the Tegean Plain with a rope as laborers of the land. "The actual chains," Herodotus adds, "with which they were tied up were still preserved in Tegea in my time, hanging in the temple of Athena Alea" (1.66).

Although the Lacedaemonians do not follow the cycle of rise and fall that interpreters of Herodotus usually see in the stories of Croesus and Cyrus, their story does fit within the structure of arrogance and punishment: arrogance that is not simply hubris but a claim, implicit or explicit, to *know better*—to comprehend the way of the world and act with confidence on the basis of this knowledge. Wise advisers (like Solon) and oracles (like Delphi) remind the successful to remain wary of their arrogance, yet these words are most often unheard or mistakenly interpreted.[34]

These tragic cycles do not, however, lead to dead ends. Learning can come through suffering.[35] Croesus could have heeded Solon; Cyrus might not have crossed the river. While the sequence of events is overdetermined—by mixed desires and longings, material forces, fate, the gods, and chance—the human agent still has some influence.[36] This insight appears in the exchange between Croesus and Cyrus when Croesus has at last recognized the wisdom of Solon's adage that we should "count no man happy" until he is dead. Croesus stands on top of the pyre, "in full consciousness of his ruin," when Solon's maxim comes to him.

> The recollection of this prompted Croesus to sigh bitterly, and to utter a groan;
> and then, breaking a long silence, he repeated, three times over, the name of
> Solon. (1.86)

Solon, Solon, Solon. Cyrus hears these words and wonders at their meaning. He inquires, badgering Croesus until he explains the meaning of his ut-
terance. Croesus's story moves Cyrus. He can imagine himself in Croesus's
position and he orders the fire to be extinguished. Yet it has grown beyond
control. (You might say it can no longer be ruled.) Cyrus cries out to the gods
to save Croesus, and as if by miracle, the skies open and rain douses the fire.
When Croesus is saved, Cyrus asks him why Croesus invaded Persia. Croesus's response suggests the lesson on the limits of political rule:

> "My Lord," Croesus answered, "it was all my own doing—to your profit, and
> to my misfortune. When I launched the invasion, however, it was with the
> full encouragement of the god of the Greeks—so the ultimate blame [*aitios*], I
> suppose, should lie with him. For would I otherwise ever have been so foolish
> as to choose war over peace?" (1.87)

Croesus's words indicate the complex understanding of *aitios* as both cause
and responsibility in Herodotus. The meaning of *aitios* shifts in these sentences from Croesus—"it was all my own doing"—to "the god of the Greeks"
to Croesus's choice (*haireetai*) of war over peace. This description captures
the same sense of doubled, overdetermined agency Oedipus famously evokes
in Sophocles's *Oedipus tyrannos*: "It was Apollo who did this but my hand
who killed him."[37] Caught up in a world of things beyond comprehension and
control, human beings are not merely pawns.[38] These stories show Herodotus
grappling with what human beings can accomplish even when the causes of
history most often lie beyond them. They also show how *aitios* works in a
world of dynamic complexity.

Such a view would seem to lead to tragic resignation. Croesus learns only
too late; Cyrus is stirred by his words but the feeling does not change the
resolved course of action.[39] Yet Croesus's final words also insist on responsibility (*aitia*) in some form: *he* did those things and the *aitios* is the god of
the Greeks. As the Proem indicates, Herodotus seems to believe that responsibility can be attributed; the narrative has, moreover, shown that Croesus's
explanation is incomplete. Yes, he did these things, and yes, the god holds
responsibility, but these are not the only factors.

Herodotus's treatment of the dynamic complexity of things thus leads to
this insight about politics: political rule involves taking responsibility. Rule
(*archê*) and responsibility (*aitios*) have an implicit link throughout the stories of book 1. Those with power and influence contribute to the historical

narrative; these also suffer the vagaries of fortune most.[40] Yet as the stories of Croesus and Cyrus illustrate, the responsibility of political rule exceeds comprehension. Or, put differently, there's no way to control all the consequences—reactions and responses—that political rule pretends to manage. Herodotus expands the world of political things to include the human as well as the non-human, fate and the gods as well as chance and mixed motivations; political complexity exceeds human capacities of sense making and intelligent response. When Croesus and Cyrus grasp for more, they attempt to simplify and reduce a much too complex world.

Not all tyrants fail, however—or at least not all single rulers. As Carolyn Dewald has shown, for example, Herodotus provides a double portrait of tyrants. On the one hand, the *Histories* depicts the defects of despotism. The speech made by the Persian aristocrat Otanes articulates an overview of some of these shortcomings in the so-called Constitutional Debate (3.80): tyrants are prone to hubris, they provoke the envy of others, they are inconsistent, they tend to act contrary to traditional customs, they frequently use violence against women, and they are prone to committing indiscriminate homicide.[41] What Dewald calls the "tyrant as despot" model in Herodotus captures this, as do the story of Deioces and one aspect of the stories of Croesus and Cyrus. These articulate a theme coursing through the *Histories*: "the tendency of powerful autocratic regimes to become more powerful still and to transgress more and more against the persons of those they rule in the process."[42]

This approach to despotism illuminates why Herodotus evinces less concern with how a ruler assumes power than with the autocratic rule that follows. Herodotus uses *tyrannos* to describe Candaules as well as many other "largely legitimate eastern potentates."[43] The outline of the lives of Croesus and Cyrus sketched thus far intimates a pattern that appears in the lives of rulers in the subsequent chapters of the *Histories* as well: monarchs with great power who overreach, which then leads to unhappiness for themselves and their people. The root of these failures is a basic misjudgment: autocracy insulates itself from good counsel; it exerts power without deliberation or discussion. Croesus misjudges and attacks Cyrus. Cyrus does the same. Yet these are not simply individual mistakes. The structure of autocracy isolates decision-makers and prevents good advice from being heard.[44]

But Herodotus also presents another approach to tyrants with his depiction of individual Greek tyrants. This is the other side of his double portrait. Although Pisistratus fools the Athenian democracy, he "did not interfere with the existing structure of offices or change the laws; he administered the state constitutionally and organized the state's affairs properly and well" (1.59). Dewald notes that Pisistratus also supervised initiatives in trade, colonization, or the improvement of Athenian political administration. Herodotus does not associate Pisistratus with the "larger systemic violence of imperial despotism."[45] In other words, Pisistratus shows how despots might act otherwise than their nature prompts.

Pisistratus distinguishes himself from other tyrants in one important respect: he heeds advice. After his first time securing the tyranny, Pisistratus flees when he hears that political rivals are conspiring against him (1.61). Once he has fled, Pisistratus consults with others and takes Hippias's advice about regaining power. Pisistratus and his sons then set about collecting contributions from communities. This equips them for their return. Later, Pisistratus also follows the oracles' advice to purify the island of Delos, digging up all the land visible from the sanctuary and removing corpses to another part of the island (1.64). Although Herodotus notes that Athens flourished even more once the Pisistratid tyranny had been overcome (5.66), Pisistratus himself highlights how tyrants can avoid some of the mistakes produced by the structure of autocracy by seeking counsel and respecting advice once given. Moreover, his most successful and lasting return to rule is built upon a collective structure of power (the contributions of other communities) that allows nonhuman forces (the forces behind the oracle and the terrains of Delos) to participate.

Counseling Wonder

Although Herodotus's narratives show the limits of political knowledge, the *Histories* does not simply present irreducible complexity. Moments in the stories I have recounted thus far point to an alternative response to the simplification and reduction seemingly necessary to political rule. The story of the Spartans' rise to prominence speaks to this theme. After Lycurgus's laws are in place, the Spartans still suffer from arrogance, invading the Tegeans and suffering the defeat described earlier. Still, they insist that they deserve to subjugate the Tegeans. They send emissaries to Delphi to ask the god if they would ever win. "Find the bones of Orestes, Agamemnon's son," the oracle replies, "and bring them back home" (1.67). At first this proves impossible, and the Spartans go again to the oracle; the oracle replies again, insisting on the need to find the bones:

> On a level plain there stands Arcadian Tegea,
> Where two winds roar, nor have any option but so to do.
> Blow is met here by counter-blow, and grief is piled on grief.
> Its life-giving earth contains the son of Agamemnon.
> Bring him home and become the guardian of Tegea. (1.67)

These cryptic words help not at all. It seems to the Spartans that they would never defeat the Tegeans.

Yet the Spartans keep searching. One Spartiate official called Lichas finally makes a discovery, "the result," Herodotus comments, "of luck and his own sharp wits [*kai suntuxiêi chrêsamenos kai sophiêi*]" (1.68). Lichas happens to enter a forge where he watches a blacksmith hammering out iron. Seeing Lichas's curiosity—for Lichas had never witnessed smithing before—the blacksmith responds with a story. If this was amazing to Lichas, the blacksmith says, he should have seen what happened in his courtyard. Digging a well there one day, the blacksmith hit upon a coffin—one seven cubits long! Opening it, he discovered a skeleton, which he measured and found to be just under seven cubits. The blacksmith then carefully covered it again with earth. Hearing this story, Lichas turns it over in his mind (*ennôsas ta legomena*, 1.68). Suddenly, it occurs to him that this body could only have been that of Orestes. "All clues seemed to point to the one conclusion," as he further reflects on the oracle's enigmatic words: the smith's two bellows were the winds; the hammer and anvil were the "blow" and "counter-blow"; and the smith's beating of the iron could stand for "grief piled on grief." The puzzle is solved and Lichas returns to Sparta to tell the news. Once the bones are returned to Sparta, their superiority in every trial of strength is never bested.[46]

This story contains the pith of an alternative to knowledge claims on which conventional political rule seems to rest. Consider this story in contrast to Sophocles's *Oedipus tyrannos*. In both stories, a party receives an enigmatic oracle and acts in response to what appear to be god-given words. Yet their responses differ enormously. The Spartans investigate, ask more questions, puzzle out the meaning. Oedipus assumes he understands the oracle and leaves Corinth on the basis of this presumption.[47] Believing that he has escaped the oracle's prophecy, Oedipus does not pause when he sleeps with a woman the same age as his mother after having killed a man in the road the same age as his father. Because Oedipus has foreclosed surprise, because he never considers that he could be wrong, this evidence does not even appear as evidence. When he solves the puzzle of the sphinx but the curse on Thebes does not lift, Oedipus never entertains the thought that he himself might be to blame.

There are many possible reasons why Herodotus tells the story of the bones of Orestes at this moment. One reading of the story, however, illuminates a kind of counsel that can be offered to those finding themselves in positions of political rule. The Spartans seek counsel, asking the oracle twice for advice. They then treat this advice as a mystery to investigate, not assuming they know the answer. The crucial shift comes not in deliberations about the

meaning of the oracle, however; it comes instead when Lichas allows himself
to be stunned by wonder (*en thômati ên horôn to poieomenon*, 1.68).[48] At this
moment, Lichas is not pursuing an answer or even considering the oracle. He
finds himself traveling in Tegea, enjoying the temporary cessation of conflict.
He happens to enter a forge. He stops, agape.

Lichas's pause and wonder contrast with the insistent forward movement
of Candaules, Deioces, Croesus, and Cyrus. None of these characters stops
to think. Moved by inordinate *erôs*, Candaules bulldozes past Gyges's objections to his scheme. Deioces proceeds with deliberate inevitability toward his
isolated tyranny.

Croesus's story is more complicated. He tests the oracles to evaluate their
accuracy, but this searching smacks more of a desire to have his preconceptions confirmed than to discover the actual truth. Croesus's confidence (*elpis*)
changes the character of his investigations (*historeôn*) (1.56). Croesus stops
only when bound to his pyre, yet he has had moments when he could have
acted otherwise, when he could have allowed himself to wonder at the dynamic complexity of the world, yet failed to do so. Twice during his imperial
conquests Croesus encounters advice that forces him to change his mind. A
stranger—some say Bias of Priene while others say Pittacus of Mytilene—
advises Croesus against building ships to attack the Greek islanders off the
coast of Asia. The islanders may be buying up horses with plans to strike
Croesus in Sardis, the visitor says. Croesus exclaims that he would love for
the islanders to try to "come against the sons of Lydia with horses!" (1.27). The
visitor then counters:

> "My Lord," came the reply, "the obvious implication of your prayer is that
> you are keen to catch the islanders while they are in the saddle, here on the
> mainland. As well you should be. But has it not crossed your mind that the
> islanders, the moment they became aware of your plan to prepare a naval cam-
> paign against them, might have offered up a corresponding prayer of their
> own? After all they would like nothing better than to catch the Lydians out at
> sea—for then they would be able to pay you back for the enslavement of their
> countrymen here on the mainland." (1.27)

The visitor offers practical advice about Croesus's tactics, but it comes embedded in a more general counsel about the dangers of presuming to know the
enemy's tactics. Croesus takes this immediate advice but does not consider its
broader implications: that uncertainty lies on both sides and the unknowable
future afflicts the strong as well as the weak. He refrains from attacking the
islanders but still invades Persia. He wins the battle but loses the war.

A similar mistake occurs when Croesus fails to heed advice from a Lydian named Sandanis about Croesus's plan to crush the power of Cyrus and the Persians (1.71). "My Lord," Sandanis tells him, "bear in mind the kind of men you are planning to attack": men who wear leather around their legs, whose native land barely yields subsistence, who drink no wine but only water, who cannot afford even to nibble a fig; men "who possess nothing worth having at all." Nothing would come of conquering such a people. Even victory would bring little, as the Persians have little worth having. Croesus does not, of course, take this advice, nor does Herodotus give us his response to Sandanis. The strategic message is obvious—to choose your targets depending on their wealth—but it also comes embedded in a wiser counsel that Croesus only later acknowledges: you may believe you act with pragmatic prudence in your pursuits, but pausing to consider your objects often prompts reconsideration. On the pyre, Croesus recalls Solon's having made light of all the splendor he had been shown and how everything he warned Croesus might happen had indeed come to pass. "Nor," said Croesus, "were his words directed at me alone, for they apply with no less force to men everywhere—and especially to men who consider themselves blessed by fortune" (1.87).[49]

Wonder acts as a counter to the onward rush of imperial expansion. This contrast appears explicitly in the Lichas episode. Moreover, this moment of wonder within the narrative of book 1 connects with a broader theme that spans the *Histories*. Drawing on the discourse of wonder that inspired contemporaneous inquiries into the natural world, Herodotus often describes his own responses to the inexplicable, the surprising, those facts and nonfacts that overwhelm his descriptive apparatus and simply astound him in terms of *thōma*, "wonders" or "marvels." The practice of wondering entails an open comportment toward the material and human world, an ability to marvel without being constrained by judgment.

Herodotus himself often exemplifies this wondering. Herodotus's wondering appears strikingly in his descriptions of Babylon, which interrupt the descriptions of Cyrus's conquests. From the beginning, Herodotus notes that Babylon is "designed like no other city known to us" (1.178); Herodotus thus marks Babylon's unfamiliarity and surprising strangeness. He describes Babylon's dimensions, offering highly particular examinations of Babylon's extraordinary walls, its one hundred gates of bronze (including the pillars and the lintels), its three- and four-story houses, and its royal palace. Herodotus notes that Babylon survives up until his time, but that he himself has not seen it and only reports what is said by the Chaldeans (1.181, 1.183). Still, Herodotus revels in the "marvels" (*thōma*, 1.194) to be found in Babylon's construction, both the physical impressiveness of its buildings and the ethical force of its customs.

Wonderful Politics

Wondering opens a more capacious understanding of what is politically possible.[50] In Carolyn Dewald's terms, telling wonders "point[s] to" reality without entirely reducing it to words.[51] Wondering thus calls attention to the limits of language and brings scrutiny to conventional categories of evaluation.
By explicitly wondering, Herodotus interjects a new layer of reflexivity into
the language of description while at the same time introducing the possibility
of new modes of understanding. Think of Lichas and his startling discovery:
it begins with delighted curiosity as he watches the blacksmith at his forge;
when he pauses in this experience he is opened to the story of Orestes's bones.

The more capacious understanding of what is politically possible allows
political thinking to move beyond the *polis*.[52] Herodotus pauses to wonder at
a variety of political organizations. Because political things are dynamic and
inexhaustible, so, too, are modes of cooperation and conflict that can go by the
name of politics. Book 1 alone offers kings and demagogues, tyrants and usurp-
ers, grassroots organizing (one way of reading Deioces) and political predes-
tination (thinking of Cyrus). When political change involves more than just
the institutions of a *politeia* but encompasses all the factors and influences that
Herodotus includes in his account of the *aitios* of the conflict between the Greeks
and the barbarians, the basic starting point of political theorizing must shift.

Herodotus's *Histories* evinces an understanding similar to the pre-Socratic
philosopher Heraclitus's apothegm that "all things are one."[53] When considering the ultimate responsibility or cause (*aitios*) of the conflict between the
Greeks and the barbarians, Herodotus prefers complexity to parsimony, in-
terconnection to separation. The *Histories* begins prior to the dyad of Greeks-
Persians that formed the conflict and dominated Greek consciousness in
Herodotus's day. Croesus exemplifies a logic of political rule that patterns a
recurrent motif in the *Histories*: success leads to excessive self-confidence;
the ruler's undoing stems from his own arrogant knowingness. This is not
simply vanity but epistemological hubris, the belief that one can know and
control the political world. The kissing cousin of such epistemological hubris
may well be the philosopher's attempt to name and thus shore up "political
things." The *Histories* displays, instead, a world of things in which political
things emerge and shift in ways even the inquirer cannot foresee. They rest
by changing, to paraphrase Heraclitus. Great becomes small, and small, great.

In such a world, conventionally understood political rule seems bound to
fail. Herodotus suggests an alternative to the modern schemes of rule dominant in the Anthropocene. Politics must begin with wonder and proceed
through the most inclusive practices possible. Just as Herodotus treats major

and minor equally, equality provides the key component of the political practices Herodotus admires most (which I treat more in the subsequent chapters). This alternative is often lying in plain sight, like the Spartans' chains in Tegea. Or it needs to be sought after and wondered about, like the bones of Orestes. Like Herodotus, Heraclitus emphasizes the importance of searching and inquiring, but the object for Heraclitus is quite hard to find. The hidden attunement is better than the obvious one. The knowledge that "all things are one" is available to only the few. Heraclitus's *logos* is mysterious and esoteric. Human beings fail to grasp the *logos* that he has illuminated; their ignorance and lack of attention cause them to miss how the deepest structure of the universe and the self are one. For Herodotus, in contrast, nature loves to show itself.[54] Fate or the gods, the natural dispositions of camels or horses, the fateful arrogance of political rulers, helmets tumbling down mountainsides, and the glow of a blacksmith's forge: these are ways that the nature of things bursts into the observer's vision. Herodotus writes what he sees and hears; his readers confront on the surface of the text Herodotus's own encounters with this varied and vibrant world. Heraclitus is an observer from outside the melee; Herodotus places himself insistently within it.

Herodotus's valorization of practical knowledge infused with wonder anticipates arguments for practical wisdom today.[55] The "Climate Leviathan" with centralized power to administer effective policies will fail.[56] Ecomodern schemes must be radically democratized to avoid creating yet another Deioces. "It is excellent to have a giant's strength," as Isabella puts it in Shakespeare's *Measure for Measure*, "but it is tyrannous to use it like a giant."[57] Projects of simplification that delimit the political and attempt to control the dynamic complexity of human and nonhuman things not only fail but also discourage the kind of attention necessary for understanding political actants in the Anthropocene. Herodotus would not endorse geo-engineering (although he would certainly marvel at it). Instead, Herodotus yokes practical wisdom and wonder. Wonder reinforces the dynamism and plasticity of practical wisdom; it infuses the latter's attentiveness with openness and respect for inexplicable difference.

Yet the stories recounted also underscore how wonder and practical wisdom are not necessarily distributed in democratic ways. Individuals may accumulate special knowledge and use it for their own ends. It is insufficient to praise local and divergent knowledge without connecting it to broader political projects to ensure its good use. The nature of things does not by itself conduce to political organizations that support its flourishing. However, Herodotus develops a reflexive and relational form of inquiry that shows how understanding the dynamic nature of things develops relationships across difference. I turn to this form of inquiry in the next chapter.

The Known World

As the Anthropocene proclaims the language of species life—*anthropos*—through a universalist geologic commons, it neatly erases histories of racism that were incubated through the regulatory structure of geologic relations. The racial categorization of Blackness shares its natality with mining the New World, as does the material impetus for colonialism in the first instance. This means that the idea of Blackness and the displacement and eradication of indigenous peoples get caught and defined in the ontological wake of geology.

KATHRYN YUSOFF, *A Billion Black Anthropocenes or None*[1]

So far my account of Egypt has been dictated by my own observation, judgment, and investigation, but from now on I will be relating Egyptian accounts, supplemented by what I personally saw.

HERODOTUS, *Histories* 2.99

Introducing his readers to a world of dynamic complexity, Herodotus does so with a clear authorial imprint. From the first sentence of the work, "Herodotus"—the narrator or author of the work—remains present: *Hêrodotou halikarnêsseos* (Herodotus of Halicarnassus) are the first words of the *Histories*.[2] Herodotus is not the impresario standing backstage; he's showing you things, dragging you away from one statue and toward another, leading you excitedly from room to room in his gallery of treasures.

Herodotus's presence has not always been popular. Much of the controversy about his work stems from animus toward the author of the *Histories* rather than concern with the *Histories* itself. Plutarch's *On the Malice of Herodotus* attacks Herodotus for his evident sympathy for barbarians—and lack of sympathy for the Greeks. Modern historians who criticize the *Histories* for errors or inaccuracies often cannot help taking the extra step of impugning Herodotus as "the father of lies." Herodotus's presence helps to explain this: his *Histories* continues to allure readers precisely because of this fascinating figure behind the curtain, yet his obscurity also allows for projection of whatever disagreements you might have with the substance of the *Histories* directly onto the author himself.

Herodotus's presence also presents a problem in light of the critique of rule treated in the previous chapter and developed across the *Histories*. Does Herodotus not "rule" the *Histories* in some sense—controlling what is said, shaping the readers' responses, grasping for authorial power in ways that imitate the tyrants he depicts? When Herodotus declares that he "knows" the first barbarian to wrong the Greeks, is this not a claim to certainty along the lines of Croesus's overconfident interpretation of the oracles? Isn't Herodotus offering his own speech or form of knowledge, and how is this not exempt from the problems evident in claims to knowledge by Croesus, Cyrus, and others?

The resemblance between Herodotus's own authorial control and the forms of rule and political control depicted in the *Histories* is the starting point for the influential reading of Herodotus in François Hartog's *Le miroir d'Héro-dote*.[3] Examining how Herodotus portrays "the other" in the *Histories*, Hartog argues that the *Histories* functions as a mirror into which the inquirer, Herodotus, peers to ponder his own identity. The eye of the inquirer sets the world in order within the context of Greek knowledge, and the construction of the past thus effects a translation of "others" into knowable, controllable entities. This construct mirrors Herodotus's own assumptions about "the other" as well as "the self"—for Herodotus, the Greeks. Hartog's approach to Herodotus and to the broader relationship between Greeks and barbarians has had great influence.

There are at least two difficulties with this reading of Herodotus, however. The first lies in the content of the *Histories*: the instability of categories is put on display from the very beginning of the *Histories*; rarely does Herodotus mention a group or people unrelated to another. The fact of interdependence in the ancient Mediterranean, the existence of a multitude of networks and connections, breaks down the sharp distinctions between Greek and barbarian. The black-and-white world of Greek and barbarian (and all the polarities and inversions this seems to imply) simply isn't the world the *Histories* displays.

A second trouble lies in the way the inquirer's itinerary unsettles the structures Hartog and others see at work in the *Histories*. Herodotus's presence as a slightly unreliable and certainly irrepressible guide to the stories he tells creates a tension with the settled structures and categories that readings like Hartog's discern. This tension appears most strikingly when the inquirer's encounters with particular practices unsettle general categories, a pattern especially visible in the narrative of Egypt. While Herodotus first presents Egypt as an inverted Greece, the details and stories he encounters speak otherwise. The inquirer begins with fixed categories and structures, but his observations, reasoning, and inquiry dissolve these divisions.[4]

The inquirer's role in destabilizing the conventional categories of understanding clarifies the difference between the undertaking of the *Histories* and that of the tyrants it depicts. It highlights how the knowledge shared by the *Histories* remains rooted in local and provisional inquiries. The *Histories* offers a portrait of the known world (*oikeomenê*), a term that Herodotus coined and that became widespread among the cartographers and geographers who followed him. The known world describes the map created by the inquirer, the lands and peoples discovered, named, and put in spatial and temporal relation to one another. Yet Herodotus's map of the world is always in process. He presents a known world that depends on the ongoing work of the inquirer, one that remains provisional and positional. There is a map, but it also bears marks of the process that created and can revise it. Alongside assertions based upon his inquiry, Herodotus presents a processual approach to knowledge that contrasts with that of his contemporaries like the Hippocratics and their claims of definitive knowledge of the world.

On my reading of the *Histories*, the construction of the known world depends upon relational thinking, a form of theorizing marked both by travel and by conversation. This relational thinking links an understanding of the nature of things to social practices of shared inquiry and the pursuit of consensus. Herodotus is not merely a tourist nor is the *Histories* merely a collection of traveler's tales. The processual approach to knowledge unsettles the tourist's assumptions about the polarity of self and other; moreover, it illuminates how relationships allow the inquirer to construct the known world—and to continue to build it so long as its inhabitants speak and listen to one another. Infused with wonder, this form of inquiry offers an approach to understanding the Anthropocene that cultivates practices of attention and mutuality. As Kathryn Yusoff reminds us, the Anthopocene can too easily inscribe a universal and abstract human (*anthropos*) in ways that efface historic and ongoing oppression. Proclaiming "the language of species life—*anthropos*," the Anthropocene "erases histories of racism that were incubated through the regulatory structure of geologic relations."[5] Hartog warns against much the same with his criticism of Herodotus's othering of non-Greeks. Yet Herodotus can respond to both dilemmas. Herodotus shows readers how travel toward and across the edges of perception requires relationships: interlocutors to question, storytellers to listen to. This form of inquiry structures possible responses to the challenges of the Anthropocene: inquiry creates constellations of relationships that produce knowledge and insight; these relationships not only chart the webs of interdependence and interaction structuring the dynamic complexity of the world but also provide a basis for concerted action within this world. Knowing is something you do with others. Social inquiry depends on the collective.

The Inquirer's Presence

Calling attention to the author's own presence in her text might appear like a move borrowed from late twentieth-century postmodern literary criticism, but Plutarch's *Malice of Herodotus* illustrates that Herodotus's presence was not unnoticed in antiquity. Plutarch's attack on Herodotus focuses on the author's choices, accusing Herodotus of dishonesty about his sources: the historian is not forthright about which sources he chooses and why; he fails to uphold the most admirable motives for his subjects; and he writes purple prose to excite readers about scatological subjects.

Yet the narrative's voice also distinguished Herodotus from his predecessors. Although "there was no Herodotus before Herodotus," as Arnoldo Momigliano put it,[6] Herodotus had antecedents, most notably Hecataeus, whom he mentions in the course of the narrative. This moment sets off the distinctiveness of Herodotus's presence in the course of the *Histories*:

> A while ago, one of the visitors to Thebes was Hecataeus, the writer [*logopoios*], who was engaged upon genealogy—a field with which personally I have never bothered. Sixteen generations he had traced back his line of descent, through his father's forebears, to a god. The priests of Zeus, however, gave him the treatment that they also gave me. . . . The priests dismissed out of hand Hecataeus and his own genealogical researches. (2.143)

From the fragments of his work that remain, it appears that Hecataeus presented his inquiries without the first-person interventions that characterize the *Histories*.[7] Although Herodotus appears to use Hecataeus's text like a guidebook,[8] traveling to the places his predecessor visited, Herodotus nonetheless distances himself from what Hecataeus has written. Herodotus insists on the primacy of what the priests show him: they count the wooden statues in the hall of kings, each of which depicts a likeness of a priest and marks a generation; this is material evidence that Herodotus explicitly adduces for his inquiry.[9] Hecataeus is a *logopoios*, a maker of *logoi*, or narratives and reasoned accounts. Herodotus contrasts this with his own role as a *histôr*, an inquirer and creator of *historiai*: an inquiry that proceeds through observation (*opsis*) and listening to the accounts of others (*akouê*) while also offering his own opinions (*gnomê*).[10]

As the discussion of Hecataeus shows, Herodotus's willingness to intervene in the narrative allows him to emphasize what methods he considers important. Following the sequence of Croesus and Cyrus in book 1, Herodotus begins book 2 of the *Histories* by describing Cambyses, the successor to

Cyrus, and his invasion of Egypt. This prompts a book-length excursus into the history, terrain, animals, and customs of the Egyptians. Herodotus begins the Egyptian narrative by recounting Psammetichus's experiment that was intended to show which was the original human race. This moment illuminates Herodotus's own approach by similarity and contrast. Before the reign of Psammetichus, the Egyptians had considered themselves the oldest race on earth; Psammetichus decided to settle the issue and conducted inquiries and then an experiment. Psammetichus gave a shepherd two newborn infants and had him bring them up "in such a way that no one ever spoke in their hearing" (2.2). They were to reside in a remote hut by themselves and the shepherd was to bring them she-goats to give them their fill of milk periodically. Psammetichus made these arrangements to listen for their first words. And so it happened. After two years of carrying out this program, one day the shepherd arrived and both children rushed to him and said, "*bekos.*" The shepherd did not immediately act but on subsequent visits the children continued to say, "*bekos.*" He passed the information to Psammetichus, who asked that the children be brought to him. The shepherd did so and they said the word in Psammetichus's presence. He tried to figure out which people called something "*bekos*" and soon discovered it was the Phrygian word for "bread." So the Egyptians concluded that the Phrygians were the oldest race.

In many ways, Psammetichus provides a vision of Herodotean inquiry. Like Herodotus, Psammetichus seeks the origins of things and consults others, not simply believing the conventional story but probing with his own inquiries. Psammetichus is provoked by his curiosity and then sets off to discover an answer. When constructing his experiment, he pursues an inquiry that prioritizes autopsy, his own seeing of the results. Moreover, as Matthew Christ points out, his inquiry resembles Herodotus's in its underlying spirit: both challenge the parochial assumptions of their countrymen.[11] Neither Herodotus nor Psammetichus flinches at contradicting regnant opinions.

Yet the Psammetichus story also illuminates the distinctiveness of Herodotean inquiry. Herodotus comments that he heard the story of Psammetichus from the priests of Hephaestus at Memphis and adds that this contradicts the "ludicrous" stories of the Greeks (2.2). Yet despite the ridiculousness of the Greek stories, Herodotus notes their existence—they imply some question about the veracity of the stories of the Egyptians. Thus, Herodotus looks for other evidence, trusting not a single source but well-reputed sources that might agree. Psammetichus seeks answers but Herodotus responds to the assertion of answers with skepticism. This difference between the two appears in a later episode again involving Psammetichus, where Herodotus questions the latter's attempts to measure the depths of the springs at the head of the Nile. Psammetichus had a rope made many thousands of fathoms long and this was let down but did not reach the bottom. Psammetichus thus concluded that the springs were bottomless. Herodotus, however, questions Psammetichus's conclusion. The rope's not reaching the bottom may well have proved the existence of strong whirlpools and countercurrents: "because the water was dashing against the mountains, this prevented them reaching the bottom when they let their sounding line down" (2.28). Although Herodotus resembles Psammetichus by seeking the origins of things and consulting with others, he goes further than Psammetichus by inquiring after disputes or contradictions. He does not just settle the question but tries to discover why some have expressed doubts about whatever conventional wisdom happens to reign.[12]

The voice of the inquirer also allows Herodotus to include disagreement while presenting his evidence so that it may be disputed. Psammetichus inquires but then concludes his inquiry with an assertion of definitive knowledge. Herodotus, by contrast, leaves open the possibility that his assertions will be contradicted. The Ionians' view about Egypt presents a useful example of this. They claim that Egypt consists exclusively of the Delta, the region defined by them as extending forty *schoeni* along the coastline from the so-called "watchtower of Perseus" to the salt factories of Pelusium, then inland from the sea as far as the city of Cercasorus, where the waters of the Nile divide to flow onward either to Pelusium or to Canobus. Herodotus questions such an assertion because it would mean there was a time that the Egyptians had no country at all: given that the Delta is alluvial, this area was formed in the not-so-recent past. If the Ionians were correct, why would Psammetichus even bother inquiring into whether or not the Egyptians were the first race since their young land would have been indication enough to the contrary? Herodotus presents his own conviction that the Egyptians have existed since the first generation of men. Even while Herodotus disagrees with the Ionians, however, he does not deny the possibility that they may be proven right:

> Such is my conclusion—and if I am right, then the Ionians must have Egypt badly wrong. Even if the Ionian thesis is correct, I can still demonstrate that the Greeks—the Ionians themselves included—are displaying basic innumeracy when they reckon the entire world to consist of three continents. (2.16)

If the Egyptians are limited to the territory the Ionians propose, the Ionians must, on Herodotus's reasoning, add a fourth continent to Europe, Asia, and Libya—because the Nile postdates these and is distinct. "What, then, does this make the Delta, if not a region distinct from Asia and Libya?" Herodotus asks (2.16).

Herodotus spells out his own views on matters of controversy in ways that air disagreement without eliding it. He shows where the reckoning of other thinkers comes up short while offering new pieces of evidence—such as the formation of the Delta—in support of his own conclusions. Still, when Herodotus arrives at conclusions, these remain tied to the observations and accounts upon which his arguments rely.[13]

The most significant moment of self-conscious presentation of his inquiry occurs in Herodotus's discussion of the flooding of the Nile. Here Herodotus pushes the limits of discovery, combining his own eyewitness accounts, the accounts of others, as well as reasoning about different possible explanations. "Neither the priests nor anyone else could help me get to grips with the nature of the Nile [*tou potamou de phusios peri*]" (2.19), Herodotus begins his account. Certain Greeks, "keen to make a name for themselves as intellectuals [*sophistai*]" (2.20), have suggested different explanations. Herodotus mentions three but deigns only one worth serious consideration. A first theory attributes the flooding of the river to the Etesian winds that blow in from the northwest and prevent the Nile from flowing onward to the sea. Yet Herodotus points out that the Nile behaves no differently even when these winds are not blowing; this explanation also has the larger implication that other rivers flowing counter to these winds would exhibit similar behavior, which is observably false. The second theory Herodotus dismisses without much discussion: this one claims that the Nile functions as it does because its waters flow in from Oceanus; Herodotus has already detailed the fallaciousness of the theory that Oceanus encircles the world (2.21, 2.23).

Herodotus finds the third theory worthy of extended treatment, and his discussion of it highlights his distinctive approach to inquiry as well as the self-conscious limiting of conclusions to evidence and provisional reasoning. The third reason "may sound by far the most plausible," but Herodotus asserts it also lies farthest from the truth. This theory proposes that the currents of the Nile derive from melting snow. This ignores the path of the Nile through Libya and Ethiopia—the hottest regions in the world—before entering Egypt, a cooler place. "Certainly," Herodotus surmises, "to any man capable of rational reflection, it would be obvious that the Nile is most unlikely to derive from snow" (2.22). Herodotus adduces three reasons in support of the temperatures at the source of the Nile: The winds from Ethiopia are hot. These countries know neither rain nor frost. So scorching is the region that its inhabitants are black.

Having criticized all other proposed theories, Herodotus does briefly state his own. "In winter," he writes, "the sun is driven by storms out of its original path and into the inland regions of Libya" (2.24). When the sun passes near to land, the land will lack water; this deviation in the sun's path explains the flooding of the Nile during winter. "In the summer months, the sun draws water out of the Nile just as much as it does out of all bodies of water," Herodotus explains, "but in winter it is the only one to suffer" (2.25). Despite Herodotus's incisive criticisms of other theories, his own is far from the consensus explanation today; but this does not negate the explicit reasoning that allows for questioning. He presents his opinion, "while leaving nothing out" (2.24).

Geography and Ethnography

The inquirer's presence in the *Histories* at least partially alleviates concerns about the inquirer's claims to mastery: by depicting his approach, allowing for disagreement, and referring explicitly to evidence, Herodotus reveals the processes of his inquiry in ways that counterbalance whatever assertions it may support.[14] Inquiry does lead to knowledge, but it's a knowledge that the inquiry explicitly links to an always provisional process. Psammetichus draws conclusions about the origins of the Egyptians or the depths of the Nile springs from his experiments; Herodotus questions this conclusiveness and raises new lines of possible inquiry. Because the inquirer's undertaking can be replicated, his authority is not unmatchable. Whereas kings and tyrants measure the world to conquer it, Herodotus describes and catalogs the world to understand it.

Yet the inquirer still sets the terms of his inquiry. Herodotus frames these undertakings and puts discrete findings into relationship with one another according to concepts and categories that are not themselves the results of inquiry or scrutiny. For example, near the opening of Herodotus's Egypt narrative, he writes this:

> Certainly, it is not only the climate which renders Egypt unique, nor the fact that the river behaves naturally in a way quite unlike any other river; there is also the fact that the Egyptians themselves, in almost all their customs and practices, do the exact opposite of mankind. (2.35)

Statements such as these form the basis of readings like those advanced by François Hartog. This symmetrical view of the world, where the Greeks inhabit the center, was common belief in Herodotus's day. According to Hartog's interpretation, this dogma results in the production of a historical text that always proceeds in terms of oppositions. The *Histories* thus creates a discourse of otherness that supports the Greeks' own identity. Even if Herodotus calls his own role as an authority into question, the inquiry he presents still reinforces these structures of understanding.[15]

Speaking of others like the Egyptians and the Scythians not in their terms but in his own, Herodotus (on this reading) encodes these others in subordinate relation to the Greeks for whom he speaks. "To speak of others," Hartog writes, "is to make it known that, over and above the variety of *nomoi* [customs], the most profound difference between 'them' and 'us' is political, a difference of power."[16] Others are present but only in the terms of the inquirer. The inquirer makes things seen, makes things known; "he makes us believe."[17]

I will return to Herodotus's discussion of Egypt, but Hartog's arguments take me to the Scythian narrative in book 4 of the *Histories*. In many ways the discussion of Scythia has a function similar to that of Egypt: Herodotus uses the invasion of Cambyses to connect his digressive delving into Egypt with the broader narrative of the rise of the Persian Empire; so, too, Darius's invasion of Scythia a generation later opens a broader discussion of its geography, customs, and history. Scythia and Egypt both mark otherness and the borders of the known world (*oikeomenê*) in the narrative of the *Histories*. Both offer opportunities to consider how Herodotus approaches this otherness— whether as would-be tyrant seeking control through knowledge or not.[18]

The Scythians inhabit the northernmost lands known in Herodotus's day. They thus present a mystery to an inquirer: few travelers have been there and few stories have migrated south to the Greek-speaking territories known so well. This distance and enigma allow for certain assumptions to shape knowledge claims about the Scythians. Following these inherited assumptions, the *Histories* appears to schematize Scythian geography and space as the land of *eremia* (barrenness) and *eschatia* (the ends of the earth). In relation to the known and inhabited world (*oikeomenê*), the Scythians occupy a position analogous to that occupied by the frontier zone in relation to the city territory. In Herodotus's global representation of the world, then, the Scythians stand in symmetrical relationship to the Egyptians: the northern boundary mirrors the southern boundary; the unintelligible and barely human civilization inverts the long-established and flourishing one. Whereas the Egyptian climate furnishes the means for wealth and prosperity, Scythian climes allow only for subsistence.

The structures of understanding used to explain strange phenomena like the Scythians have broader implications for understanding Herodotus's inquiry. Seen through this lens, cultures that may appear merely varied are actually systematically organized; they outline a broader representation of the world with geometrical proportions. Climate provides an example of this proportionality. Cold explains everything to the north while heat serves the same purpose to the south. Ionia, for example, is located between the extremes:

> Now, so far as I am aware, there is no other region, not in the whole span of the
> inhabited world, where the skies are a more beautiful shade of blue, nor the
> climate finer, than the one in which the Ionians, who share in the Panionium,
> have founded their cities. Compared to Ionia, the countries which lie further
> to the north are oppressively cold and wet, while the more southerly regions
> suffer from an excess of heat and a lack of water. (1.142)

Yet the temperateness of Ionia prevents it from having the wonders that come
only in extreme conditions. So Herodotus comments that outside Greece, at
the ends of the known world, one encounters truly remarkable phenomena:

> Just as fate has blessed Greece with by far the most beautiful mix of seasons, so
> also has she endowed the furthermost reaches of the inhabited world [*oikeo-
> menês*] with the most beautiful things. (3.106)

> It is probable, however, that the ends of the earth, encompassing the rest of the
> world as they do, and bounding them in, do possess things which strike us as
> exceptionally beautiful and rare. (3.116)

Each climate has its own kind of excellence: one of extremes (the edges of
the earth) and one of balance through mixture (Ionia and, more generally,
Greece). Although Herodotus never spells out the climatic theory implicit
here, it appears to operate as a "self-evident grid,"[19] as his description of soft-
ness as associated with wealth and hardness with poverty suggests.

At the heart of these traditions about the strange edges of the earth and
their relation to Greece lies the concept of the inhabited world (*oikeomenê*).
The Scythian narrative brings Herodotus up against an empty space (*erêmos*),
the terminal boundaries beyond which no other inquiry had proceeded. To
conceptualize the difference between the territory inquiry has charted and
what lies beyond this, Herodotus uses a term that would dominate subsequent geographic writing: *oikeomenê*, meaning "inhabited land." The *oikeomenê* is discovered land; what is not inhabited is still unknown, shrouded in
mystery. The edges of the inhabited world are the site of its extremes: India
(3.106), Arabia (3.107), the Ethiopian territories (3.114). Territory beyond the
inhabited world is the subject of only speculation. The Ister is well known because it flows through inhabited (*oikeomenês*) territory in contrast to the Nile
(2.34). The territory east of India is uninhabited "and no one can say what sort
of land exists there" (4.40).

The *oikeomenê* is not just the inhabited land but the *known* land. What
is *oikeomenê* is safe, civilized, legible. In the tradition prior to Herodotus,
the *oikeomenê* functions as a center against which the strangeness of others,

positioned on the edges of the inhabited world, is contrasted. Yet this raises the question: is the inhabited land static or dynamic? That is, what precisely is the status of this knowledge of the world, to be able to say it is inhabited or not? Does this not depend on a set of claims about how the inhabited world is known, how easily it can be comprehended? Even while Herodotus places the Scythians on a grid that marks their strangeness, the processual knowing of Herodotean inquiry makes *oikeomenê* a provisional category dependent on the ongoing research of the inquirer.

The Known World

The inhabited world marks a known world, but processual knowing calls attention to how knowledge about this world is provisional and always subject to revision. Knowledge about the world is thus dynamic and complex like the world itself. According to Hartog, Herodotus's travels "served him not so much to construct his representation of the world as to confirm and complete it."[20] In other words, Herodotus worked "like a Lévi-Strauss of antiquity," completing a picture of latent structures within the world he explored. This reading of Herodotus helps to call attention to the conventional assumptions in the background of the *Histories*, assumptions about the relationships among cultures that Herodotus often seems to promote or at least never seems to shake. Yet as critics of Hartog have also suggested, this view also sets up a static view of political communities as well as of the inquirer's own work. To understand the kind of knowledge that the historian develops and displays, you need to probe behind the grids and polarities that were both his inheritance and his point of departure. This means seeing how the inhabited world is marked not only by borders and separations but also by networks and intermixtures.[21] It also means seeing how the inhabited world is a construction of the inquirer rather than a given which he simply reinforces.[22]

Mapping the world as filled with geometrical proportions requires fixed ethnic and cultural identities rooted in their place, but the *Histories* resists such stable identities from its very beginning. As Carolyn Dewald argues, the very first set of stories implicitly introduces the theme of radical ethnic transformation in which "the Same unexpectedly *becomes* the Other and the Other the Same."[23] In the Proem of the *Histories*, Io, a Greek princess, is taken to Egypt and becomes a goddess and mother of an Egyptian god. Europa, a Tyrian princess, is taken to Crete and has the continent of Europe named after her. Later Herodotus describes how the Greeks sail to Colchis and take the princess Medea, from whom the Medes got their name later in her wanderings (7.62). Each of the three women is the daughter of a king in her native country; all three "become cultural icons of the countries of their eventual appropriation." Three peoples essential to the course of the *Histories*—Greeks, Egyptians, Medes—appear as "profoundly interrelated through the mutual exchange of their women."[24]

The Ionians provide a stunning example of intermixture as well as unpredictability. Located between Greece and Asia, the Ionians are the first victims of aggression from the east. Yet the Ionians' own aggressions when they first established their settlements also participate in this process. Beautiful as their country is and positioned to experience the perfect mixture of climate, the Ionians also fail to live as their Greek neighbors to the west: given multiple chances to claim their freedom, the Ionians decline or fail.

Herodotus's treatment of Egypt also undermines the inherited structures of knowledge that treat *oikeomenê* as a static category. Although Herodotus introduces his account of Egypt's customs by describing how they invert the Greeks', his frequent examples of how the Greeks have adopted Egyptian customs call into question the inversion concept, suggesting that the actual truth about the relationship between Egyptian and Greek customs is much more complicated. The Egyptians are not just more knowledgeable about their own history, but their inquiries best the Greeks', as the story of Psammetichus's inquiry into the original people of the world illustrates. Herodotus comments that the rites as well as the name of Dionysus were imported from Egypt. "Almost all the names of the gods came to Greece from Egypt" (2.50). The Egyptians may have the reputation of shunning other customs, yet they incorporate an Ethiopian knife in their sacred preparations of a corpse and also honor Perseus in the Egyptian city of Chemmis.

The mixing of Egyptian customs has an analogue in the political mixing that contributes to Egypt's continuing existence. When Psammetichus is exiled by the other eleven Egyptian kings for appearing to fulfill an oracle that he would come to rule alone, Greeks help him (2.151). When some Ionian and Carian freebooters are swept off-course and forced to land in Egypt, Psammetichus realizes that they may be part of the oracle. He befriends them and persuades them to rally in his support. With these allies he overthrows his fellow kings. As a reward, Psammetichus offers the Ionians and the Carians property on the banks of the Nile; they later teach some Egyptian children to be fluent in Greek, and so all interpreters in Egypt, to Herodotus's day, trace descent from these children.

The Egyptians present mixtures in terms of customs and politics that destabilize the rigid understanding of the inhabited lands. This destabilization thus implies a more dynamic concept of *oikeomenê*. Whereas in the conventional understanding, the *oikeomenê* is mapped according to a Greek space of shared knowledge, the Egypt narrative suggests that the *oikeomenê* depends on the practices of the inhabitants themselves—and thus not the master plan of the Greek historian and his "geometrization of space."[25] Speaking of Egypt, Herodotus declares, contrary to the Ionian theories he has just been discussing, that Egypt is "simply that which is inhabited by the Egyptians" (2.18). The Egyptian *oikeomenê* is what the Egyptians inhabit—not a specific place or a specific position in relation to the Greeks but rather wherever they are when they act like Egyptians. Egyptian practices of inhabitation unsettle the conventional assumption that Egyptians are simply the inverse of Greeks; Herodotus's particular details prevent the universalizing impulse from containing his account.[26]

The Scythians' nomadism also resists the assumption that continuous, static dwelling forms the basis of *oikeomenê*. Their lands are desolate and void of any signs of inhabitation. Darius's brother and adviser Artabanos anticipates this when he warns Darius against the invasion prior to its beginning, calling them "impossible to approach" (4.83). Coes, the commander of the Mytilenaeans fighting alongside Darius, amplifies this warning as the Persian forces are about to finish crossing the Ister:

> "O King, you are about to invade a land," Coes said, "where there is not a trace of tilled fields. Nor are there any cities built there [*ouden oute polis oikeomenê*]." (4.97)

Coes regards the Scythians as lacking any inhabitation, as without an *oikeomenê*. This makes them unconquerable and strange. Rather than inquiring into the Scythians' practices, Coes and others call them strange and leave off further questioning.

By contrast, Herodotus calls attention to how the Scythians inhabit their territory in a dynamic way. The Scythians are Scythians wherever they reside. When they invaded and conquered the Lydians, they did so without losing their integrity as Scythians, something that the Persians almost failed to do themselves. In one crucial respect, moreover, the Scythians stand for a value that Greeks (and Herodotus) respect: freedom. This becomes clear during the Persian invasion of Scythia. After Darius has left behind the Ionians to guard his rope-and-boat bridge spanning the Ister, the Scythians circle behind him to approach the Ionians.

> "Men of Ionia," they said, "the gift we come bearing you, if you will only hear us out, is freedom. We have learned that you were instructed by Darius to stand guard over the bridge for sixty days, and no more—and that once that deadline is past, and supposing that he has still not appeared, you are all to head for home. That being so, why would he censure you simply for doing as

you were told? We will not blame you either. Just wait here until the prescribed number of days is up, and then be off." (4.133)

The Ionians agree and the Scythians depart. The Persians wage unsuccessful battle and finally decide to return. Again the Scythians circle back before the Persians can reach the bridge. They are astonished and furious to find the Ionians still there—despite the requisite number of days having passed.

> "Your sixty days are up, Ionians, so it's wrong of you to be here still. Previously it was fear that kept you here, but if you dismantle the bridge now, you can leave straight away without any worries, with the gods and the Scythians to thank for your freedom." (4.136)

The Scythian speech prompts a debate among the Ionians, who decide to stick with Darius in order to preserve their tyrannies at home. (I discuss this episode further in the following chapters.) The Scythians are unstinting in their criticisms. Herodotus comments:

> The Scythian opinion of the Ionians is that they make the worst and most cowardly free people in the world, but that if they were to think of them as slaves, they would have to say that no master could hope to find more loyal and submissive captives. (4.142)

As this episode suggests, nomadic power may well provide the surest path to the attainment of freedom.[27] Not only do the Scythians escape the domination of others; they rule themselves according to their own customs. The Scythians thus construct their own *oikeomenê*, one that resists the conventions about inhabitation that appear at first glance to structure the *Histories*. Herodotus puts both in play.

Once inhabitation becomes the work of a given people rather than a concept imposed by an outside inquirer, the nature of inquiry shifts. The inquirer can now wonder at strangeness rather than relegate it to the category of "other." To shift north to Scythia again, although the Scythian territory is "utter desert" and the Scythians "know nothing of agriculture," Herodotus also notes how the nature of the country supports the Scythians' "most admirable abilities," namely their ability to evade aggressive forces like the Persians by not having established settlements or architecture worth protecting (4.46). The "nomadic power" of the Scythians is not a strange and inexplicable force (a "contradiction in terms")[28] but rather a marvel worth admiring and, perhaps, learning from. The Scythians have adapted to the riverine environment they inhabit (4.47), creating customs, such as cooking their sacrificial victims—horses, usually—atop a fire of bones, that do not depend on extravagant resources (4.61). Herodotus notes that much like the

Egyptians (although unlike the Persians) the Scythians seek to protect their customs from external influence (4.80).

Itinerant Mapping

The extent and texture of the known world depend on where you stand. Seen from one vantage point, the *Histories* appears to rely on inherited conventions about self and other, known and strange, that structure understanding. But from a different angle, the particular encounters described in the *Histories* frequently undermine and contradict these settled categories. Rather than depict the Egyptians and the Scythians as singular, unified entities, Herodotus relates the practices that make these peoples who they are. Their identity stems not from their placement in a set of symmetries and inversions but rather from their customs and habits, modes of settlement and eccentricities. The *oikeomenê* comes about through their inhabitation.

This shift in the meaning of *oikeomenê* also transforms the work of the inquirer. From the beginning Herodotus regards history as dynamic: great cities become small, and small become great. This sense of dynamism structures his inquiry. As Alex Purves puts it, Herodotus's "descriptions of space and geography always have the idea of movement working through them."[29] The accounts of the Egyptians and the Scythians exemplify this, from the slow accumulation of the Nile Delta to the Scythians' viper-quick guerrilla tactics as they evade the Persians. Such movement also appears in the inquirer's work. Herodotus is constantly on the move, and as he travels, the borders of the known world, the *oikeomenê*, shift. Herodotus shows us how the *oikeomenê* is constructed not only by inhabitants but by the pathways created through his own inquiry. The mapping of the *oikeomenê* follows the itinerary of the inquirer and remains a dynamic process, provisional and unending.

To give a sense of the inquirer's itinerant mapping, let me return to the opening descriptions of the various explanations for the conflict between the Greeks and the barbarians. As Herodotus describes the trips across the Mediterranean between Phoenicia, Troy, Egypt, and elsewhere, he relies on the geographical model of the *periplus*, the mapping of the coastline by early travelers, to plot the coordinates of the stories told. The chronology develops in spatial terms as the historian places himself on imaginative journeys to these places. Croesus's story unfolds, as Purves comments, "as a kind of geography through which Herodotus travels on his journey through the 'small and large cities of mankind.' "[30] That narrative tracks various locations to form networks—from Scythia to Lydia to Athens to Sparta to Persia. These networks in turn make up the substance of the inquirer's assertions about the *oikeomenê*, an area that becomes known through the connections disparate places form to one another through the travels of the inquirer. Herodotus is the shuttle interweaving the warp and weft that form the fabric of the places described in the *Histories*. The inquirer poses a question that sets the itinerary for the construction of the known world that follows.

This itinerary becomes most explicit in the Egypt narrative, where the particular texture of the historian's itinerant mapping appears, layered with first-person observation (*opsis*), listening to the accounts of others (*akouê*), and the inquirer's own opinions (*gnomê*).[31] Recall when Herodotus relates the story of Psammetichus's experiment to determine the original race of men. After having told the story, Herodotus places it in the context of his travels and inquiry:

> This account of how the children were brought up was not, however, the only topic I heard about in Memphis, during the course of my conversations with the priests of Hephaestus. Indeed, the reason that I then went off to Thebes and Heliopolis was because I wanted to know if the priests there would concur with what I had been told in Memphis: the scholars in Heliopolis have a reputation for being the best informed in Egypt. Now, except for the gods' names, I have no desire to pass on any details of what I heard from the dimension of the divine, for in my opinion all men are equal when it comes to a knowledge of the gods. When and if I do touch on the subject, it will only be because I am obliged to by my narrative. (2.3)

This rich passage has many dimensions: you see how Herodotus reports conversations as the bases of his stories; Herodotus also uses these conversations as bases for further inquiry; these inquiries, moreover, turn on reputations for wisdom, themselves the implicit product of conversations and un-recounted inquiries. Herodotus further chooses what he will relate from his travels; the map of the known world, in this additional sense, depends on the discretion of the inquirer (cf. 2.47). These inquiries do not rest in a single location but rather impel travel. What becomes known depends, then, on the position and experience of the itinerary the inquirer pursues.[32]

The first advantage of travel lies in being able to confirm or disconfirm *with your own eyes* what you have been told. Herodotus asserts that it is beyond dispute that Egypt's land is increasing because of the Nile: "It should be self-evident even to someone who has not been told it," Herodotus writes, "so long as he has a brain, and eyes to see" (2.5). Herodotus uses his own eyes and brain when he sails to Tyre in Phoenicia to clarify stories he heard about Heracles. There he could see with his own eyes the sanctuary of Heracles and the rich dedicatory offerings. Seeing these things, he discovers a further contradiction in the Greek consensus. The Tyrians say their shrine was established at the same time as the founding of Tyre, yet when Herodotus visits Thasos, he finds a sanctuary of Heracles built by the Phoenicians, five generations before Heracles son of Amphitryon was even born in Greece. Herodotus concludes that the Greeks are foolish—they are "forever making claims without first researching them" (2.45). To take another example, Herodotus can inform the ignorant Greeks about the flying snakes of Arabia because he visited a place not far from the city of Bouto to learn more about them (2.75).

Seeing does not always bring enlightenment, however. When Herodotus seeks the sources of the Nile, "a mystery which nobody with whom I came into discussion about the matter, whether Egyptian or Libyan or Greek, ever professed to have fathomed" (2.28), he pushes to the bounds of human exploration and can go no further:

> There was no further information to be had from anyone; nevertheless, insofar as I was able to push the limits of discovery, I pushed them. Initially I did this as an eyewitness [*autoptês*], by traveling as far as the city of Elephantine; beyond there, however, I was dependent for my enquiries upon what I heard from others [*to d' apo toutou akoêi êdê historeôn*]. (2.29)

The sources of the Nile still confound inquirers; Herodotus demonstrates that a gumshoe's footwork can only go so far. In contrast to the Nile, the Ister is well known; many people live and thus have traveled around its sources (2.34). What is known depends on the itineraries of the inquirer as she maps the world. Every map comes with fingerprints, reminders of the particular traveler who followed its constitutive itineraries.

Travel brings the inquirer into new relationships which hold possibilities for further knowledge, but this does not mean that local knowledge is all-encompassing. When Herodotus wants to find out why the Nile floods during the summer solstice, not one of the Egyptians with whom he speaks can help him (2.19). Greeks have attempted explanations and the Egyptians offer nothing to improve them. Herodotus can offer his opinion and reasoning but his forms of evidence limit his ability to do anything more.

By explicitly describing the *process* of developing knowledge about the inhabited world, Herodotus thus displays the mapping of the known world, the *oikeomenê*, as processual in a sense that complements his descriptions of how particular peoples inhabit their lands. People inhabit the world in dynamic and complex ways; understanding of this world is established through an ongoing process of inquiry. This understanding is itself dynamic: the geography and networks Herodotus illuminates become related through his itinerary of inquiry. Thus, any map of the *oikeomenê* is not "secure knowledge," as some might have it, but processual knowing, not a thing but an activity.[33]

It's worth noting how Herodotus's understanding of the *oikeomenê* as processual knowing differs from the methods of his contemporary inquirers, the writers associated with the Hippocratic tradition. Although the Hippocratics bring a spirit of unfolding inquiry to their examination of the human body, maintaining the provisional nature of their claims and limiting generalizations to experiment-based inference,[34] their descriptions of the nonhuman world, in particular the terrains of inhabitation (*oikeomenê*), repeat static notions of environmental determinism at odds with Herodotus's open-ended approach. This idea—that the physical environment determines the nature of human society—appears in the Hippocratic essay *Airs, Waters, Places*, which discusses the effect of winds, waters, and geography on the health and physical character of human beings, attempting to show that the ethnic characters of Europe and Asia depend on their physical environments. Although there are elements of such thinking in Herodotus, such as the famous comment that "soft lands breed soft men" (which I discuss in the next chapter), Herodotus focuses on change and how people can transform their environments (such as Cyrus's draining of the rivers obstructing his conquests) and how these environments themselves can be dynamic actors (such as the rivers of Scythia). While the author of *Airs, Waters, Places* does acknowledge the importance of nonenvironmental factors, there is very little of Herodotus's emphasis on the practices of inhabitation by the denizens themselves. Moreover, there is no treatment of how the author came to this knowledge: the knowledge is presented as self-evident or well-known truth; in contrast to the case studies and experiments described in the more explicitly medical sections, this knowledge comes detached from any experience that might explain it.

Herodotus's understanding of the *oikeomenê* follows the itinerary of the inquirer rather than a particular grid or set of assumptions about environment, climate, or ethnicity. In this sense, the mapping of the *oikeomenê* illustrates a broader pattern across the *Histories*, a pattern that appears already in the Herodotean critique of tyrants' knowledge. Herodotus is keen to undermine all determinative structures, every system that one might use to explain the whole. As Dewald observes: "Throughout the *Histories* people come to grief because they think they understand the structures that shape the world they inhabit, when they really have no idea of them."[35] My readings of Candaules, Croesus, and Cyrus in the previous chapter support this reading. The Egyptians, by contrast, with their robust traditions of history and inquiry—introduced deftly by Herodotus with the Psammetichus story at the beginning of the narrative—seem less susceptible to the hubris of knowledge. They see how understanding depends on process; they give evidence for their claims, pointing to the rows of statues as tangible markers for their genealogy.

Relational Inquiry

The distinction between what he has seen for himself (*autopsis*) and what he has heard and recounts illuminates another dimension of Herodotus's inquiry: its relational quality. While displaying his processual understanding of the *oikeomenê* as the known world of the inquirer, Herodotus also articulates relationships with his sources. Herodotus is a valuable teacher, as Ryszard Kapuściński puts it, for showing that relationships underlie all the knowledge of the inquirer.[36] The inquirer undertakes her *historia* through listening to others (*akouê*) as well as seeing for herself (*opsis*). Throughout the *Histories* (and especially in the Egypt narrative), Herodotus gives an account of the sources of his evidence. Most often these sources are other people: Egyptian priests, local residents in a place Herodotus visits, or groups of people such as "the Spartans" or "the Phoenicians." What Herodotus hears from others leads him to confident knowledge as well as further questions. When he visits Dodona he can conclude: "Thanks to what I heard at Dodona, I know for a fact that it was the original practice of the Pelasgians to accompany every sacrifice with prayers to the gods" (2.52). At other times, Herodotus is left with questions, such as when he describes asking about the sources of the Nile.

Herodotus's inquiry is relational: it depends upon often-unmentioned relationships with other inquirers, storytellers, informants, and ordinary citizens. One key term in Herodotus's vocabulary of inquiry is "consensus" (*homologein*). Although Herodotus doesn't say precisely how he establishes consensus, ascertaining this general sense of things allows him to describe the particular nature of a knowledge claim while adverting to its origins. Consensus can also prompt further inquiry by the historian himself, as this moment in the Egypt narrative attests:

> Now up until this point I have drawn for my reports exclusively upon what the Egyptians themselves have to say; but henceforward I will relate the consensus of both native and non-Egyptian sources as to what happened in the country, supplemented by some observations of my own. (2.147)

Herodotus himself constructs this consensus, drawing together disparate sources. Yet even when Herodotus can identify a consensus, the consensus still needs supplementing by the historian's own observations (*opsis*).

At times when Herodotus cannot look for himself, he reasons about the consensus or tries to discern which consensus merits following. The *Histories* begins with the abduction of Helen as one possible starting point for the war between the Greeks and the barbarians (1.3). When Herodotus converses with the Egyptian priests, the relation allows him to pursue further questions on the matter (2.113). Inquiring about the stories in regard to Helen, Herodotus hears from the priests about the landing of Alexandros (Paris) at the Canobic mouth of the Nile, where his attendants fled to the sanctuary of Heracles for asylum lest they suffer because of Alexandros's deeds. Their accusations against Alexandros eventually find the ear of Proteus of Memphis, who demands that Alexandros be brought before him so that Proteus can "examine him and find out what he might have to say for himself [*hin eideô ti kote kai lexei*]" (2.114). Outraged by what he discovers, Proteus orders Alexandros to depart, leaving Helen in Egypt.

You can imagine Herodotus listening to this story, comparing it with the Greek consensus with which he had been raised. So he writes:

> According to the priests, that is the way Helen came to Proteus. And it seems to me that Homer had also heard this version of the story. But since it was not as appropriate for epic composition as the other one which he adopted, he rejected it, but did reveal here and there that he nevertheless knew this version, too. (2.116)

Herodotus continues by examining particular passages from both the *Iliad* and the *Odyssey*, showing how Homer might have already known the stories of the Egyptians even while choosing to exclude them. Here Herodotus also describes Homer's activity as similar to his own: Homer listens to stories and selects what works for his theme; the Homeric epics are also built on relational inquiry, even though Homer does not display this process as explicitly as Herodotus does.

Seeing the mapping of *oikeomenê* as a process of knowing through relational inquiry highlights a significant difference between the qualities of knowing pursued by Herodotus and by those in positions of political rule. This reading of the importance of *oikeomenê* to the work of inquiry also opens space between Herodotus and the character within the *Histories* to whom he is most frequently compared: Solon. While Solon is presented as a ruler, his counsel, as described in chapter 1, speaks of moderation and humility in a world of dynamic complexity. Solon enters the story with gravity, and his wisdom seems to encapsulate a general theme of Herodotus's narrative. A long tradition of interpretation has associated Herodotus and Solon, yet perhaps the chief reason for their comparison is that they are both travelers. Travel and observation were characteristically Greek—Odysseus, who "wandered much, . . . who saw the cities of many men and knew their mind," figured this tradition, as we saw before—and became formalized in the practice of *theoria*.[37] Herodotus describes three great reasons for Greeks to travel to Egypt: to trade, to fight in war, and to see the sights of the country for themselves (3.139). The last of these is *theoria*.

Theoria is a beautiful thing, and it resembles Herodotus's practice as developed in this chapter but with some important differences. Solon's travels and commitment to spreading his wisdom anticipate Herodotus's own itineraries and publication of the *Histories*. Yet when Solon visits Croesus as part of his *theoria*, he asks no questions. Like Herodotus, Solon seeks to see things with his own eyes, yet he elicits no stories from Croesus. Solon himself is the one who tells the memorable stories of Tellus and of Cleobis and Biton.

Another notable practitioner of *theoria* recounted in the *Histories* adds a second dimension of connection and difference between Herodotus's itinerant mapping and *theoria*. Like Herodotus, the Scythian Anacharsis goes abroad and sees a great deal of the world (*gên pollen theôrêsas*), "demonstrating great wisdom along the way" (4.76). On his return trip, he stops at Cyzicus, where he discovers the citizens celebrating a "splendid and magnificent" festival for the mother of the gods. Anacharsis vows to the mother goddess that if he returned to his own land safely, he would sacrifice just as he saw the Cyzicans doing and would also institute a nightlong festival for her. He returns and celebrates the rites of the goddess in their entirety, "with a drum and with images tied upon him." Herodotus continues:

> But one of the Scythians saw him doing this and told the king, Saulios. The king himself then went to the same place, and when he saw Anacharsis performing these rites, he shot him with an arrow and killed him. And because Anacharsis had gone abroad, visited Hellas, and practiced foreign customs, if anyone even now asks the Scythians about him, they deny knowing about him at all.

"This illustrates the danger of *theoria*," Andrea Nightingale writes with mild understatement.[38] Like Herodotus, Anacharsis inquires into the practices of others, showing particular interest in religious beliefs. Yet while Anacharsis mimics what he has observed, Herodotus performs the inquiry itself. *Historia* incorporates *theoria* but also reflects on the activity of theorizing itself.[39]

The relational inquiry Herodotus undertakes when mapping the *oikeomenê* has an element of observation similar to *theoria*, yet its underlying logic differs. This suggests a third dimension of similarity and difference. Although

Solon and Anacharsis seek wisdom through observation, they still seem to operate within the inherited structures of understanding Herodotus destabilizes, reinforcing the division between Greeks and barbarians as well as the radical otherness of the one to the other. Whereas the "tourism" of *theoria* takes in spectacles, the relational inquiry of the *Histories* leads Herodotus to strike up conversations. Like Herodotus's *historia*, *theoria* emphasizes encountering the foreign and the different, yet Herodotus's relational inquiry adds practices of attention and reflection.[40]

Like *theoria*, however, this relational inquiry is infused with wonder. Wonder distinguishes the historical inquirer from those bent on developing understanding that can then be applied to political rule. Norma Thompson has suggested that "the process of self-definition and description by storytelling" is the theme of Herodotus's politics: Herodotus's storytelling makes his readers aware of their own stories and thus the foundations of their political communities; Herodotus's greatest accomplishment lies in understanding these stories without destroying them.[41] Working through his own firsthand experiences allows Herodotus to place himself in the middle of the storytelling enterprises of diverse human communities, not judging from an external position of authority but rather illuminating a particular community's substance from within. By "telling wonders," in Rosaria Munson's phrase, Herodotus attempts to communicate, in the human terms he knows, what is a wonder precisely because of its incommunicability. Naming these as wonders, however, Herodotus marks the actual fact or nonfact as nonidentical to his description. Wondering creates a relationship between familiar and unfamiliar while leaving the otherness intact.

How Herodotus assembles and tells stories further illuminates the more basic openness to others characteristic of Herodotus's approach—the necessity of wonder and how its orientation differs from the imperatives of political rule. Understanding and telling stories require gathering these stories from the concrete practices and objects that form a community's life. While Thucydides obscures his practice of historical inquiry, Herodotus shows us its basis in seeing, hearing, measuring, and comparing; moreover, Herodotus calls attention to the different stories that cast significance on varied aspects of political life.[42] Yet if Herodotus simply evaluated the stories of others on the basis of his perspective, these stories would reduce to a single narrative; Herodotus's own terms and stories would dominate the different terms and stories he encountered. To succeed in mapping the world's complexity without completely reducing it, then, inquiry requires a certain kind of relationship toward the material and human world, an openness to difference. This openness to difference is best characterized as wonder: a way of displacing the narrator's categories of understanding—or at least holding them in abeyance—and inviting others to do the same. While Herodotus leaves his narrative with fingerprints and his maps with remainders, wonder encourages others to participate in the bottom-up and open-ended construction of knowledge he puts on display.

This understanding of Herodotean inquiry adds a second dimension to the practice of wonder described in the previous chapter. By destabilizing the conventional boundaries of understanding, Herodotus's practices of wondering deauthorize the privileged-observer perspective, thus opening deliberations to varied and differently situated participants. Communication across difference can become more possible with the awareness of that which exceeds categories of understanding. By "telling wonders" Herodotus attempts to bridge the divide between the familiar and the unfamiliar, between what seems easily described and encompassed and what resists accounting. Herodotus does not reduce the vibrant and multiform objects of his inquiry to one mode of understanding; rather, he sets up his text as a conversation between located inquirer, variably different objects, and audience. The text is "circumscribed by the relation between the narrator and his addressee," as Roxanne Euben writes,[43] yet the logic of wondering opens up the text to new voices by virtue of its inclusive entailments.

3

The Practice of *Nomos*

And as always, when one seeks to go backward in time, one must rely on mythology—
Greek, if possible. . . . If *nomos* comes across as an element of an ethical history of international law, its real conceptual role is to render the collective comparable once again.
In other words, *nomos* is a more juridical and more erudite version of the term cosmo-
gram, which I have used to imagine the diplomatic assembly of the peoples struggling
for the Earth.

BRUNO LATOUR, *Facing Gaia*[1]

For if someone were to assign to every person in the world the task of selecting the best
of all *nomoi*, each one, after thorough consideration, would choose those of his own
people, so strongly do humans believe that their own *nomoi* are the best ones. Therefore
only a madman would treat such things as a laughing matter. . . . Well, then, that is how
people think, and so it seems to me that Pindar was right when he said in his poetry
that *nomos* is king of all.

HERODOTUS, *Histories* 3.38

While Herodotus illuminates and maps the dynamic complexity of the world
through his inquiry, he also takes a human perspective. The *Histories* does
not treat the phenomena described and investigated apart from the question of how human communities might take up and use the stories, theories,
and questions that form the substance of the narrative of the *Histories*. The
writing of the *Histories* speaks directly to the human communities it catalogs
and chronicles. This chapter takes up the varieties of political community
depicted within the *Histories* and the central term, *nomos*, Herodotus uses for
describing these varieties. By reconstructing Herodotus's theory of *nomos*, a
term that captures "custom, law, and culture," I excavate how *nomos* names
the essential practice of political communities that inquiry both reveals and
seeks to instruct. *Nomoi* (plural of *nomos*) for Herodotus, depend on activity;
different instantiations of *nomoi* emerge through the iteration and duration
of human practices. *Nomoi* are also subject to change, and Herodotus's attention to *nomoi* suggests how inquiry might shape them.

Inquiring into *nomoi* within the dynamic complexity of the world leads
Herodotus to a distinctive view on the broader ecologies that support various political regimes. *Nomoi* arise in responsive interaction with nonhuman forces or actants—what you might call the interrelationship of human

communities and "nature" or the "environment." Both of these terms are, however, deceptive: Herodotus does not regard these ecologies as outside or apart from the *nomoi* which human beings constitute, modify, and sustain; unlike Herodotus's contemporaries, moreover, Herodotus believes *nomoi* can shape as well as be shaped by other things. Human beings do not exist except in relation to nonhumans; Herodotus makes this relationality integral to his account of *nomoi*. The *Histories* describes how human beings can develop *nomoi*—understood as customs, cultures, and laws—in relation to the unpredictable and abundant world of things which Herodotus's inquiry reveals.

Among these various *nomoi*, Herodotus also identifies persistent forms that promote flourishing.[2] While different *nomoi* have various optimal forms, Herodotus identifies equality (*to ison*) as crucial to all of them. Herodotean equality does not involve leveling all actants, human and nonhuman, however; it stands instead for proportionality. The proper proportion requires practices of yielding and balance, paying attention to the rhythms of fluctuation and change that Herodotus views as persistent and inescapable in the world he describes. Human constructions of equality can approximate the forms of equality Herodotus sees in the world of things; these can then organize *nomoi* for the greatest possible collective power. Equality, not man, is the measure of all things.

The Herodotean perspective on *nomoi* begins from the practices of peoples in relation to the world of things that affect and are affected by them. Not only does Herodotus deny the singularity of the *polis*, but his approach to *nomoi* proffers examples of flourishing political communities that are not Greek. The implicit theory of *nomoi* illuminates how Persians, Scythians, and Egyptians—as well as Greeks—organize themselves for collective power. Whereas the concept of *politeia* focuses attention on structures, *nomos* emphasizes practices.

This organization for collective power speaks directly to the crises of the Anthropocene. The Anthropocene itself names a recognition of inadvertent collective power exerted across generations with unintended consequences. As Dipesh Chakrabarty puts it, "humans have become geological agents very recently in human history."[3] Human beings have always been biological agents, yet this agency assumed geological import when numbers and technologies were deployed at a collective scale previously unreached. *Nomoi* describe these numbers and technologies; the *Histories* places human efforts at collective activity at the center of its account. It thus empowers responsible and beneficial ownership of the consequences of these actions.

Moreover, and unlike Latour and other New Materialists, Herodotus advances a human-centered account of *nomoi*. For Herodotus, human beings are world makers. As Clive Hamilton writes, "a new world-in-the-making, the Anthropocene world, is being disclosed."[4] While calling attention to the role of nonhumans in making these worlds, Herodotus still focuses on what humans have done and can still do. With Andreas Malm, Herodotus would ask, "Have humans constructed it or not?"[5] *Nomoi* consist of practices that human beings undertake; with *nomoi* human beings can reinforce the world they've made or make it anew. *Nomoi* provide hope in an increasingly uninhabitable world that human beings could do otherwise.

Nomoi in the World of Things

While studies of Herodotus's political thought are sparse, nearly all focus on the so-called "Constitutional Debate"[6] in book 3 of the *Histories*.[7] Book 3 continues the exploits of Cambyses following book 2's excursions to Egypt. Cambyses soon dies, however, creating a power vacuum. In the Constitutional Debate, Herodotus transcribes a discussion he purports took place among a group of seven Persian elites after they had taken power from a usurping group, the Magi, whose reign began just as Cambyses, son of Cyrus, died of a self-inflicted wound to the leg. After the seven defeated the Magi, they gathered to debate how to rule. Three Persians argued for a democracy, oligarchy, and monarchy, respectively, as the new political order they should adopt. For many interpreters, these arguments offer the first comparative approach to political regimes in ancient Greek political thought.[8] They also anticipate many of the key concepts and arguments that would take root and flower in the centuries to follow.[9]

Herodotus's presentation of the debate does not clearly favor one particular regime. Although some commentators have taken Herodotus's treatment of democracy as showing his regard for it as the most choice-worthy regime,[10] both the particular moment of the narrative and its place within the whole of Herodotus's *Histories* resist such a view. Herodotus illuminates the various conventions and contingencies that make different political regimes possible and desirable. Combining interrelated and interdependent physical, intellectual, and cultural factors to show the appropriate political regime for a given situation, Herodotus develops a view of the political regime as always situated within and in responsive interaction with a dynamic world of things.

In the first of the speeches, the Persian noble Otanes introduces democracy with a flourish: the rule of the many, he says, has the fairest of names—*isonomia*. *Isonomia* might best be translated "equality of law."[11] Everyone makes the law and everyone is subject to it:

What about majority rule, on the other hand? In the first place, it has the best
of all names to describe it—*isonomia*. In the second place, it is entirely free
of the vices of monarchy. It is government by lot, it is accountable government, and it refers all decisions to the common people. So I propose that we
abandon monarchy and increase the power of the people, because everything
depends on their numbers. (3.80)[12]

Otanes elaborates the meaning of *isonomia* through its three constituent parts:
rule by lot, accountability procedures, and making all resolutions refer to the
public.

While Otanes speaks as a Persian, these three components of a regime
took fullest form in the Athens of Herodotus's day.[13] "Rule by lot" meant that
nearly all political offices were filled by lotteries. As a result, there were no
strong institutional identities; governments were stable for only short periods, usually no longer than a year, with iteration in office relatively rare.[14] The
agenda-setting Council of 500 was filled by lot, the administration of law was
in the hands of the People's Courts (chosen by lot), and juries had extensive
discretionary scope.[15] Accountability procedures meant that all government
officials were required to give an account of their tenure both before (*doki-
masia*) and after (*euthunai*) their terms of office.[16] They were also liable to recall and punishment (*eisangelia*). Orators could be held to account for advice
through other laws (*graphê paranomôn*). All resolutions referred to the public: each of these measures lay within the power of the people as embodied in
the Assembly (*ekklêsia*) and the law courts (*dikasteria*).

Otanes's allusions to Athens also bespeak the contingency of the Athenian
democracy—and of successful democracies more generally. At this point in
the narrative, Herodotus has already narrated many stories about how Athens
became Athens. Its distinct topography, including coast, plains, and hills, created the possibility for three different factions (1.59). When these came into
conflict, Pisistratus, the famous Athenian tyrant, took power in large part because of his ability to trick the Athenians using their own customs. In one of
these instances, Pisistratus returned from having been driven out of power by
dressing a tall and strikingly beautiful woman in a full suit of armor, placing
her in a chariot, and declaring that Athena herself was bringing Pisistratus
home to her acropolis (1.60). The Athenian democracy came about only once
the Pisistratidae were overthrown, a defeat instigated by the chance event of
the capture of their children, which threw them into such confusion that they
were forced to accept terms (5.65). Cleisthenes, who emerged as the leader
after the Pisistratidae were deposed, enlisted the common people in the creation of the organizational structure that became emblematic of democracy.

The example of Athens suggests the accidents and contingencies that inform any particular regime. Indeed, *isonomia*, the word Otanes uses to describe democracy, does not necessarily equate with the democratic institutions Otanes lists.[17] Equality of law could well exist within an oligarchical regime: power is distributed in the state on the basis of equality, yet the authority to issue law and be bound by it could well exist in representative systems with strong executives, as many modern political regimes demonstrate. When Otanes concludes that "everything . . . is contained within the multitude," this points to the indeterminate nature of democracy. Majority rule, *isonomia*, rule by lot, accountability procedures, and popular sovereignty name components that may or may not be sufficient. Herodotus makes his readers extraordinarily aware of the particular conditions that create a democracy as well as the paradoxes involved. Athenian democracy arose in a dynamic ecology of geography, history, personality, and contingency.

The subsequent speech by Megabyzus responds directly to Otanes's claims about *isonomia* and the multitude. This speech ostensibly advocates an oligarchy, yet much of it focuses on the negative aspects of empowering the people (*dêmos*). The people cannot be easily subdued, let alone directed or governed. They are like "a stream swollen in the winter," overflowing all boundaries and swamping all political control.[18] They lack education and have never seen anything good or decent. Let the enemies of Persia be ruled by democracies, Megabyzus declares. The Persians themselves should choose the best men to rule.

This speech is full of critiques of democracy common during the fifth century BCE, and many commentators pass over this speech to focus on Darius's. Yet the choice of language here is important. The image of a stream swollen in winter is Homeric. It describes the irresistible vehemence of heroes, and Theognis employs it to indicate the overflowing, impulsive mass of people.[19] With this metaphor, Megabyzus invokes a broader sociological phenomenon: Megabyzus describes the *nature* of crowds.

Megabyzus's claim about crowds has support elsewhere in the *Histories*. One of the first acts of Athens as a democracy is to punish and enslave the neighboring Boeotians and Chalcidians for aiding Cleomenes in his attack against them (5.77); Athenian democracy seems not to extend respect for the *dêmos* to others. Nor is the Athenian *dêmos* predictable: I have already recounted the story of the Athenians' being tricked by Pisistratus; Herodotus offers a corresponding story later, describing how the Athenians fell for the claims of Aristagoras of Miletus when he inveigled them to join the Ionian revolt against the Persians. Herodotus comments: "This seems to suggest . . . that a crowd [*pollous*] is more easily fooled than a single man" (5.97). Even the Persians, who with Cyrus can collectively preserve their status as rulers (9.122; discussed further later in this chapter), also hold that rule by one man is necessary to drive people past their natural inclinations (7.103). Herodotus raises the question of the nature of crowds but doesn't answer how they can be directed or their actions predicted.

The metaphor of the swollen stream suggests a *natural* tendency, one that can perhaps be diked or dammed but only so far. At the foundation of Megabyzus's argument for an oligarchy, then, stands the idea that this structure would provide the most effective crowd control. The Constitutional Debate is an oligarchy already in action. The best men deliberate and vote on the proper course to take. There's no consideration of what the Persians in general think or of rivalries within the group. And the assembled seven arrive at an acceptable answer that allows the Persian Empire to survive.

Darius speaks after Otanes and Megabyzus. His speech builds on the diverse variables introduced by the previous speakers by adding another dimension: history. "Where does freedom come from?" asks Darius after he has argued for the inevitability of monarchy. Answering his own question, Darius points to the founder of the Persian Empire, Cyrus, who freed the Persians from the Medes. The *nomos* of the Persians is monarchy. Ignoring the criticisms of Otanes and Megabyzus, Darius indicates the particular appropriateness of this regime for the Persians. It is the ancestral tradition and the source of their freedom.

Alongside his praise of monarchy for Persia, Darius introduces a *historical* argument that considers contingency—namely, that regimes change with time, despite commitments otherwise. The Constitutional Debate as a whole illustrates the importance of historical contingency: Otanes's speech alludes to the Athenians, who had only recently freed themselves from a tyrant; Megabyzus observes the inherent fickleness of the people, which Herodotus notes throughout the *Histories*; Darius warns against introducing more contingency through rapid innovation. Taken all together, the Constitutional Debate creates a moment of potential discontinuity when the assembled consider a radical change to their customs of governance. Although Darius's argument succeeds, Herodotus's attention to contingency suggests that it could have been otherwise.

The Constitutional Debate itself puts the contingencies that shape political reflection on display. In the mouths of Otanes, Megabyzus, and Darius, the regime categories appear much less separable in practice than in theory. As the narrative continues, Otanes loses the appearance of a committed democrat. When his proposal is not selected by the seven, he withdraws from participation, in effect refusing to "rule and be ruled in turn"; later, Darius calls on Otanes to command the invasion of Samos, where Otanes orders the massacre of the Samians, disobeying Darius's instructions (3.141, 3.147). Although Megabyzus disappears from the proceeding narrative, Darius's trickery wins him the kingship, undercutting the conventions by which they had agreed to decide the future ruler but also emphasizing again the contingencies involved in creating any political regime.

Translating *Nomos*

On my reading, the story of the Constitutional Debate in Herodotus limns an approach to *nomoi* that neither opposes them to a stable *physis*, or nature, nor sees them as completely determined by that nature. Herodotus insists that humans can act; at the same time, however, the world of things exceeds the boundaries of the human and demands a chastened view of what can be accomplished by human action. The ingredients of a political regime include apparently natural phenomena (such as the nature of crowds) as well as contingencies (such as Darius's successful plot to win the kingship). Herodotus's presentation, moreover, suggests that different *nomoi* could obtain if the arguments had gone otherwise. Otanes's decision to exclude himself from the regime further indicates that multiple constitutions could serve the Persians well.

Viewed more broadly across the *Histories*, *nomos* in Herodotus is various and multiple. Herodotus stands poised between the polarizing thought of the Sophists, who pitted *nomos* against *physis*; the often deterministic approach of the Hippocratic writers, who saw *nomos* as a product of environment; and the codification and formalization of *nomos* as a law, which began in earnest during Herodotus's time of writing.[20] Each of these concurrent developments appears reflected in Herodotus's usage of the term *nomos*, and surveying the twists and turns via three possible translations of the word helps to place and comprehend the general features of *nomos* in the *Histories*. *Nomos* can be translated as "law," "custom," and "culture"; studying how each captures aspects of *nomoi* in the *Histories* illuminates their deeper logic and thus how the practice of *nomoi* can take different forms.[21]

NOMOS AS LAW

While acknowledging that *nomos* did not always denote something like "law," Martin Ostwald has argued that Cleisthenes introduced a significant and definitive change to *nomos* when Athens became a democracy. Prior to Cleisthenes, *nomos* was merely descriptive, stating the "traditional form or customary pattern" followed by a given practice without accounting for that practice's origins.[22] This changed when Cleisthenes used the term *nomos* instead of *thesmos* as the official term for "statute": the general name for social norm took on the meaning of law; *nomos* now gained a prescriptive and not just a descriptive meaning.[23]

Although Ostwald's account has provoked response,[24] the sense of *nomos* as an enacted law with both descriptive and prescriptive force has a place in Herodotus's usage. Herodotus recognizes Solon for making the *nomoi* of the Athenians, laws that he put in place for the Athenians at their request. Solon then went abroad for ten years, during which time the Athenians vowed to abide by these same *nomoi* (1.29). Although Solon referred to these laws as *thesmoi* rather than *nomoi* in his poems,[25] by calling them *nomoi* Herodotus connects this legislative activity with the other senses of *nomos* in the *Histories*.[26]

Herodotus also uses *nomos* to describe the reforms in Sparta initiated by Lycurgus. Before Lycurgus, the Spartans experienced the worst *nomoi* (*kakonomotatoi*, 1.65) of nearly all the Hellenes. The conversion to good *nomoi* (*eunomien*, 1.65) occurred when Lycurgus went to the oracle at Delphi and the Pythia spontaneously proclaimed him a god. Some say, Herodotus reports, that the Pythia then dictated the laws to him; the Lacedaemonians say, however, that Lycurgus brought these new institutions from Crete and implemented them in place of the old. Herodotus comments: "Having changed all the institutions, he was careful to see that the new rules and precepts would not be violated" (1.65). Once put in place, these *nomoi* needed protection much as they did for Solon. The example of Lycurgus thus shows, as Ostwald puts it, "the enactment of *nomoi* in the political sense of 'statutes' or 'regulations.'"[27] Moreover, Herodotus declares that the entire political and social order of Sparta prevalent in his own time stemmed from Lycurgus's reform of *nomoi* as law.[28]

NOMOS AS CUSTOM

Yet while *nomos* carries the sense of law in these instances, it more frequently denotes something less precise and more diffuse. When Herodotus quotes Pindar that "*nomos* is king," Donald Lateiner argues that something like "custom" is meant—and, moreover, that Herodotus means to promote a relativistic approach to custom.[29] Lauren Apfel describes how the *Histories* offers a "Herodotean bazaar" of customs, the presentation of which suggests an incipient pluralism: Herodotus recognizes a "fundamental diversity" in the world; his inquiry allows him to map the many-colored nature of *nomoi*.[30]

As "custom," then, *nomos* describes various, usually informal practices and habits seemingly inherent to the different peoples that Herodotus surveys.

When Herodotus quotes Pindar, the broader context informs a translation of *nomos* as "custom" and not simply "law" in the more positivistic sense described earlier.[31] Before his downfall and death, Cambyses returns to Memphis after retreating from an unsuccessful campaign in Ethiopia. There he observes the Egyptians celebrating and believes they are rejoicing at his miserable failure. He asks the celebrants the reason for their festivities, and they try to explain that they honor the epiphany of Apis. Cambyses refuses to believe them and asserts that they are lying and will be put to death. Not only does Cambyses kill them, but he summons the priests to bring him Apis—"a calf born of a cow which can then no longer conceive any more calves" (3.28)—and stabs it with his dagger in the thigh, laughing at the priests and the other Egyptians. As Herodotus reports: "The Egyptians say that right after this incident, Cambyses went completely insane because of his crime, though he had not been entirely in his right mind before, either" (3.30). Indeed, Herodotus recounts other deeds testifying to his madness, all of which involve heedless violation of *nomoi*: having his brother murdered; marrying one of his sisters and murdering the younger one; killing his honored servant Prexaspes's son; attempting to assassinate Croesus; and mocking and deriding the cult statue in the sanctuary of Hephaestus. After this list, Herodotus sums up:

> I am convinced by all the evidence that Cambyses was seriously deranged. Otherwise he would not have endeavored to mock what is sacred and customary. For if someone were to assign to every person in the world the task of selecting the best of all customs, each one, after thorough consideration, would choose those of his own people, so strongly do humans believe that their own customs are the best ones. Therefore only a madman would treat such things as a laughing matter. (3.38)

To adduce further proof, Herodotus tells the story of Darius's summoning of the Hellenes and the Indians to his court to ask them how much money they would take to eat and burn the bodies of their dead, respectively. Each group refuses, the one with silence and the other with outcry, denying that they would ever do such a thing. Herodotus concludes:

> Well, then, that is how people think, and so it seems to me that Pindar was right when he said in his poetry that *nomos* is king of all. (3.38)

Nomos here describes a diverse set of rules, conventions, observances, habits, and policies. Many of Herodotus's other uses of *nomos* fall under this meaning:

wearing hair long (1.82); not believing the gods have human qualities (1.131); considering an animal unclean if it has a single black hair (2.38); not acquiring or keeping houses (3.100); regarding the absence of thunder in winter with amazement and considering it a portent (4.28); drinking only from vessels made in their own lands (5.88); naming as king the elder son of the deceased king (6.52); appointing the king's successor before going to war (7.2); identifying certain deeds as ungodly (8.106); and joining battle without first performing sacrifices (9.41). Herodotus treats these and other examples of *nomoi* as peculiar and interesting, if idiosyncratic, practices of the peoples he observes and tells stories about. Unlike laws, these do not result from specific enactments. Unlike cultures, as I detail below, they do not fit into larger coherent patterns.

NOMOS AS CULTURE

Understanding *nomos* as custom does not, therefore, obviate all critical evaluation of these *nomoi* and their suitability. As Donald Lateiner puts it, "the arbitrariness and diversity of *nomoi* do not themselves invalidate them . . . because each set functions admirably for its community."[32] This translation of *nomos* moves in the direction of "culture" and away from "custom." "Culture" suggests a certain regularity and pattern to a set of customs, a discernible logic beneath the appearance of diversity. If the sense of *nomos* as infinitely variable custom shows Herodotus's affinities with the Sophists, translating *nomos* as "culture" highlights Herodotus's closeness to the Hippocratic writers.

As culture, *nomos* cannot assume infinite variety; it arises in relationship to a particular place and people.[33] "Culture" is more organic than "custom"; it cannot be adopted arbitrarily. Perhaps the most famous example in Herodotus comes in the episode involving Demaratus and Xerxes late in the narrative of the *Histories*. Xerxes succeeds Darius and continues his aggressions against the Greeks. Demaratus is a former king of Sparta who fled to Persia after failing to secure the throne. Anticipating his invasion, Xerxes asks Demaratus if the Hellenes will submit or resist. Demaratus replies:

> In Hellas, poverty [*peniê*] is always and forever a native resident, while excellence [*aretê*] is something acquired through intelligence and the force of strict law [*apo te sophiês katergasmenê kai nomou ischurou*]. It is through the exercise of this excellence that Hellas wards off both poverty and despotism. (7.102)

This short passage contains multiple registers. First, Demaratus alludes to the power of environment, describing how "poverty" (*peniê*) always abides with the Hellenes. This might suggest weakness and a lack of resources, but Demaratus juxtaposes this with the cultured practice of excellence (*aretê*), which counterbalances poverty's destructive pressures as well as the threat of despotism. *Peniê* means you must work for your living and brings with it the threat of debasement; however, the culture of the Hellenes has created the conditions for such work to elevate them to excellence. The concept of *nomos* joins virtue (*aretê*) and freedom from despotism. Virtue preserves freedom by promoting the best embrace of the laws. This freedom thus depends on a particular set of factors: the environmental determinants as well as the interactive cultural response that can be developed to achieve virtue.

As culture, *nomos* is shaped by environment while also being an anthropogenic response to it. *Nomos* names the practices developed through interactive responses of humans and nonhumans: influences, conditions, and so forth. Unlike the Hippocratics, however, Herodotus does not see environment as determinative. As Rosalind Thomas puts it, "There is a complex interplay . . . between physical environment and *nomoi*, customs or laws, but at every stage *nomos* is crucial."[34] Returning to the discussion of Demaratus and Xerxes, notice that there are terms of both nature and culture: the poverty of the Hellenes stems from their natural environment as well as their *nomoi*; the Hellenes' superiority does not, then, appear unchangeable. This fits what Albrecht Dihle calls "Ionian ethnography" and the more Sophistic view with which Herodotus ends.[35] *Nomos* affects all the Hellenes; it does not merely describe a custom they have adopted. "The simple environmental explanation (poverty of land, poverty of spirit) is deliberately put in second place," Thomas writes "next to the humanly constituted *nomoi* of the Spartan life-style."[36]

The Practice of *Nomos*

The different translations of *nomos* as "law," "custom," and "culture" can make it appear as if the *Histories* lacks coherence. Yet one important common thread unites these meanings of *nomos*: they depend upon the practice of those living with them; *nomoi*, in other words, exist insofar as they are actively taken up by people.[37] Expansive and rather nebulous as a term, *nomos* captures both the written laws physically inscribed on stelae as well as the principles or beliefs according to which one acts. Yet for Herodotus, *nomoi* are never merely beliefs or ideas but always materialized in practices: a social order exists as a cosmos of material artifacts; it lives as its constituent agents sustain or modify it. Thus, while a *nomos* was something held as an idea, it was also "something that did not easily change."[38] *Nomoi* depend on reiteration yet are also substantial such that people act "according to *nomoi*" (*kata nomous*), "make *nomoi*" (*nomous poiousi*), and practice *nomoi* (*nomoisi chreontai*).[39]

"Change of specific customs (*metabolê*)," writes Henry Immerwahr, "is of particular interest to Herodotus."[40] The "Battle of the Champions" between the Spartans and the Argives over Thyrea explains why Argives always cut their hair short while the Spartans let theirs grow long (1.82). Or Cyrus follows Croesus's advice about turning the Lydians into shopkeepers and changes the Lydians' customs through force (1.55). Whereas previous translations of *nomoi* see these laws, customs, and cultures in synchronic terms, seeing *nomoi* as practice highlights how Herodotus explains *nomoi* in diachronic terms, showing the processes that produce and change *nomoi* across time.[41] Ethnography is closely integrated with history; *nomoi* provide a key to understanding the logic of change integral to law, custom, and culture.[42]

Herodotus remarks on the *nomoi* of countless nations and peoples, but the most extended inquiry into *nomoi*, one that illustrates how practice across time is fundamental to an understanding of *nomoi*, comes with the story of the Persians, which spans the whole of the *Histories*—from Cyrus to Cambyses to Darius to Xerxes. The example of the Persians highlights how *nomoi* exist through practice, that *nomoi* are not a passive environment so much as the substance of the expression of a people. *Nomoi* provide the basis for collective power, yet *nomoi* can also become alienated from the people when tyrants attempt to control them. Herodotus favors *nomoi* that preserve collective power and shows through his account of the Persians how once emancipatory *nomoi* can decline and vitiate the power they first constituted.

Herodotus calls attention to the overall change of Persian *nomoi* by inserting a story about Cyrus—the progenitor of the Persian Empire—in book 9, at the very end of the *Histories* after the Persians have suffered definitive defeat four generations following Cyrus's death. This final pendant of the *Histories* recounts an exchange between Artembares, an eminent Persian, and Cyrus about the former's proposal to emigrate from the country they inhabited at the time—which he describes as "small and rugged"—and to take over "somewhere better." Cyrus is not impressed with the proposal, telling the Persians to go ahead but to be prepared to become subjects instead of rulers on the grounds that "soft lands tend to breed soft men" (*phileein gar ek tôn malakôn chôrôn malakous andras ginesthai*). "It is impossible, he said, for one and the same country to produce remarkable crops and good fighting men" (9.122). The Persians admitted the truth of Cyrus's argument, and as Herodotus writes: "they chose to live in a harsh land and rule rather than to cultivate fertile plains and be others' slaves."

Back in book 1, Herodotus describes how Cyrus initiates the Persians' liberation in a way that anticipates the final story of the *Histories* and its emphasis on the practice of *nomoi*. While the Persians are still subjected to the

Medes, Cyrus convenes an assembly of the Persians and first has them clear
and prepare for cultivation a tract of wild land covered with thornbushes.
After they have done this, Cyrus then orders them to come back the next day,
bathed and refreshed; upon their return Cyrus provides a feast for them as
they recline in a meadow. Cyrus asks them which day they prefer, and they
declare the first day terrible but the next one pleasant and good. Cyrus then
discloses his plan:

> "Men of Persia," he said, "listen to me: obey my orders, and you will be able to
> enjoy a thousand pleasures as good as this without ever turning your hands
> to servile labour; but, if you disobey, yesterday's task will be the pattern of in-
> numerable others you will be forced to perform. Take my advice and win your
> freedom." (1.126)[43]

Although Cyrus asks that the Persians heed him, he appeals to their collective
judgment—to take his advice and win their freedom. Cyrus's persuasiveness
depends on this judgment (which itself depends on their experience); at this
point he stands only as a potential liberator, powerless except for his rhetoric.
The Persians respond with collective affirmation, welcoming "with enthusi-
asm the prospect of liberty."

The final pendant in book 9 of the *Histories* thus calls attention to the collective affirmation of *nomoi* described in book 1 while also showing the great shifts
the Persians have undergone in the generations since their liberation. Collective power realized through *nomoi* has declined as tyrannical autocrats have asserted control over the laws, customs, and culture of the Persians. The Persians
during Cyrus's time protect their freedom by opposing potential enslavers, yet
they do not develop *nomoi* that encourage their own power. Although Cyrus
appeals to the people and persuades them to free themselves, neither he nor the
people create any institutions to support the recurrence of this persuasion and
collective decision-making. When the Persian Empire grows and subsequent
leaders use force to weaken the collective power of the Persian people to practice their *nomoi*, the freedom this facilitated declines. Once unbridled from
collective nomistic practices, tyrants can violate *nomoi* at will. For example,
Herodotus describes how before Cambyses fell in love with his sister it was not
at all the custom of Persians to live with their sisters. Wanting to marry his sister, however, Cambyses insisted that the royal judges discover a law that would
allow it. The tyrant's act perverts the *nomos* and arrogates influence over *nomoi*
to the monarch and away from the collective power of the people (3.31).

The juxtaposition of Cambyses's violations of the collectively established
nomoi and the Constitutional Debate illuminates how the latter crystallizes a
moment between a time when Persian *nomoi* retained their relevance and the

period of their decline. The Constitutional Debate presents would-be rulers' radical views of the malleability of *nomoi*. No proposal discusses the readiness of the Persian people to accept any given form of rule or their desire for participating in rule if such participation were demanded. When the governing *nomoi* are undermined, as was the case under Cambyses, then the contingency of—and human agency behind—*nomoi* become apparent. This also opens up the possibility that rulers like Cambyses can violate *nomoi* and thus destroy the freedom won through collective work like that spearheaded by Cyrus.

The assumptions within the Constitutional Debate prove all the more surprising because of their contrast with the accounts Herodotus gives of the development of the political regimes in Athens and Sparta, respectively. In both of these stories (which are told in book 1), Athenians and Spartans take up and sustain the new *nomoi* introduced by lawgivers. When seen as a contrast to Herodotus's discussions of *nomoi* and people, the perspective adopted by the participants in the Constitutional Debate is more like Cambyses's deranged disregard of customs than it may have first appeared. Like Cambyses, the participants in the debate largely ignore previous *nomoi*; like Cambyses, they also presume that the *nomoi* they wish to create should (and will) become the *nomoi* of the land. (It may well be most accurate to say that tyrants threaten *nomoi* entirely: their unpredictability and willingness to violate the customs of the land, including their own, bespeak a dangerous rejection of the conditions and substance of *nomoi*. Collective power cannot sustain such tyrannical onslaughts.) The speeches in favor of rule of the majority and oligarchy proceed abstractly. Only Darius's speech advocating monarchy refers to previous *nomoi*. While Otanes mentions the outrageous arrogance of Cambyses as a reason not to adopt a monarchy, he does not speak to the desire of the Persian people for participating in a democracy (3.80). When Megabyzus criticizes Otanes's position, he asserts that "nothing can be both more unintelligent or insolent than the worthless, ineffectual mob" (3.81)—but without any reference to the Persians. (I wonder: would Cyrus have referred to his fellow Persians as "the mob"?) Darius's speech is the one that speaks most from the context of the Persian Empire, noting that their freedoms came from the monarchical form that Cyrus had adopted (3.82):

> Well, then, in my opinion, since we were freed by one man, we should preserve that form of government. Moreover, we should not let go of our ancestral traditions, which are fine just as they are, for that would not be the better course. (3.82)

Darius thus advocates respect for *nomoi*, conserving the authority they already have for reasons of their past success. Yet paradoxically, Darius retells the story of Persian freedom as the triumph of a single man—Cyrus—rather than as a collective act of the Persians. As if to confirm this interpretation, once the seven have voted for Darius's proposal—a procedure that is itself dissonant with Persian *nomoi*—the people are never consulted. They are instead subjected to him: "The power of Darius pervaded everything and everywhere in his realm" (3.88).

Following their liberation with the help of Cyrus, however, the Persians can no longer affirm their *nomoi*. While Darius claims the need to respect *nomoi*, he positions himself as a tyrant accountable to no one. The debate among Darius, Megabyzus, and Otanes continues the tyrannical approach to *nomoi* begun with Cambyses; the explicit contrast between Xerxes, the latest instantiation of this tyranny, and the pendant story of Cyrus and Artembares at the end of the *Histories* serves to remind readers of the collective power enabled by *nomoi* that the Persians have lost. The Persian narrative thus raises the question of what kind of political order can sustain *nomos* as *basileus* and the power it promises.

Equalizing Politics

These different accounts of *nomoi* in the *Histories* illuminate how the variety of *nomoi* within the *Histories* also figures a variety of political formations. While collective power arises under political conditions of cooperation, this cooperation has different textures and inflections depending on the *nomoi* of the inhabitants. The *nomoi* of the Persians permit a king; the *nomoi* of the Egyptians that Cambyses violates require the sanctity of bulls; the *nomoi* of the Lacedaemonians demand obedience unmatched by the Athenians. Although Herodotus revels in the differences among all these *nomoi*, a logic unites the *nomoi* of the Persians, the Egyptians, and the Hellenes: collective power depends upon the common practice of *nomoi*.[44] In the examples discussed so far, both the Persians and the Hellenes show how this power requires collective practice of *nomoi* and how various *nomoi* can either sustain such power or vitiate it. The Persians liberate themselves with Cyrus yet do not create *nomoi* to support their own freedom. The Spartans, by contrast, create *nomoi* that they freely choose to obey and thus maintain their collective power.

In addition to this pluralistic approach to *nomoi* that looks beyond any particular Greek *polis* as the only form of political organization, the *Histories* introduces a particular temper of political practice that explains the flourishing of a given regime: equality.[45] Equality takes various forms, which Herodotus calls *isonomia*, *isêgoria*, and *isokratia*. These provide organizing principles for political communities, ways of expressing (and criticizing) what Josiah Ober calls the people's "capacity to do things."[46] Herodotus's pluralistic approach broadens the political formations that may realize equality, yet he also points to the superiority of particular formations of equality for creating and sustaining collective power. Political communities flourish when constituted with attention to equality even while their constitutive *nomoi* can vary; however, the equal power (*isokratia*) and equal speech (*isêgoria*) of the Athenians appear to provide the best arrangement of *nomoi* for maintaining collective power.

The differences among *isonomia*, *isokratia*, and *isêgoria* express subtle variations in Herodotus's approach to equalizing politics. Of these three, *isonomia* has received the most attention. The predominance of *isonomia* has led some researchers to ignore the fine gradations between this concept and Herodotus's discussions of *isokratia* and *isêgoria*. But as I show in what follows, these distinctions are vital for illuminating how equality can function in different regimes and thus how regimes made up of different *nomoi* can express collective power in similar forms yet through diverse content.

Isonomia characterizes, first of all, an opposition to tyranny, but as Gregory Vlastos and other commentators have pointed out, opposition to tyranny captures only one-half of *isonomia*.[47] *Isonomia* also involves "equality of law," as the second part of the compound, *nomia* from *nomos*, indicates. The importance of *isonomia* for understanding Herodotus's possible political teaching appears in the various structures it entails, the different formations of *nomos*. The resulting variety affords different instruments of political prophylaxis against future tyranny.

As Vlastos has noted, *isonomia* emerged from pre-Socratic reflections on justice and equality in the cosmos.[48] This background sense can inform consideration of the role of equality in Herodotus's treatment of *nomoi*. In the first use of the term, medical writer Alcmaeon defines health as "equality (*isonomia*) of the powers."[49] *Isonomia* thus points to the possibility of equilibrium. The health of the polity depends on a multitude of factors, not all of which lie within the domain of political control or power. Thinkers such as Empedocles, Parmenides, and Anaximander saw natural events united in a common law of *isonomia*: equality can prevent injustice; the earth owes its stability to this equality. For Anaximander, "the boundless itself, being perfectly blended, must be in a state of dynamic equilibrium."[50] *Isonomia* does not prescribe specific actions, yet it provides a metric for maintaining balance and harmony, a rule of equality that can maintain conditions of political flourishing.

Isonomia was a "buzzword" of the Athens contemporary to Herodotus, yet in the *Histories* it does not have positive associations or connotations.[51] After the first mention of *isonomia* in Otanes's speech, it appears twice more in the context of Ionian tyrants: Maeandrius, the man appointed by the tyrant of

Samos, Polykrates, to superintend the territory during his absence; and Aristagoras, the deputy ruler of Miletus who helps incite the Ionian revolt against
the Persians. In both instances, *isonomia* is introduced much as it was proposed by Otanes. And similar to what happened in the Constitutional Debate, *isonomia* does not take root: Maeandrius drops his proposal to institute
isonomia after a townsperson demands an accounting of the money under
his control (3.142); Aristagoras departs after having converted Miletus to what
Herodotus calls "a theoretical state of *isonomia*," but leaves generals in charge;
soon the Ionians have tyrants installed once again (5.37). Combining Otanes's
speech and the narrator's redescription (in terms of *dêmokratia*) of it as well as
these incidents suggests a skeptical view of the term. Although *isonomia* appears in the context of antityrannical speeches and actions as a political order
meant to take the tyranny's place, these examples indicate that *isonomia* names
a political regime much more easily talked about than actually practiced. None
of these regimes lasts. Indeed, *isonomia* never really exists in the *Histories*.[52]

But *isonomia* is not the only principle of equality in the *Histories*. Just
as different situations support various *nomoi*, equality as a *nomos* varies in
Herodotus's account. According to the language of the *Histories*, the Athenian
democracy is not *isonomic*.[53] "Herodotus never spoke of Athenian *isonomia*,"
Mogens Hansen observes.[54] *Isonomia* is used only in Otanes's speech and in
the accounts of the efforts of Maeandrius and Aristagoras. Instead, the Athenian democracy following Cleisthenes's reforms has its own corresponding
language of equality: equal voice (*isêgoria*) and equal power (*isokratia*). The
differences among these *iso-* compounds illuminate important distinctions
among the qualities of collective power depicted in the *Histories* as well as how
this power can come into being.

After the Athenians free themselves from their tyrants, Herodotus explains
their strength in terms of *isêgoria*:

> Thus Athens went from strength to strength, and proved, if proof were needed,
> how noble a thing equality before the law [*isêgoriê*] is, not in one respect only,
> but in all. (5.78)

This sole use of *isêgoria* in the entire *Histories* seems worthy of notice, but
few commentators have examined it.[55] The logic of *isêgoria* appears different
in important respects from that of *isonomia*. The emphasis is not on something institutionalized but rather a broader political culture: according to the
context of Herodotus's usage, *isêgoria* creates the conditions where everyone
strives for what is best for himself, with the assumed reward being theirs; yet
while each pursues his own cause, this leads to the strength of the whole. Unlike *isonomia*, *isêgoria* is not instituted; Herodotus does not use the typical

language of institution or dissolution (which does arise when he describes *isokratia*) but instead invokes *isêgoria* as a general, abstract term. *Isêgoria* displays itself in the activity and accomplishments of the Athenians, unlike the noble-sounding principle of *isonomia*, which appears unconnected with concrete political acts. *Isêgoria* refers to the agora where the Athenians transact their daily business; it stems from the mundane activities of democratic life.

Although there is no obvious logical connection between *isêgoria* and the defeat of the Boeotians and Chalcidians,[56] Herodotus notes that the proof of *isêgoria*'s strength comes in all respects. The military victories offer only one piece of evidence among many possible examples of support. The context of this assertion shows another, broader set of reasons why *isêgoria* supports collective power: namely, the Athenian people's ability to gather and respond to urgent matters. After Cleisthenes has enlisted the people, he retires from the city of his own accord. Cleomenes, the Spartan king intent on restoring the tyranny, marches into the city. Banishing seven hundred Athenian households specified by Isagoras (the would-be tyrant of Athens), Cleomenes seeks to dissolve the Council and place powers in Isagoras and his three hundred partisans. But the council resists, and when Cleomenes occupies the Acropolis, the whole of Athens unites against them (5.72). This event amounts to a reinstallation of the democracy but without a specific leader standing behind it. Just as the passage praising *isêgoria* notes how the Athenians were previously in servitude, their expelling of Cleomenes and his Spartans contrasts with the inability of the Athenians to respond coherently against previous tyrants such as Pisistratus, who triple-duped them to gain his power (1.59–64). Perhaps the Athenians learned something in the intervening years. The Athenians at the moment when Herodotus praises their *isêgoria* have proven their ability to rule themselves; they have asserted a more robust collective power; and they have accomplished this through equal participation in public life by seemingly all parties. *Isêgoria* denotes equality to participate in public life; its strength lies in the collective power it unleashes. As Yoshio Nakategawa puts it, "The most important characteristic of *isêgoria* consists in rousing a sense of community, a sense that the Polis is not a tyrant's possession but every citizen's own property."[57]

Herodotus introduces another name for its equality: *isokratia*. As I recounted earlier, when the Athenians free themselves from their tyrants, they demonstrate their strength with immediate conquests of the Boeotians and the Chalcidians. The Spartans begin to wish to restore the Athenian tyranny lest the Athenians come to match their own strength and influence. To discuss this, the Spartans summon their allies, and Socleas, a Corinthian, speaks against the restoration:

"Upon my word, gentlemen," he exclaimed, "this is like turning the universe upside-down. Earth and sky will soon be changing places—men will be living in the sea and fish on land, now that you Spartans are proposing to abolish popular government [*isokratias kataluontes*] and restore despotism in the cities. Believe me, there is nothing wickeder or bloodier in the world than tyranny." (5.92)

Socleas proceeds to describe the horrors of the tyranny in Corinth, illustrating his claim against it. Much like *isonomia* and *isêgoria*, *isokratia* is set off in contrast to tyranny. But again Herodotus does not treat these as identical terms.[58] The narrative context suggests an initial distinction: *isokratia* involves not the individual's pursuit of his own cause that redounds to the good of the whole but instead the equal power of each individual that leads to collective strength. *Isêgoria* is the soccer match where each player has an important but different role; *isokratia* is the hoplite army where every man has identical equipment and moves in lockstep. Socleas implies that the Spartans also exemplify this *isokratia*: the Spartans' abolition of *isokratia* would turn the world upside down because this would involve destroying their own principle of political organization and power.[59] Both Athens and Sparta exhibit *isokratia* through the power devolved on individual citizens; this stands in contrast to the concentration of power sought by tyrants.

Socleas's story offers a negative illustration of what *isokratia* involves that also elucidates what arrangement of equality *isokratia* effects. Periander, one of the tyrants Socleas describes, learned his bloody ways from Thrasybulus, the tyrant of Miletus. Periander sent a representative to Thrasybulus to ask his opinion on how best and most safely to govern his city. Inviting the envoy to walk with him from the city to a field where wheat was growing, Thrasybulus conversed with him, asking questions about why he had come while cutting off all the tallest ears of wheat he could see and throwing them away, until the finest and best-grown part of the crop was ruined. The representative returned to Periander with this story of apparent madness, but Periander grasped its meaning immediately: Thrasybulus had recommended murdering all the people in the city who stood above the rest; Periander took the advice and "from that time forward there was no crime against the Corinthians he did not commit" (5.92).

Isokratia, this story seems to suggest, involves planting a field where no wheat grows taller than the rest. Before genetically modified crops, this might seem impossible, but here the analogy breaks down: specific educational regimes can create such conditions, as the Spartans demonstrate; the customs and culture (or *nomoi*), in other words, can sustain equality and prevent a Periander from ever arising.[60] Croesus's advice to Cyrus back in book 1 about what to do with the rebellious Lydians offers a complementary example: turning them into shopkeepers, Croesus recommends, puts them all on an equal level of commerce and exchange. None will distinguish himself by attaining political power because none will pursue it in the first place. Ironically, this can create conditions ripe for tyranny from the outside even while it prevents it from within.[61]

Socleas's likening of Athens, Corinth, and Sparta indicates that *isokratia* does not belong solely to democracy, since each of these *poleis* differs slightly from the other.[62] Corinth's form of equality was not as open as Athenian *isêgoria* appears to have been.[63] After the fall of the Cypselids, the Corinthians instituted a board of eight *probouloi*, or advisers, and created a council. This allowed for people to participate in deliberation with equal strength to the board of *probouloi*. Sparta possessed a similar structure, with its provisions for a *gerousia* of thirty men, including the two kings, and a popular assembly. The Athenian democracy after the Cleisthenean revolution also balanced a council with an assembly of equal strength. Yet all three shared a predominant bicameral principle of governance. The nomistic institutions persisted—oligarchic in the case of Corinth and Sparta, democratic in the case of Athens—and *isokratia* tempered these toward equitable balance that allowed for collective power.

Herodotus's other usage of *isokratia* in the *Histories* adds another layer to this analysis. Surveying the customs of the Issedones, one of the distant tribes in the Scythian region, Herodotus describes them as practicing *isokratia*:

> Issedonian customs are said to be as follows. When a man's father dies, all his relatives bring livestock to his house. They sacrifice the animals and chop the meat up into pieces—and then they also chop up their host's dead father, mix all the meats together, and serve them up as a special meal. What they do to the head, though, is pluck all the hair off, clean it out, and then gild it. Then they treat it as if it were a cult statue, in the sense that the dead man's son offers it magnificent sacrifices once a year, just as in Greece sons commemorate the anniversary of their father's death. In other respects, however, the Issedones too are said to be a moral people, and women have as much power as men in their society [*Allôs de dikaioi kai houtoi legontai einai, isokratees de homoiôs hai gunaikes toisi andrasi*]. (4.26)

The absence of any other information about the Issedones' governance makes comparison to Athens, Corinth, and Sparta on this dimension impossible, but it is nonetheless a remarkable moment. Herodotus emphasizes equality of men and women in a way that resonates throughout the *Histories* and connects *isokratia* to *nomoi*. Only their ritual funeral practices single out men. *Nomoi* depend not just on male citizens but are the substance of life for all the people who practice them.[64] From the story of Candaules in book 1 to Xerxes's pursuit of his brother's wife in book 9, Herodotus gives example after example highlighting how men and women cooperate to practice *nomoi* and thus sustain collective power. Although Herodotus does not advance these stories to argue for a symmetrical sharing of political office, his expansive notion of the world of political things means that the activities of women as well as men contribute to the temper of equality.[65] Herodotus's stories of *nomoi* across diverse peoples imply, argues Carolyn Dewald, "that any society functions because of the reciprocity that exists between women and men."[66]

Extrapolating from Herodotus's references can allow for a general understanding of how equality tempers (or might temper) the various political regimes depicted in the *Histories*. Returning to the language of Alcmaeon, equality consists in the yielding and adjustment necessary for maintaining balance. Equality was closely associated with democracy, as Herodotus's redescription of Otanes's speech in these terms indicates (6.43), yet associating equality with a specific regime misses its broader applicability and relevance for considering different political regimes. These are general terms and not particular to the regime type of Athens. Persians, Ionians, Athenians, and Spartans can all have some variety of one of the three, although each has its specific emphasis. *Isonomia* names a principle of political equality; *isêgoria* invokes the need for deliberation and the effectiveness of equal voice in promoting individual efforts for the common weal; the equal power involved in *isokratia* prevents the rise of tyrants while promoting strong collective action. In each of its varieties, equality serves the establishment of collective power by aligning particular *nomoi* with popular participation.

Ecologies of *Nomos*

The reading of the Constitutional Debate with which I began, however, suggests that human beings are not wholly responsible for their *nomoi*. *Nomoi* supporting collective power have the form of a cooperative achievement, but this cooperative achievement takes place in the dynamic world of things (as elaborated in chapter 1), where chance and contingency as well as nonhumans hold great influence. Just as diverse *nomoi* texture the political lives of peoples in various ways, a world of things affects and interacts with these *nomoi*. *Nomoi* cannot be separated from the actants of the world of things; just as nonhuman as well as human things make human life, these actants are the material of which *nomoi* consist. Collective power is not simply a human achievement, because *nomoi* depend on conditions beyond (and below and around) *nomoi*. A few examples discussed already are the poverty of the Persians (which in turn diminishes and threatens their original *nomoi*) as well as the poverty of the Hellenes; the history of relations between Athens and Sparta that leads Cleomenes to intervene on behalf of the Athenians' liberation from tyrants; and the barren lands of the Scythians that facilitate their nomadic freedom.

The survival of the Greeks also depends on the gods. Although Herodotus emphasizes the human practices that create and shape religious rituals and beliefs, he also notes the important role of nonhuman, divine agents. Imagine these as yet-unknown forces coursing through the Anthropocene. Herodotus's attention to these forces appears most famously in his statement about the Greeks' victory over the Persians:

> They [the Athenians] chose that Hellas should survive in freedom; and after rousing to that cause all the other Hellenes who had not medized, they repelled the King with the help of the gods. (7.139)

Herodotus does not name these gods nor describe how the Athenians invited them to help. "The gods" fill explanatory space simply because the Athenians could not have accomplished what they did alone.

Alongside Herodotus's openness to the unpredictable interventions of the gods, he also recognizes the significance of more "natural" causes. An ecological approach to *nomoi* thus highlights how Herodotus draws from his Ionian inheritance by accepting the power and importance of nonhumans in dynamic interaction with humans while maintaining an agnostic openness to the gods' existence and influence. Rosalind Thomas and others show how Herodotus emerged from the context of early Greek science and its concern with the vitality of matter.[67] Herodotus's use of words such as *historiê* and *physis* suggests his "distinctively Ionian Greek connections."[68] In particular, Ionians such as Thales, Anaximander, and Anaximenes brought about "a general increase of awareness and the application of intelligence to things" upon which Herodotus appears to build explicitly.[69]

Like his Ionian counterparts, Herodotus *inquires* into the kinds of materials that form the world. This inquiry reveals the interactions between human *nomoi* and nonhuman ecologies. Herodotus's examination of Egypt provides a useful example: Herodotus begins with the seemingly permanent dimensions such as the soil, the seacoast, the mountains, the Nile, and other topographical features. These features inform "the situation of the Egyptians" (2.14): for example, the ease with which they can grow crops and the agricultural patterns that result. Only after accounting for these elements does Herodotus turn to the *nomoi*—the cultural practices, customs, and laws—of the Egyptians (2.35). Although each aspect of the material world can change, these alterations take place in different ways and on different timescales than the changes wrought by humans (e.g., the silting that forms the Nile Delta occurs over an exceedingly long expanse of time). Herodotus notes that the *nomoi* of a people, in contrast, can change through influence: the Egyptians again and again influence the beliefs and practices of the Greeks and other peoples. The names of the gods came to Hellas from Egypt, for example, although the practice of making statues of Hermes with an erect phallus originated with the Pelasgians (2.50–51).

Herodotus's attention to nonhuman factors goes farther than an appreciation for the formative role of geography. *Nomoi* do not simply "rest" on top of inert environments; instead, the ecologies of *nomoi* are living, dynamic systems, and the natural world is a player in Herodotus's drama. When a violent storm arises to destroy a pair of bridges Xerxes has constructed to bridge the Hellespont for his invasion of Greece, Xerxes responds to this nonhuman power by assigning blame and punishment:

> Xerxes was infuriated when he learned of this; he ordered that the Hellespont was to receive 300 lashes under the whip, and that a pair of shackles was to be dropped into the sea. And I have also heard that he sent others to brand the Hellespont. (7.35)

"Bitter water, your master is imposing this penalty upon you for wronging him even though you had suffered no injustice from him," Xerxes has his men say as they strike the Hellespont. "It is for just cause, after all, that no human offers you sacrifice: you are a turbid and briny river!" (7.35). Herodotus highlights this power of the natural world with a contrasting episode immediately prior to Xerxes's lashing: on the road through Lydia to Sardis, Xerxes discovers a plane tree that so impresses him with its beauty that he endows it with golden ornaments and entrusts it to one of the Immortals, the elite corps of Persian troops, as its guardian (7.31).

Geography also plays a dynamic role in the *Histories*. Anticipating the Syrian conflict with which I began, Xerxes's uncle Artabanus warns him that the land and the sea are his two greatest enemies (7.49). This has both a passive sense and an active sense. These features are impassive obstacles for the Persian forces: try as they might, the massive Persian forces cannot drink all rivers dry (7.21) or divert rivers in their path (7.128). Yet these two features exert active force as well. As the Persian fleet under Mardonius subjugates Greek cities following the Ionian revolt, they sail close to the shore of the mainland up to Acanthus, from which they attempt to round Mount Athos (6.44). Yet as they proceed around the mountain, a strong north wind quickly makes navigation impossible; the wind batters them badly and wrecks about three hundred ships, killing more than twenty thousand men. Suffering these losses as well as more in their victory over the Byrgoi, Mardonios retreats to Persia. Oceans, rivers, mountains, and storms do not just form an environment in the *Histories*; they *act* within the course of history.

Nomoi consist of different repertoires of responsive interaction with nonhuman forces like mountains, oceans, and rivers; the ecologies of *nomoi* thus include all such actors and forces within the domain of the *nomoi*. As Rosalind Thomas notes, a striking feature of early medical and scientific writing was "the combination of interest in nature and in the human world, with theories to link them."[70] Unlike the Hippocratic writers of his era, however, Herodotus does not entertain a unidirectional relationship where climate determines political regime.[71] Herodotus offers a moderated version of this strong materialist thesis. The interaction among human and nonhuman goes all the way down. For Herodotus, human beings are biocultural creatures, in Samantha Frost's illuminating language. The term "encapsulates the mutual constitution of body and environment, of biology and habitat."[72] The Scythians offer an example of what this mutual constitution looks like in the *Histories*.[73] Whereas the Hippocratics treated the Scythians as determined by their climate such that sexual incapacities were regarded as a natural condition, Herodotus avoids attributing the physical character or cultural practices of a people to the climate and geography. As Philip Kaplan writes, Herodotus instead "suggests that their nomadism is a *response* to the geographical conditions of the lands north of the Black Sea, not an inevitable product of those conditions."[74] Yet this response is *interactive*: the Scythians' nomadism means they do not engineer the environment but rather adapt to it, which in turn means also allowing the geographical conditions to evolve with minimal human influence.[75]

The closeness between Herodotus and the contemporary Hippocratic writers is most visible on the question of *nomoi*, and the comparison serves to accent the distinctiveness of Herodotus's ecological approach to *nomoi*. For the Hippocratic author of *Airs, Waters, Places*, geography determines what *nomoi* are characteristic of a given people:

> The small variations of climate to which the Asiatics are subject, extremes both of heat and cold being avoided, account for their mental flabbiness and cowardice as well. . . . Such things appear to me to be the cause of the feebleness of the Asiatic race, but a contributory cause lies in their customs; for the greater part is under monarchical rule. When men do not worry so much

about warlike exercises as about appearing warlike, they do not run the same risks.[76]

The Hippocratic author contrasts this condition with those of Europeans (including the Greeks):

> Indeed, this is the reason why the inhabitants of Europe are more courageous than those of Asia. Conditions which change little lead to easy-going ways; variations [lead] to distress of body and mind. Calm and an easy-going way of living increase cowardice; distress and pain increase courage. That is one reason for the more warlike nature of Europeans. But another cause lies in their customs. They are not subjects of a monarchy as the Asiatics are and, as I have said before, men who are ruled by princes are the most cowardly.[77]

For the author of *Airs, Waters, Places*, climate informs custom while custom then shapes the constitution of its inhabitants. At first glance, it might seem that Europe and Asia differ completely in every respect, including in their ability to be free. Yet as Rosalind Thomas comments, both "may possibly become courageous so long as they are autonomous."[78] A well-ordered constitution would have the effect of creating a well-ordered people—although given the Hippocratic author's concomitant suggestion that the effects of the soft Asian environment cannot be circumvented completely, the effect would be somewhat muted.

Although the Hippocratic author of *Airs, Waters, Places* thus seems to preclude collective power among certain peoples, Herodotus's account points to the possibility of different cultural responses—*nomoi*—as conducive (or obstructive) to this power. Herodotus's pluralistic approach to *nomoi* forms the basis of a pluralistic approach to politics. Rather than operating at the level of continental generalization, Herodotus's travels take him to particular peoples and particular practices of political freedom. Herodotus views *nomoi* as *iterated interactions* (repeated practices) among a multitude of agents and forces. Responsive interaction attentive to the particular features of all those things proves most successful. To take another example, when Herodotus speaks of the Ethiopians, he continues the idealizing tradition dating from Homer, describing them as tall, attractive, and long-lived. Yet instead of ascribing these attributes to their environment, Herodotus explains them in terms of the Ethiopians' use of a uniquely salubrious spring, one whose liquid was so light that nothing could float on top of it (3.22). This is neither the only possible use for its waters nor a recent or arbitrary custom. Culture (*nomos*) explains the Ethiopians' practice while the mechanism is biology.

Herodotus's openness to the grand variety of customs might suggest relativism about *nomoi*. Unlike the Hippocratics, Herodotus identifies *nomoi* as a practice of collective power where human agents can responsively interact with nonhuman agents, be they geographies or the gods. Yet this respect for *nomoi* does not lead Herodotus to praise all *nomoi* alike. Equality in general and *isêgoria* in particular provide examples of *nomoi* that Herodotus finds worthy of praise. Herodotus's famous comments about the Babylonian customs he finds admirable and those that repulse him underscore this point. The Babylonians' marriage lottery falls into the first category and involves auctioning off the most attractive brides and then using the proceeds from this auction to pay men to marry the less attractive ones (1.196). Also admirable is how the Babylonians turn medical treatment into a matter of public concern:

> Because they do not consult doctors, when someone is ill they carry him to the main square [*tên agorên*], where anyone who has personal experience of something similar to what the ill person is suffering from, or who knows someone else who has, comes up to him and offers him advice and suggestions about his illness. They tell him what remedy they found effective in their own case, or what they saw working in someone else's case, which enabled them to recover from a similar illness. No one is allowed to walk past a sick person in silence, without asking what sort of illness he has. (1.197)

Herodotus describes this as the Babylonians' "most sensible" (*sophiê*) custom after their marriage lottery. Both create conditions of equality: the marriage lottery redistributes contingent differences of attractiveness among the whole populace to create more equality (albeit while reinforcing conventions of attractiveness); similarly, by bringing their problems to the agora for all to investigate in common, the Babylonians' approach to medical treatment models *isêgoria* with a content different from the Athenians'. Placing people in need of medical advice in the public square to "crowd-source" their treatment seeks the wisdom of crowds rather than relying on the power of experts. These practices of equality support collective power, unlike the custom Herodotus finds most objectionable. Herodotus regards as "disgraceful" the custom that requires every woman of the land to sit in the sanctuary of Aphrodite and have sex with a strange man. Wealthy women act "snobbish" and "drive to the sanctuary in covered carts," surrounded by a large retinue of attendants. Attractive and tall women go home quickly, but unattractive women often must wait three or four years. Unlike the customs Herodotus praises, this one calls attention to differences and does not empower the populace.[79]

Herodotus's preference for *nomoi* that support collective power also distinguishes him from his contemporaries like Antiphon and Protagoras. Like Herodotus, Antiphon suggests that the conventions of *nomos* vary according to people;[80] yet unlike Herodotus, Antiphon takes the further step to praise whichever *nomos* best accords with nature, *physis*. The *sophisticated* person will use justice (*dikaiosunê*), for example, to his own advantage, ignoring the societal variations.[81] Herodotus provides examples of characters that might fit Antiphon's model, people like Deioces, who fosters dependence on his own judgment and thus accrues enormous power. Yet Herodotus does not praise these uses of *nomoi* for individual advantage. Instead, the most praiseworthy *nomoi* are those that support collective power. Herodotus evinces a fundamental concern for the life of peoples. These peoples make history and they create the wisest *nomoi* for ensuring social reproduction.[82]

Herodotus's praise of the collective draws him close to Protagoras. Protagoras, as Cynthia Farrar has argued, introduces a protodemocratic approach to *nomoi*, praising the *polis* as necessary to life and *nomoi* as the constitutive elements of the *polis*.[83] Like Herodotus, Protagoras does not claim to know nature or the truth about the gods. Human communities must establish their own customs to produce order.[84] But unlike Protagoras, Herodotus emphasizes practices of equality that span the variety of human communities around the Mediterranean. *Isokratia* and *isêgoria* could exist (in some nomistically inflected form) anywhere: the Babylonians have their versions in the marriage lottery and crowd-sourced medical treatment; the Athenians shine; the Issedones, at the northern edges of the earth, are partway there. Protagoras's agnosticism resembles Herodotus's, but Herodotus's respect for collective power—for developing the capacity of people to do things—leads him to praise specific *nomoi* over others.

Herodotus's preference for *nomoi* tempered by equality thus exists alongside a respect for the pluralism of *nomoi* as different repertoires for living in the world's dynamic complexity. This ecological understanding of *nomoi* thus goes beyond even modern thinkers like Montesquieu, who allow for the importance of terrains, geography, and so forth.[85] Unlike Montesquieu, Herodotus wonders at the potency of nonhuman forces, from rivers and storms to the gods in their many guises. This wondering is crucial; it allows Herodotus and his audience to imagine causes beyond themselves. Human beings' hands are not the only forces controlling the tiller. Here a contrast with Carl Schmitt's *The* Nomos *of the Earth* suggests the distinctiveness of Herodotus's concept of earthly flourishing.[86] Diagnosing a crisis in modernity before the advent of the Anthropocene, Schmitt proposes *nomos* as the configuration in which "the orders and orientations of human social life become apparent."[87] Yet Schmitt, like most thinkers of modernity, considers this *nomos* only in the singular. His thought is ultimately Hegelian in its totalizing, yet it lacks attention to what Theodor Adorno called the "cross-grained, opaque, [and] unassimilated material" that stands outside universal history.[88] Schmitt directs human thinking to the elemental order of its terrestrial being but views this order as unchanging and universal.

In contrast, the *Histories* depicts an abundance of diverse and distinct political communities. Herodotus thinks diversity as a whole yet without losing sight of the wondrous and uncanny differentiation within it, the "strange multiplicity," in James Tully's phrase,[89] of plural communities. These communities practice distinctive *nomoi*, which in turn facilitate, in better and worse ways, the collective power constitutive of (but entirely sufficient for) flourishing. While distinct, these communities are also deeply interrelated (prefiguring what Timothy Morton calls "the mesh").[90] Herodotus illuminates in particular the networks of connection and influence that crisscross the ancient Mediterranean. The Greeks would not be Greek without the Persians, not simply because they required an "other" for the formation of their "self," but because Greeks and Persians have always been in a relationship, even if only indirectly. Only when aggression and hostility enter this relationship does it become troubling.

4

Narrating Inquiry

That we know global warming is our doing should be a comfort, not a cause for despair, however incomprehensibly large and complicated we find the processes that have brought it into being; that we know we are, ourselves, responsible for all its punishing effects should be empowering, and not just perversely. Global warming is, after all, a human invention. And the flip side of our real-time guilt is that we remain in command. No matter how out-of-control the climate system seems—with its roiling typhoons, unprecedented famines and heat waves, refugee crises and climate conflicts—we are its authors. And still writing.

DAVID WALLACE-WELLS, *The Uninhabitable Earth*[1]

Anyway, that is what happens as a result of the cold. But there is one thing that puzzles me (this may be a digression, but then this account has sought out such digressions ever since its beginning): what stops mules from being born anywhere in Elis, which is not a cold place? There is no other obvious reason for it.

HERODOTUS, *Histories* 4.30

Herodotus does not answer the ostensible question of his inquiry—who began the conflict between the Greeks and the barbarians?—in a straightforward way. Nor does Herodotus take up and work through the ethical and political questions that arise in the course of his narrative in conventional philosophical or theoretical terms. Herodotus offers a display of his inquiry replete with digressions and asides, ineffable wonders and discoveries. This inquiry leads readers to consider the dynamic complexity of things (*peri phuseôs*), to witness the historian's processual mapping of a known world (*oikeomenê*), and to confront the diversity and importance of *nomoi* to various political communities. This chapter returns to the *how* of the *Histories* to examine how Herodotus communicates his inquiry. I argue that the form of the *Histories* creates a new genre of ancient political thought and that this form possesses a distinctive meaning and set of effects for its readers both in antiquity and in the Anthropocene.[2]

The *Histories* challenges readers to consider the nature and function of stories and storytelling. What do stories *do*? Like everything in the *Histories*, stories have various and multiple forms. Within the narrative of the *Histories*, they appear first of all to illustrate the tentative conclusions drawn by the inquirer about why something occurred or who deserves responsibility (*aitios*). Yet the stories don't play only this specific role within the argument. Stories can

offer context that may or may not prove necessary for an evaluation of the characters or events. Stories can entertain and divert, looping away from the causal
sequence of events to offer piquant contrasts like a sprig of *tenadam* on a cup
of Ethiopian coffee. Some stories seem to offer themselves to multiple interpretations; others seem practically disposable, asides without greater significance. Stories are told simply to be entered into the historical record.

Most treatments of the stories told by Herodotus analyze their function
within the narrative of the *Histories*.[3] Considering the effects of these stories
on their audience, however, leads to broader inquiry into how these stories
direct the reader toward particular activities. Stories affect readers. Herodotus
does not address an empty room. Perhaps the most vociferous ancient reader
of Herodotus, Plutarch, offers one set of reactions and thus a way to measure
and assess what Herodotus's stories do. Plutarch's criticisms are the response
of a particular reader; he thus employs an analytical lens analogous to what
today goes by "reader response" criticism. Reading the stories of the *Histories*
with a specific readership in mind calls attention to the open-endedness of
many of these stories' meanings; it also emphasizes the emotional and affective work that these stories undertake. Herodotus tells stories not simply to
illustrate, contextualize, or entertain; he also tells stories to move his readers,
to stir up reaction, reflection, and response.

Herodotus's contemporary readers were also members of particular political communities. As the predominant Greek power at the time of Herodotus's
creation of the *Histories*, Athens and the Athenians stand as one particular
collection of readers meriting extended consideration. Herodotus's glancing
references to the founding family of democratic Athens, the Alcmaeonidae,
as well as his critique of the founding story of the tyrannicides, have prompted
much commentary.[4] Here Herodotus's discussion of *isonomia* also reenters.
On my argument, the stories concerning Athens chasten and complicate the
stories Athens tells about itself. The *Histories* shows how Athenian democracy
did not come about through the great acts of particular founders; Herodotus's
various stories imply much broader popular agency standing behind political
success and flourishing. By resisting a single story or a conventional narrative
arc, Herodotus invites manifold participants to the process of political life. He
opens political space for competing stories and thus expands the possibilities
for participation in public life.

Put into the broader context of its readers in antiquity, then, the inquiry
on display in the *Histories* appears directed toward a participatory response.
The dual tasks set forth in the Proem of book 1—to prevent deeds from fading
from memory with time and to identify the responsible party for the conflict
between the Greeks and the barbarians—capture the *what* (i.e., the content)

of the *Histories*, but these opening lines also denote the *how*. Herodotus describes the form of the *Histories* in a particular way, as a "showing" (*apodeixis*) of his inquiry (*historia*). The *Histories* presents a performance, a display or demonstration of the inquiry undertaken. This performance of the story of the inquiry that forms the *Histories* holds open a space for wonder and reflection about its own limits. It contains an implicit theory of narrative—what I call a "narratology"—that shows how to tell a story well and truthfully in a world of dynamic complexity.

The narratology of the *Histories* has an amplitude, to use Walter Benjamin's term, instructive for the Anthropocene. Written about events in the recent past, the *Histories* did not offer news to its readers; when one reads the *Histories* today, it has even less of a claim of breaking stories or imparting time-sensitive information. Yet the amplitude of its stories distinguishes them.[5] This amplitude appears through Herodotus's narration of his inquiry and the worlds it evokes. Formed through wondrous and irreducible bricolage of so many stories and reflections, conversations and observations, the narrative of the *Histories* constructs a provisional and unfinished portrait of what is known (and unknown) in this world, a human world abundant with overlapping customs and cultures and laws. It anticipates ecological writing in the twentieth and twenty-first centuries with its call to wonder and even love toward nonhuman animals. The Anthropocene requires such narrative forms, forms that can both elicit a practice of inquiry appropriate for the dynamic complexity of the world the inquiry chronicles and infuse that inquiry with the desire to act on behalf of that world in pursuit of earthly flourishing.

At a second level, the *Histories* shows how to write a political story. As David Wallace-Wells emphasizes, stories of the Anthropocene are still being written. Herodotus addresses the Athenians and questions the stories they tell about themselves. Herodotus shows the contingency of their successes and reminds the Athenians of the collective efforts that achieved them. This corrective angle can also be empowering, however. Herodotus proffers a vision of intellectual exchange and inquiry that supports the democratic life that the Athenians bear on their standard. Much like human beings in the Anthropocene, they are the authors of their present situation. "And still writing."[6]

The Stories of the *Histories*

The *Histories* not only teems with stories; it also raises the question of what a story can do. Sometimes a story is just the shadow of a story: sometimes Herodotus hints at a story without telling it, as when he mentions that he is familiar with the Mysteries in Egypt but will not betray what he knows about them (2.171). Sometimes a story covers the entirety of the *Histories*, such as the story of Cyrus, who appears in the middle of book 1 and returns in every subsequent book, explicitly and implicitly, influencing the course of events through his actions as well as the memory of him. Sometimes a story seems completely irrelevant to the trajectory of the narrative—yet delightful and diverting all the same. One of my favorite stories fits this last description, the story of Rhampsinitus and the thief (2.121). Of this story, Herodotus comments that he finds it "incredible" yet he tells it nonetheless.

King Rhampsinitus, they say, possessed great riches in silver, so great, in fact, that none surpassed him in his day or after. To protect all this money, he proposed building a vast stone chamber. The builder, however, had designs on the king's treasure. When he constructed the chamber, he inserted in the wall a stone that could be removed. Time passed and the builder fell ill; when he sensed the end approaching, he called his two sons and told them about the stone. He had done it for their sakes, he told them, so they might always live in affluence.

After the father died, the sons were not slow to set to work. At night they went to the palace, found the stone in the wall of the treasury chamber, removed it with ease, and plundered the treasury. When the king next paid a visit to the chamber, he was astonished to find that his treasure was diminished yet he could find no signs of entry. On each successive visit, he found that more money was gone. (The thieves kept on plundering more and more.)

At last the king determined to set a trap near the vessels containing the money. When the thieves came that night, one of them was caught in the trap. Knowing he was lost, he called to his brother to cut off his head so that when his body was discovered, nobody would recognize the son of the chamber's builder. The brother was persuaded. He returned the stone to its place and went home with his brother's head in his arms.

The next morning, the king returned to his chamber and marveled to see the body of the thief in the trap without a head while still no signs of entry appeared. He commanded that the body of the dead man be hung up outside the palace wall and set guards to watch it. If some person was seen weeping or lamenting near the place, he ordered, they should be seized and brought before him. Then he waited.

The mother of the thieves heard of this exposure and demanded that her surviving son get his brother's body back, threatening him that if he failed she would denounce him to the king as the robber. The son tried in vain to persuade his mother to let it rest but she insisted. At last he yielded and devised the following scheme. He filled some skins with wine and loaded them on donkeys. He then drove the donkeys to the place where the guards were watching the dead body. As he approached the guards, he pulled two or three of the skins off and untied the necks. The wine poured out freely and he began to beat his head and shout. The guards saw the spilling wine and rushed to catch it. The son pretended anger and then let himself be pacified. He chatted with the guards and gave them one of the skins. The guards persuaded the son to remain and drink with them. He let himself be persuaded. The drinking went on and the guards grew drowsy. Eventually they fell asleep on the spot. The thief waited until the middle of the night and then took down the body of his brother. Then he shaved off the right side of all the guards' beards to mock them and carried the body of his brother home.

The king was furious about the news of the theft of the thief's corpse. Now there was nothing more that he wanted than to catch the thief. So—and Herodotus notes that he finds this unbelievable—he installed his daughter in a room with instructions to accept all men without discrimination. But if they wanted to sleep with her, they had to tell her the cleverest and the worst thing they had done. If she discovered the thief in this way, she would grab him and not let him go.

The thief understood what the king was up to. He wanted to prove himself more cunning than the king, so he cut an arm off a fresh corpse and took it with him under his cloak when he went to see the king's daughter. In reply to the question she asked everyone, he told her that the worst thing he had done was decapitating his brother and the cleverest had been getting the guards drunk so he could rescue his brother's body. Hearing this, the king's daughter seized hold of him but she grabbed the corpse's arm and the thief ran out the door.

When the king heard the news of the thief's latest caper, he was impressed with his resourcefulness and daring. He sent heralds everywhere and offered the man immunity and a generous reward if he would present himself. The thief believed the offer and went to the king. Rhampsinitus was so taken with him that he gave him his daughter to marry and proclaimed him the most intelligent man in the world.

The story of Rhampsinitus and the thief may seem familiar even if you have not read Herodotus. As Wolf Aly has shown, many stories in Herodotus "bear all the tell-tale signs of narratives which have passed from mouth to ear to mouth again."[7] The tale of Rhampsinitus and the thief has a parallel in *Der Meisterdieb*, collected by the Brothers Grimm in southern Germany in the early nineteenth century. Such typicality as a folktale does not mean these stories have no historical basis, yet certain features may have eroded away or have been dramatized as the stories were told and retold.[8]

The *Histories* itself is a product of a preexisting storytelling tradition that Herodotus interweaves with his own collection of information. "Story" most often translates *logos* in the *Histories*; prior to Herodotus these *logoi* were collected and disseminated by *logoipoioi*, makers of *logoi*. Herodotus gestures to this history when he mentions knowing about Aesop "the storyteller" (*logopoios*, 2.134), who descended from a courtesan who may have built a pyramid of Ethiopian stone in honor of Mycerinus the king of Egypt. Chief among these *logoipoioi* stands Homer: the *Odyssey* and Odysseus have a strong imprint on the first four books of the *Histories*; when Herodotus approaches the actual Persian Wars, beginning with the revolt of the Ionians against the advancing Persians (which takes place in book 5), the *Iliad* becomes a model. As Alan Griffiths writes of the *Iliad*: "That great poem functioned as the ground bass underlying all Greek cultural expression up to and far beyond Herodotus's own day, and it is the authoritative familiarity of Homer that makes this style both attractive to Herodotus and acceptable to his audience."[9]

Herodotus retells the stories of others but from particular angles. One angle of approach involves having a particular character tell a story. This is a frequent Homeric technique as well—allowing characters to play roles such as "the wise adviser" or "warner." Such speeches are often embedded in the context of a debate where characters point to other examples to underscore their points. In other words, stories function within these stories in similar ways to how stories function in the *Histories* as a whole. In the *Iliad*, Phoenix urges Achilles to return to the battle by telling the story of Meleager (9.543–605). Similarly, Achilles attempts to persuade Priam to take food despite his grief by pointing to the story of Niobe (24.602–17).[10] Recall the Corinthian Socleas, who tells the story of Periander recounted in chapter 3. Or consider the Spartan king Leotychidas, who cautions the Athenians with the story about his countryman Glaucus: "I would like to tell you about something which took place in Sparta," he begins. A man, Glaucus, was renowned for his integrity "more so than any other man then alive in Lacedaemon." Yet when entrusted with money by a Milesian, Glaucus kept the money for himself and denied having been given the money in the first place. Asked to swear an oath, Glaucus visited the oracle at Delphi for permission to lie. The oracle denied him his request and Glaucus returned the money to the Milesian. Still, Leotychidas concludes:

> But here is the point of the story, the reason why I mentioned it to you, Athenians: today there is not a single descendant of Glaucus alive, nor is there a single household that is considered to stem from Glaucus. He has been utterly and completely eradicated from Sparta. (6.86)

It may be tempting to associate this "lesson" with Herodotus, but it's also distanced from the narrator. You would not say that Homer speaks through Achilles.[11] Herodotus has his characters use stories in ways that suggest what function stories might play, but he does not directly say what his stories should mean or do.

While they may not deliver digestible lessons, Herodotus's own retellings of inherited stories do illuminate particular angles within his own storytelling. The story of Gyges and Candaules in book 1 takes up a familiar tale. As Herodotus tells the story, Candaules coerces his bodyguard Gyges into hiding himself in Candaules's wife's bedroom so that he might see her naked. When Candaules's wife discovers Gyges, she presents him with an ultimatum: give up his own life or kill Candaules and take the throne. Gyges chooses to save himself and begins a new line of Lydian rulers, one that eventuates in Croesus. In Plato's *Republic*, Socrates also recounts the tale of Gyges. In Socrates's telling, however, Gyges is not a bodyguard but a shepherd. With the power of invisibility granted by a magic ring he discovers in an ancient burial site, Gyges enters the king's palace unseen, seduces the queen, kills the king, and wins power for himself. This telling, as Griffiths puts it, suggests the "naïve fantasy world of the folktale."[12] Herodotus's omission of the magic ring and insertion of Candaules's forcible persuasion indicate a different purpose from Plato's: Herodotus's telling emphasizes the excess of the tyrant (recall how Candaules is described as overcome with *erôs*) as well as the inability of would-be tyrants to completely control their situation and thus the impossibility of rule. The *Histories* focuses on the broader social or political problem rather than the psychological angle of the *Republic*.[13]

There are other moments when Herodotus deploys stories that resonate across the narrative, stories that create a structure of meaning that remains implicit but nonetheless present. The Gyges story also figures one of these motifs, what Griffiths calls "The Awful Dilemma." When Gyges is discovered by Candaules's wife, she presents him with an agonizing choice: die himself or kill the king. This kind of dilemma has its originating text in Agamemnon's choice at Aulis: sacrifice his daughter or be abandoned by the Achaeans. Herodotus reworks this story across the *Histories*, from Arion's choice to be killed or attempt a death-defying swim for freedom (1.24) to the thief of Rhampsinitus, who must kill his brother and desecrate his corpse or be killed himself (2.121). The reiteration of the Awful Dilemma motif underscores a sense of the human predicament that informs Herodotus's inquiry. One finds oneself in situations not of one's choosing where exiting such situations inevitably involves loss or sacrifice. (In a way, this amplifies the impossibility of political rule motif as well.) Reducing these stories to apothegms about the "human predicament," however, obscures their complexity and openness: each story has a structure of meaning that exists through the particular details but not as a general truth; it only approaches generality as it appears again and again. Working through the particulars of the world as she explores it, the inquirer exemplifies precisely this truth.

The ring composition offers another structure of meaning that links different stories from across the *Histories*. Rosalind Thomas points out a straightforward example in the account of Croesus's expansionist plans (from book 1). As king of Lydia, Croesus inquires about possible allies as he prepares for war (1.56). This inquiry leads Herodotus to describe the major Greek ethnic groups: the Dorians and the Ionians (1.56–58). Croesus soon learns that the Athenians and the Spartans are the most powerful among the Greeks. Herodotus then inserts the stories of these cities' development: factional strife in Athens and Pisistratus's three periods of power; the Spartans' good governance under Lycurgus.[14] What appears as digression to the modern reader in fact functions structurally to show how narratives nest within one another. Thomas notes that the main narrative continues, but these subnarratives will prove no less important as Athens and Sparta regain prominence in the *Histories'* later books. The priority of one narrative over another does not present itself as obvious; readers are left to discern which stories are salient for understanding which plotlines.

While some of Herodotus's flashbacks follow the kind of structural logic that Thomas's account suggests, this does not explain every "digression." Not all the stories hang together; the lack of coherence accents the tension between any general inferences and the particular grain of the *Histories*. In other words, you cannot deny an irreducible distance between the many *logoi* and the overarching *logos* of Herodotus's *Histories* (if there is such a *logos*).[15] Some detours from the chronological narrative seem entirely random while others appear to have treatments disproportionate to their importance. Most famous among the latter category is book 2's treatment of Egypt, occasioned by Cambyses's conquest. In these sections, Herodotus goes beyond the necessary context setting to explore (among other wonders) accounts of the flooding of the Nile, the Egyptians' reverence for animals, and the far-lying lands where the most beautiful human beings in the world, the Ethiopians, live. Yet Egypt has a place in the "main narrative": it becomes germane in relation to Cambyses, whose own relevance lies in continuing the deterioration of Persian *nomoi* that in turn facilitates his invasion of Greece.[16] Other flashbacks and parenthetical comments seem much less apposite, as when Herodotus pauses to wonder at particular marvels, such as circular boats made of leather that float down the river to Babylon (1.194). These moments of extranarrative comment or diversion serve to resist the collapse of Herodotus's inquiry into a single story, a history about which you could say "history instructs us." Instead, the *Histories* is polyvocal, in J. Peter Euben's term, speaking with multiple voices and emplotting multiple narratives.[17]

Displacing the main narrative—through structural ring-composition features and disproportionate or disruptive flashbacks and insertions—Herodotus shows how the many stories of the *Histories* contain both an internal logic and a diversity that resists this logic. These stories do not teach simple lessons. Although Herodotus links various stories through particular structures of meaning, these exist in tension to other seemingly extraneous stories. Just as many arguments come through the mouths of specific characters, the particular details and characters of each story locate whatever truths they hold to a place in the narrative or a situation that elicits the story in the first place.[18]

Responding to Stories

Reading Herodotus as a "moral historian" seems to offer a contrasting approach to what I have sketched thus far. The "moral history" mode of analysis seeks above all to draw lessons from historical narrative. This style of historiography flourished in the Hellenistic period, starting a few generations after Herodotus; some readers have also employed it to interpret the *Histories* itself. In this vein Charles Fornara writes that Herodotus "injected into the record of Persian, Lydian, and Greek history an importance reaching beyond the facts in themselves. History became moral and Herodotus didactic."[19] There are, in the words of Thomas Harrison, "ultimate" lessons to be drawn from Herodotus's *Histories*; its usefulness has a definite and determinable quality.[20]

The moral reading of Herodotus has an illustrious predecessor in Plutarch, who impugned Herodotus because the *Histories* lacked moral integrity.[21] The *Histories* was not sufficiently moralistic for Plutarch.[22] Although I would contest Plutarch's flat-footed and tendentious reading, his interpretive approach opens a broader avenue toward considering the reader's response as integral to the meaning of the *Histories*. This in turn clears a middle ground between readers who see in Herodotus "moral history" and those who insist on more openness in his text. "Moral history" is a kind of reader's response—a response that takes up the didactic implications of the text with particular attention to how it might inform a moral life.[23] Anticipating readings of Herodotus as a moral historian, Plutarch focuses on Herodotus's formulations of praise and blame, accusing Herodotus of contradiction for wanting to preserve the glories of the past while questioning the motivations of its key actors. Plutarch's reading highlights particular aspects of the *Histories* to which ancient readers most likely responded. Plutarch emphasizes the subtleties of Herodotus, in particular his deception and beguilement of readers. Plutarch also notes the presence of the incongruous, of *atopoi* (out-of-place) elements, as characteristic of Herodotus. These elements include how Herodotus frequently conjectures about the motives of the actors whose heroism he notes. Plutarch models one individual's response; his commentary, Emily Baragwanath points out, "illuminates in a more general way the question of the character and range of responses we might reasonably expect on the part of an ancient reader of the *Histories*."[24]

Plutarch notes Herodotus's account of the liberation of the Athenians by the Spartans as one particularly egregious act of malice on the part of the author. "He may not be able to deny the Spartans their liberation of Athens from its tyrants," Plutarch writes, "but he can blot out and defame a fine deed by reporting a shameful reaction."[25] Herodotus does indeed note that the Spartans changed their minds: they discovered that those banished by the Pisistratid tyranny, the Alcmaeonidae, had conspired with the Pythia (the Delphic oracle) to advise the Spartiate, the leaders of the Lacedaemonians, whenever they came to consult the oracle, to set Athens free. "Endlessly barraged by this one message," the Lacedaemonians complied and drove out the Pisistratidae despite having had close ties of friendship until that moment. Plutarch points to a passage describing a moment when the Spartans discovered how the Athenians had attempted to mislead them:

> However, the Athenian preparations for revenge against Aegina were checked by fresh trouble from Lacedaemon: the Lacedaemonians had found out about the trick the Pythia had played on them and the Pisistratidae, and how the Alcmaeonidae had engineered it. They were doubly upset, first because they had driven men who were their friends and allies out of their homeland, and second because the Athenians had never shown them any gratitude for having done so. (5.90)

Herodotus implies inconsistency in the Spartans, according to Plutarch. The Spartans' good deed is blemished. Plutarch is furious.

Plutarch's objection calls attention to a characteristic of the *Histories* with broad implications. Plutarch's anger highlights the frustration provoked by Herodotean complexity. One cannot simply identify heroes and villains. The Spartans' liberation of the Athenians may appear heroic but Herodotus complicates the story. The Spartans seem to free the Athenians out of piety yet their piety is unquestioning—they simply obey the oracle and thus are led astray. This event accentuates both the strength and the limits of Spartan simplicity.[26] Plutarch complains about Herodotus's depiction of the Spartans' change of mind, but he omits another reason that Herodotus offers: namely, that the

Spartans had heard prophecies warning them that the Athenians would be a source of great damage to them (5.91). Here again Herodotus portrays the Spartans as obeying oracles without considering the difficulties of interpretation. Yet this lesson itself has another wrinkle given how frequently the *Histories* calls attention to mistaken interpretations of oracles.

Plutarch objects to how Herodotus undercuts the Spartans' heroism, but this heroism itself is not straightforward. The Spartans' liberation of Athens is also not entirely their own work. It depends, as I described in the previous chapter, on the contingency of the Pisistratidae's children being captured, the inspired leadership of Cleisthenes, and the Athenians' collective act of banishing Cleomenes and Hippias one final time. Fate intervenes, Herodotus comments, which might also suggest that perhaps the Alcmaeonidae didn't bribe the Delphic oracle after all (5.65). Herodotus sets up the story as one of the Spartans' liberation of the Athenians but then adds layer upon layer of complexity to this ostensibly singular act.

Moreover, the Spartans' change of mind to which Plutarch objects does not only suggest a lack of heroic decisiveness. You could also read it as a demonstration of social learning. Although the Spartans simply obeyed the first oracle instructing them to liberate the Athenians, now they take their doubts to an assembly of their allies (5.91). They confess that their policy has taken a wrong turn, admitting how they succumbed to "bogus oracles." They point to the Athenians' ingratitude and excesses, as evidenced by their attacks against the Boeotians and the Chalcidians. "So yes, we made a mistake," the Spartans continue, "but now, with your assistance we aim to try to make up for it" (5.91). Yet the Spartans do not simply retaliate. They summon their allies and seek consensus (*koinôi logôi*). And when Socleas's speech turns collective sentiment against the Spartans' wishes, the Spartans accept what this consensus brings.

You might protest that Plutarch's objections really amount to a refusal of historical complexity. There is some of this—and readings that reduce the *Histories* to "moral lessons" often commit the same foul. Yet Plutarch's response opens the wicked problem of arriving at any lesson or straightforward character within the *Histories*. The overlapping and intersecting stories that form the fabric of the narrative may simply be ignored, as Plutarch seems to prefer; but these stories might also force less prejudiced readers to pause, drawing them into a process of reflection and reevaluation. As I showed in chapter 2, Herodotus seems intent on complicating conventional assumptions: barbarians are not simply Others and Greeks the Same; the *Histories* instead invites reconsideration.

Plutarch's reading of Herodotus also illustrates how your position as a reader prompts certain kinds of response. Plutarch's apparent desire to rescue those Greeks impugned by the barbarian-loving Herodotus had a lot to do with his Boeotian and Corinthian ancestors as well as his more general moral stance. Plutarch lived in a time when bias and flattery were at their worst; his writing reacted against this.[27] As A. J. Bowen comments, "Plutarch's romantic puritanism was not at ease with Herodotus' catholic and generous relativism."[28] Plutarch's objections concern not just content; Herodotus's style raised Plutarch's suspicions. "Herodotus is an artist," Plutarch concludes, damning with faint praise: "His tale reads well."[29] The surface-level delights prevent readers like Plutarch from probing more deeply; the complexity also disrupts readers intent on finding a friend or an enemy.

At the same time that Plutarch's example demonstrates the provocative features of the *Histories*, the *Histories* challenges any simplistic "moral history" reading to account for its own position. The lessons drawn from within the *Histories* depend on standpoints outside them: assumptions about what can be learned from ancient books; convictions about what needs to be learned; presuppositions about how learning takes place. Moreover, Plutarch serves to illustrate how the *Histories* prompts reflections on where you stand when reading the *Histories*.

Herodotus and Athens

Plutarch's response to Herodotus also illuminates another aspect of reader response to the *Histories*. One stated intention of the narrative is to identify the *aitios*—the cause or responsible party—for the conflict between the barbarians and the Greeks. As Gregory Nagy has argued, the *Histories* has a distinct juridical aspect. *Historia* can be traced to traditions of juridical prose, especially in the context of inter-*polis* arbitration; its "juridical sense" shapes the whole of the narrative.[30] Plutarch signals this juridical sense when he describes Herodotus's "pretending to speak in defense on behalf of the Alcmaeonidae against the very charges he had had first to lay against them." He continues: "First you prosecute, then you defend; and against famous men you bring false accusations, which then you withdraw."[31] As Baragwanath points out, Plutarch illuminates how opposing accounts possess explicit connections to different versions of the story told to the historian.[32] Herodotus puts you in the position to judge.

Being placed in such a position of judgment would have been familiar to many of Herodotus's readers. It echoes the situation of jurors in the law courts (*dikastêria*) or citizens in the Assembly (*ekklêsia*) of democratic Athens; Herodotus puts these fifth-century readers in the accustomed and practiced position of assessing speakers' debates in a variety of contexts, both formal and informal. Plutarch thus signals a response that Herodotus may well have intended: to promote reflection and even a commitment one way or the other from his readers; to demand in this way a responsibility from the readers to take a stand on the conflicting accounts Herodotus puts into play.[33] Herodotus takes up his fifth-century audience's expectations that a judgment could be made, that truth could be grasped; he positions his readers to make these judgments as they encounter the text.

Adopting this position on reading Herodotus shifts the conversation about Herodotus's relationship to Athens, which many have taken as a primary audience for the *Histories*. While it continues to matter *what* the *Histories* say about the Athenians, *how* it does so inflects this content. And this *how* also speaks to the new genre of ancient political thought Herodotus's *Histories* models for readers in the twenty-first century and beyond. The *Histories* can teach how to make better judgments in the Anthropocene.

The story of the shield signal following the battle of Marathon demonstrates the kind of questions that Herodotus puts to his Athenian audience and thus the kind of thinking the *Histories* evokes. Marathon is the first victory of the combined Greek forces against the invading Persians. On the heels of this exciting Greek victory, Herodotus returns to an episode during the battle that had led many to impugn the Alcmaeonidae. As the Persians sail off from their defeat, they head for Athens hoping to find the city undefended (6.115). As Herodotus retells the story, the Alcmaeonidae—the family of Pericles's father—were later blamed for having contrived a scheme to display a shield and signal to the Persians aboard their ships that encouraged them to sail swiftly toward Athens. At this point in the narrative, Herodotus continues with the aftermath of Marathon, but a bit later he returns to the story to defend the Alcmaeonidae as "vehement tyrant haters" who would never cooperate with the Persians (6.121). Herodotus details the Alcmaeonidae's work to liberate Athens and in the process explains how they came into prominence through their wealth, gained first from Croesus and then later from marrying into the wealthy family of Cleisthenes, tyrant of Sicyon (and namesake of the Cleisthenes who would participate in the liberation of the Athenians). In Herodotus's roundabout way this leads to a story about how the tyrant Cleisthenes of Sicyon arranged a series of contests for the marriage of his daughter, Agariste. These contests involved a year of testing the merit, valor, disposition, education, and character of potential suitors. Out of all these tests, Hippoclides, son of Tisander, "preeminent among the Athenians in both wealth and good looks," stood out—until the final night.

> After the meal, the suitors competed with one another at singing and at public speaking. As the drinking progressed, Hippoclides had a clear lead over the others, but then he told the pipe-player to strike up a tune, and when the musician did so he began to dance. Now, although Hippoclides liked his own dancing a lot, Cleisthenes was beginning to look on the whole business askance. After a while, Hippoclides stopped momentarily and asked for a table to be brought in. When the table arrived there, he first danced a Laconian dance on it, then some Attic figures, and finally stood on his head on the table and waggled his feet around. Hippoclides' uninhibited dancing of the first and second sets of figures had already put Cleisthenes off having him as a son-in-law, but he kept silent because he did not want to scold him. When he saw him waggling his legs around, however, he could no longer restrain himself. "Son of Tisander," he said, "you have danced away your marriage." The young man replied, "Hippoclides doesn't care!"—and that is how the proverb arose. (6.129)[34]

Plutarch alludes to this story when he refers to Herodotus's "dancing away the truth," but Plutarch, as usual, tends to see Herodotus from only one direction. This risks ignoring the amplitude of the narrative itself—and thus the complicated judgment Herodotus invites his Athenian audience to make.[35] As Benjamin writes, Herodotus's storytelling "achieves an amplitude that information lacks": his stories do not come with explanation but rather preserve themselves by being capable of multiple interpretations; stories have a life beyond their original telling because they can serve multiple contexts and possess multiple meanings. The story of Hippoclides is not simply one of an idiotic reality show contestant in ancient Sicyon. In the context of Herodotus's defense of the Alcmaeonidae, the story suggests that they were lucky, that their subsequent fame and fortune stemmed in part from the foolishness of others. Or you might claim that Hippoclides shows that pleasing oneself (through dancing or otherwise) is inimical to winning political power. Or you could argue that Hippoclides's nonchalance is an admirable quality given that he, unlike the Alcmaeonidae, was unwilling to kowtow to tyrants. Multiple readings avail themselves.

What might the Athenians have made of this story? It doesn't seem right to assert with Charles Fornara that Herodotus's treatment is "not admiring but objective."[36] "Objectivity" is misplaced on polyvocal stories. Herodotus does not deal in unequivocal statements. He does link Pericles with this amusing and potentially critical story, yet the single mention of Pericles seems to foreground his noble birth:

> The marriage of Megacles [who was chosen instead of Hippoclides] and Agariste produced the Cleisthenes who fixed the tribes and established democracies at

Athens. He was named after his mother's father, the tyrant of Sicyon. As well as Cleisthenes, Megacles also had a son called Hippocrates, who became the father of another Megacles and another Agariste, named after Cleisthenes' daughter. This Agariste, the daughter of Hippocrates, married Xanthippus the son of Ariphron. When she was pregnant she dreamt she gave birth to a lion, and then a few days later she bore Xanthippus a son, Pericles. (6.131)

Interpreters have long discussed the meaning of this dream of the lion; Hermann Strasburger argues that the lion can symbolize sovereignty but also savage, uncontrollable violence and destruction.[37] Any critical interpretation must also acknowledge Herodotus's earlier praise for the Alcmaeonidae, which credited them for their role in saving Athenian freedom (6.123). But for my purposes, the ambivalent depiction of the Alcmaeonidae has broader relevance in connection with the questions Herodotus raises about equality and the Athenian *polis*. You could argue that Herodotus's use of *isêgoria* and *isokratia* and not *isonomia* to describe Athens offers a veiled critique of the emptiness of the rhetoric of *isonomia* (and even its institutions) in the Athens of his day. This critique may connect with Herodotus's revision of the founding legend of the tyrannicides: as the song of Harmodius associates the slaying of tyrants with making Athens *isonomous*, so Herodotus believes these acts only exacerbate Athens' suffering under the tyrants (5.55 and 6.123). Herodotus may also have intended to include Pericles and the Athenian Empire in his criticisms, as the *Histories* associates *isonomia* with leaders' using the term in potentially manipulative ways and with imperialism as antithetical to the popular movements that support freedom. One possible reading of these controversial passages, then, is that Herodotus poses not only the question of the potential treachery of the Alcmaeonidae to his Athenian audience but also whether or not Pericles had begun to resemble many of the tyrants depicted in the *Histories*.[38]

In her brilliant reading of the Hippoclides story, Leslie Kurke provides further support for this interpretation.[39] This story, as Kurke shows, can be read as a beast fable. Indeed, it has undeniable resonances with the Indian tale of the Dancing Peacock.[40] Viewing this story as a recasting of an Indian beast fable into Greek history illuminates specific aspects of Herodotus's telling that in turn speak to the project of his storytelling: first, Herodotus adds a repetition of the other suitors as "puffed up" with pride, linking this story to the previous story of Alcmaeon emerging from Croesus's treasure, swollen with gold dust; second, Herodotus preserves the theme of luxury, prominent in the Indian fable, but concentrates it in a single Sybarite, Hippoclides, at the top of his list of suitors; third, Herodotus's prominent placement of this Sybarite calls attention to this "conversion from fabular animals to human characters";[41] fourth, at the moment of climax when Hippoclides responds, Herodotus effectively winks by using the fabular formula *hupolabôn eipe*, "saying in response." All these connections between Herodotus's tale and the original beast fable carry forward, on Kurke's argument, the general work of low fable in an Aesopic vein: to demystify and explode a tyrant's epic pretensions. Hippoclides's punch line is "an exquisite display of nonchalance that earns him a very un-Homeric form of eternal fame"; the tyrant's pretensions, in turn, "are ironized and exposed as absurd."[42] Hippoclides is the ordinary man made a hero, while both Cleisthenes and Megacles—"hapless" according to Kurke, despite his luck in winning with a second-place finish—are the butts of the joke.[43]

As Robert Fowler memorably puts it: "The story would have gone down a storm in Athens."[44] Kurke's analysis calls attention to Herodotus's deployment of the "low" genre of fable to mock the elitist pretensions of the Alcmaeonidae. The suggestion that they were tyrant haters is put in comic relief by Hippoclides's true indifference to the power and wealth tyrants can offer. Herodotus likely draws from popular stories told against the Alcmaeonidae, as Rosalind Thomas has argued; Herodotus's emplotting his critique in the form of a fable underlines its origins as precisely *not* from the Alcmaeonid family tradition. Yet here Fowler's statement has a second, important sense: the storm stirred up in Athens would have stemmed in large part from the irreducible complexity of the story itself, its amplitude. As Kurke points out, the intensity of debate about the meaning of these passages suggests Herodotus's success at crafting "an indirect, coded message to those in power (Pericles, Athens)."[45] The meaning on the surface appears to flatter, but its ripples and depths invite further thought and interpretation.

Narrating Inquiry

Like the uninhibited Hippoclides, Herodotus too stands on his head, inverting both the stories of Athens and the enterprise of writing itself. Deborah Steiner argues that writing in fifth-century Athens did not just criticize the Athenian democracy in content; it also constituted a withdrawal in form.[46] When Herodotus employs the low forms of comedy and fable, he embraces the textual mode of those who rejected or were excluded from Athenian politics. In doing so, however, Herodotus does not offer a straightforward critique of the leadership of democratic Athens. Although the Aesopic message seems sarcastically critical, it does not speak unambiguously; it must coexist, for one, alongside Herodotus's earlier direct praise for the Alcmaeonidae's role in saving Athens. The form of telling this story provokes deliberation in its audience. It refuses to reduce the dynamic complexity of the world to black-and-white argument;

Herodotus offers instead a strategy that provokes his readers to think. There is here a broader invitation to deliberate—what Kurke calls "bouleutic deployment"[47] of this strategy—that speaks to the entire project of the *Histories* and its particular form of political engagement and education.

Stepping back for a minute, it's worth noting that Herodotus wrote in an age of rhetorical self-awareness. His contemporaries, the Sophists, called attention to their own modes of argument, experimenting with various ways to present the truth or, alternatively, convince others in ways that made no attempt at truthfulness.[48] The foregrounding of the *how* of *historia* emerges from this context: the challenges of memorializing the past given limited and often-conflicting information; the shortcomings of previous accounts; and, perhaps above all, the self-consciousness of the historian as he crafts a narrative of his inquiry.

Unlike the Sophists, Herodotus does not present his inquiry as arguments; he puts this inquiry into a story. At the same time, Herodotus distinguishes himself from storytellers like Hecataeus, emphasizing that he presents not merely a collection of stories but an inquiry (5.36). The task of memorializing comes twinned with that of inquiring into the *aitios*. Nagy provides a useful distinction here: Herodotus is a *logios*, a master of speech whose authority rests in the force of the display (*apodeixis*) he presents; this is distinct from being a *logopoios*, or mere storyteller, one who simply retells the stories in circulation.[49] Yet as we have seen, Herodotus's display includes reflection on the *how* of his inquiry, the mode and means of this display (what Nino Luraghi calls "meta-*historiē*").[50] Herodotus is a *histōr*, or inquirer, who seeks to distinguish himself while investing his poetic explorations with a commitment to truth. The display is not merely a display but a demonstration of an inquiry.

Yet Herodotus's stories remain central to his project; the *histōr* coexists with an unrepentant *logopoios*. Herodotus's stories include the high and the low, radically extending the persons and objects that can count in his account. His stories reflect the dynamic complexity of the world itself. The polyvocality of the *Histories* holds an amplitude evident in the abundance of interpretations they can yield. The amplitude of stories in turn affords a quality of indirection that straightforward inquiry does not. Unlike the high forms of epic and tragedy, the "Aesopic bricolage" of the *Histories* undermines the authority of the author by identifying him with the storytelling slave; *historia* is not just provisional and located but also spoken by a lowly character outside the traditional hierarchies of influence and esteem.

Even in the absence of explicitly fabular stories, moments in the *Histories* reveal their complications when seen as the work of both a *histōr* and a *logopoios*. The stories within the *Histories* illuminate the story of the whole of the *Histories*—the story of Herodotus's inquiry. As David Branscome puts it, Herodotus sets himself up as an inquirer rivaling other inquirers such as Solon, Demaratus, Aristagoras, the Athenians in their speech about Marathon, and Xerxes.[51] Recall the difference between the Spartans' two reactions to the oracles about first liberating the Athenians and then resisting their rise to power. The first response—unquestioning obedience—leads them to the unwanted situation of having failed in their task while empowering the rival Athenians. The second response prefigures a Herodotean approach: first, the oracles left behind by the departing Pisistratidae are discovered; then the Spartans deliberate about their potential meaning, seeking consensus about the next course of action; finally, when Socleas convinces the assembly not to follow the Spartans' suggested course, the Spartans comply. This process of material inquiry, deliberation, and good judgment outlines how Herodotus proceeds in his own historical inquiry.

The Athenian debate about who should receive honors for their role in the battle of Marathon also highlights how Herodotus narrates his inquiry in contrast to other inquirers depicted in the *Histories*.[52] A decade after the victory at Marathon, the Greeks again face the invading Persians. After the Spartan defeat at Thermopylae and the naval victories at Artemisium and Salamis, the land forces meet on the plains of Plataea. The Tegeans and the Athenians dispute who should hold the left wing in the battle; each points to past success as evidence for why they should take the prime position. The Teageans argue that they have commanded the left wing as allies of the Lacedaemonians ever since their king and general Echemus fought and killed Hyllus, the leader of the invading Heracleidae. The Tegeans point repeatedly to their achievements—their *erga*—both in the past and in the present. They thus employ a form of Herodotean evidence, although only in support of their position.

In response, the Athenians attempt to undermine the Tegeans' arguments by describing these deeds (*erga*) as mere words (*logoi*). The Athenians begin with this distinction:

> We know that this meeting has been convened to prepare for battle against the barbarians and not for speeches [*logoi*], but since this man from Tegea has put before you accounts of valiant deeds that each of us has accomplished in both ancient and recent times, we are forced to demonstrate to you that the most prominent positions belong to us as our ancestral right rather than to the Arcadians, because we are truly valiant. (9.27)

In addition to contrasting words and deeds, the Athenians invoke Herodotean terms of demonstration and the true account. As they continue, the Athenians also take up the idea of *aitios*. They deserve to command the left wing because they acted *alone* in their past actions—not merely fighting alongside the Lacedaemonians but fighting apart from others, simply as Athenians.[53] They hold responsibility.

Similar to the Tegeans, the Athenians adduce examples in support of their position. They received the Heracleidae alone. They buried Polynices and his Argive supporters. They repulsed the Amazons who invaded Attica. They proved themselves "inferior to none" in the Trojan War. Yet these past victories only prepare for the most important recent demonstration of their desert:

> So let that be enough talk about deeds performed long ago. And even if there were nothing else for us to show as our achievement—as if any of the other Hellenes had as many successes as we have had—our accomplishment at Marathon certainly makes us worthy to hold this privilege and others besides: there we alone of the Hellenes fought the Persian all by ourselves and not only survived such a remarkable endeavor, but won a victory over forty-six nations. (9.27)

Ergon appears four times in these lines; it points to the evidence that the Athenians put on display. As if to emphasize the sheer quantity of evidence the Athenians have adduced, the whole camp of the Lacedaemonians shouts to acclaim the Athenians as more deserving.

Readers of the *Histories* would have been prepared for another reaction. Herodotus has already narrated a different version of the battle of Marathon. In his account (6.102–16), the Plataeans bring their entire military force to aid the Athenians as they await the Persians' arrival at Marathon. The Plataeans command the left wing. During the battle, the Persians break through the middle of the Greek line, but the Greeks still emerge victorious, with "the Athenians and the Plataeans prevailing on the wings" (6.113). Herodotus offers the backstory for why the Plataeans joined the Athenians, describing their particular history of cooperation (6.108): the Plataeans went as suppliants to the Athenians, seeking help against the Thebans; the Athenians eventually defeat the Thebans and expand Plataean territory at the Thebans' expense. Herodotus comments there: "That then is how the Plataeans had offered themselves to the Athenians and thus gained their protection. And now they had arrived to help the Athenians at Marathon" (6.109).

That said, in the very section where Herodotus notes the Plataeans' presence alongside the Athenians—where "the Athenians and the Plataeans [were] prevailing on the wings"—he emphasizes the Athenians over and against the Plataeans. In the first half of this sentence, the Athenians and the Plataeans are the subject; in the second half, however, the Athenians stand alone:

In their victory there, they allowed the barbarian troops that they had routed to flee and then, drawing both of their wings together, they fought those enemy troops who had broken through the center; in this encounter, too, the Athenians were victorious, and as the Persians fled, the Athenians pursued them and cut them down until they reached the sea, where they called for fire and started to seize the ships. (6.113)

Herodotus thus introduces ambivalence into his own account of the victory at Marathon. The Athenians win with the assistance of the Plataeans but they also are victorious through their own efforts. This episode comes right before the shield incident that Plutarch found objectionable; Herodotus doubles a sense of ambiguity about the Athenians' involvement and responsibility, refusing the kind of hagiographic portrait that Plutarch and, I might imagine, many of Herodotus's contemporary Athenian readers wanted.

The *Histories* thus presents a more complicated explanation of victory at Marathon than do the Athenians. Moreover, this complication arises in the course of the inquiry's narration. Herodotus does not simply tell readers that the Athenians were wrong; rather, he prepares readers to witness the simplification that took place in the Athenians' speeches and the ignorance of recent history in their auditors. The sequence of events matters. Herodotus's historical narration allows readers to recognize the political uses of the past even while grasping how the past consists of stories gathered and analyzed by the inquirer. There is no single past, and the complexities of history vitiate—although they do not preclude—attempts to use the past in an instrumental way. At the same time, Herodotus's narration of his inquiry demonstrates what makes any account of the past persuasive and calls into question the cogency of speeches like the Athenians' prior to Plataea.

Narrating inquiry thus positions readers to recognize the limited inquiries and arguments of the characters within the *Histories*. The mode of this narration also prevents readers from simply accepting Herodotus's narrative as the final word. By narrating his inquiry rather than simply presenting its results, Herodotus can offer stories while neither reducing historical complexity to a single conclusion nor passing off narrative as a truthful representation of historical reality. These moments all introduce reflexivity into the narrative as well as into the reader's response: Herodotus both calls attention to his own emplotting while also forcing the reader to recognize this feature of the inquiry, positioning the reader to make her own judgments about the historical narratives on offer. As I showed in chapter 2, Herodotus thus undermines the authoritative narrator that would otherwise tyrannize the reader. As Carolyn Dewald writes: "The *histōr* seems to join us in the audience and respond as we might to what unfolds before our eyes."[54] The firsthand experience of historical inquiry, now shared with others, affects the inquirer's craft, the inquirer himself, and how you interpret and understand both. What's more, this *histōr* is also a *logopoios*, a storyteller who speaks through irreducible fables and half-hidden truths. These competing forms have consequences for potential translations of Herodotean inquiry beyond his ancient context.

Nomos and Narrative

In the middle of his essay "The Storyteller," Walter Benjamin recounts the story of the Egyptian king Psammenitus from book 3 of the *Histories*. Psammenitus had been beaten and captured by the Persian king Cambyses, and Cambyses sought to humble his prisoner. He ordered that Psammenitus be placed on the road along which the Persian triumphal procession would proceed. Cambyses then arranged for Psammenitus to see his daughter and other Egyptian girls pass, dressed as maids going to the well with their pitchers. All the Egyptians lamented and bewailed this spectacle, but Psammenitus only bent down in silence to the ground. Cambyses now sent the son of Psammenitus with two thousand other Egyptian boys, bound with ropes around their necks and bits in their mouths. Psammenitus saw his son being led to his death, but while the other Egyptians cried and shouted with anguish, Psammenitus behaved just the same as he had with his daughter. Then, however, after the boys had gone by, an elderly man passed by, one of Psammenitus's former drinking companions who was now a pauper, possessing nothing except whatever alms he could beg from the army. When Psammenitus saw him, "he burst into a flood of tears, called out to his friend by name, and beat himself on the head" (3.14). What does this story mean?

Herodotus's stories open new worlds. From this story, Benjamin writes, we can see "the nature of true storytelling":

> The value of information does not survive the moment in which it was new. It lives only at that moment; it has to surrender to it completely and explain itself to it without losing any time. A story is different. It does not expend itself. It preserves and concentrates its strength and is capable of releasing it even after a long time.[55]

Herodotus offers no explanation; he leaves the story to speak for itself. It speaks through the structures of meaning and implication that crisscross the *Histories*; by virtue of its evocative telling, which demands a response from readers; through its role as part of the narration of inquiry itself and Herodotus's subtle reminders that he has summoned these stories and imparted what coherence they possess. The stories of Herodotus entertain, divert, adduce evidence, offer dueling and never-resolved reasons, complicate, and instruct. They possess an amplitude that information lacks. This amplitude is essential for depicting as well as evoking the complexity and dynamism characteristic of the nature of things. This amplitude is essential for approaching, understanding, and engaging in political life.

As Benjamin points out, stories do not exist apart from the world in which they are told. The amplitude of stories depends in large part on the life of the storyteller, the tradition of telling and retelling that Herodotus joins with his *Histories*. This fact may cause grief in a world so full of information, where social inquiry moves increasingly toward mathematical abstraction and where political discourse is dominated by experts. As I described in chapter 1, Herodotus offers reasons to doubt any promises of mastery; the complexity of the world eludes such grasping.

Psammenitus burst into a flood of tears. It can't be accidental that Herodotus includes an overwhelming affective response. As I have argued, Herodotus sought response to his writing too. Plutarch's acerbic response marks one possibility. Although the distance and strangeness of these stories may not render them less stirring to a twenty-first-century audience, Herodotus's orientation toward not just communicating but *eliciting* wonder, curiosity, and even a desire to know presents a challenge to writers in the Anthropocene. How do you write to evoke collective response? How do you not only shame but startle, not only convince but inspire? Herodotus's *Histories* provides a model.

By performing its inquiry explicitly, the *Histories* also mimics the process of placing something "into the middle" for discussion—*es meson*—that arises repeatedly throughout the *Histories* as the best possible approach for deliberation. This also intimates how the *Histories* figures a *nomos*—a practice of inquiry and performance that elicits particular responses from its audience. The *Histories* practices a form of inquiry that convenes a diversity of things around a middle ground where earthly flourishing might be pursued. As John Lombardini has argued, to place affairs *es meson* "creates the conditions for popular government" because this "recreates the public sphere."[56] Putting something into the middle creates a common space of appearances; it means "that which is held in common" and "that which is public."[57] Putting political matters *es meson* is consonant with the practices of equality Herodotus calls *isonomia*, *isêgoria*, and *isokratia*; indeed, it seems most of all an *isegoric* act, placing a multitude of different participants on equal footing as complex personalities who live their polyvocal stories. As I have shown, the *Histories* models the value of openness, perhaps even "a model of the value of openness for the democratic grounding of deliberation."[58]

The *Histories* takes up practices of *es to meson* in its very form of narrating inquiry.[59] In other words, the *how* of the *Histories* demonstrates what *isêgoria* might look like outside Athens. It offers a possible *nomos* of deliberation about collective life. Herodotus's roots in oral culture show themselves both in his thinking through what Leslie Kurke calls "embodied discourses and practices"—the characters of Gyges or Hippoclides, the plotlines of a rise and fall or reciprocity—and in his preservation of competing and often even contradictory stories from various sources. Not only does Herodotus place himself in a particular position and set of relationships as an inquirer, but his stories also proceed from different locations and vantage points. As Kurke puts it, Herodotus's text thus forms "an open agora of logoi, jostling one another, with the histor as our sly tour guide among them."[60]

The spatial model of *es meson* finds its textual analogue in Herodotus's *Histories*. As Marcel Detienne describes it, the *meson* was "the common point for all those gathered in a circle around it."[61] Words spoken here constituted a common interest. Although this has often been taken as exclusive to the Greek *polis*, Herodotus's virtual agora includes non-Greeks and even nonhumans. It summons a multitude of human and nonhuman things as participants in the series of events called, broadly, "the Persian Wars." In doing so it dramatizes the meaning of *es meson* and enacts the political practices most conducive to collective flourishing.

In Euripides's *Suppliant Women*, Theseus declares: "Freedom is this: who has some useful counsel and wants to bring it *es meson*?"[62] With its open agora of *logoi*, the *Histories* brings its counsel *es meson*. It thus puts in motion a possible *nomos* of *es meson* by virtue of the public display (*apodeixis*) of the inquiry it offers. Herodotus's narration puts the logic of *es meson* on display; this in turn supports practices of freedom and earthly flourishing. This inquiry convenes the dynamic and complex nature of things, the itinerant inquiries of the historian as she maps the *oikeomenê*, and the practice of *nomoi*. The narrating of inquiry integrates these discoveries and revelations into an open-ended and response-provoking performance. Herodotus's performance of inquiry, in turn, shapes a new *nomos*, a practice performed by the readers and auditors of the *Histories*, that can support the free regimes depicted in it in their pursuits of earthly flourishing.

5

Freedom and Earthly Flourishing

> From a Gaian viewpoint, all attempts to rationalize a subjugated Earth with man in charge are as doomed to failure as the similar concept of benevolent colonialism. They all assume that man is the possessor of this planet; if not the owner, then the tenant. The allegory of Orwell's *Animal Farm* takes on a deeper significance when we realize that all human societies in one way or another regard the world as their farm. The Gaia hypothesis implies that the stable state of our planet includes man as a part of, or partner in, a very democratic entity.
>
> JAMES LOVELOCK, *Gaia*[1]

> You know well how to be a slave but have not yet experienced freedom, nor have you felt whether it is sweet or not. But if you could try freedom, you would advise us to fight for it, and not only with spears, but with axes!
>
> SPARTANS TO THE PERSIANS IN HERODOTUS, *Histories* 7.135

Ancient Greek political thought reflects and reflects on the birth of politics. As Melissa Lane suggests, politics in the ancient Greek imagination fundamentally concerned the relations among those in the political community; this implies that different political communities could organize different structures for mediating these relations.[2] The excellence or virtue of a people varies depending on regime and arises in tandem with another political value developed to capture the transferal of familial or social relationships into a nascent political sphere: *eleutheria*, or freedom.[3]

The specific origins of *eleutheria*'s emergence as a concept remain contested,[4] but the Persians Wars form the key moment for its articulation in political terms. Kurt Raaflaub argues that the Persian Wars acted as "freedom wars" wherein the concept gained a new political meaning in contrast to the domination and loss of political autonomy threatened by the attacking Persians.[5] In the sixth century BCE, communal independence did not yet appear as a political problem, yet when the Greeks created a league to secure themselves against the Persians, *eleutheria* served as a rallying cry, becoming the distinguishing characteristic of their political forms (in contradistinction to tyranny). The Greeks conceptualized the Persian Wars as a struggle for freedom against political servitude, and, Raaflaub writes, "a noun (*eleutheria*) was created to express this concept and Zeus Eleutherios was the first to receive thanks after the victory of Plataea."[6] Compressing this period into a single play, Aeschylus's *Persians* explicitly celebrates the Greeks' victory in terms of freedom.[7]

Once understood only as a private status to distinguish free men from their slaves, freedom thus gained political meaning during this period, and in two ways: it served both to articulate a collective refusal of enslavement to a tyrant and to indicate the ability of a *polis* to rule itself free from foreign control.[8] Christian Meier argues that *eleutheria* "underwent a distinct shift in the direction of politicization."[9] *Eleutheria* became understood as a public good created and sustained politically; citizens began to view the social world as "constituted by citizens acting in their capacity as citizens," that is to say, as *political*.[10] In this way the Greek political identity of the *poleis* arose. "Citizens were expected to act as citizens (*politai*) . . . and this expectation was now given institutional form."[11] As my reading of Herodotus will suggest, this was not solely a Greek achievement.

Herodotus's treatment of *nomos* as a practice involving different tempers of equality to realize collective power sets the stage for understanding the various accounts of freedom just below the surface of the *Histories*. Although some readers have been tempted to see the *Histories* as praising only an Athenian conception of freedom, I argue against such a view for multiple reasons. First, as I showed in chapter 3, Herodotus adopts a pluralistic approach to *nomoi*, appreciating how the practices of different peoples arise in responsive interaction with nonhumans among and around them. Second, these particular *nomoi* form the basis of different kinds of freedom. I focus here on four primary forms of freedom, associated with four different peoples: Persian freedom, Scythian freedom, Spartan freedom, and Athenian freedom. Herodotus's emphasis is on the *collective* basis of this freedom. All these consist of practices of collective power articulated and expressed by *nomoi*. All four of these peoples are free when they rule themselves, freed from external domination by foreign powers or internal domination by a tyrant. Yet the distinction between internal and external freedom does not get to the heart of Herodotus's account. The collective basis of freedom rests on *nomoi*. Freedom for Herodotus depends on *nomoi* in two specific ways: *nomoi* form the basis of freedom, the essential ground upon which freedom arises; *nomoi* also limit freedom by creating the substance through which freedom exists, meaning that particular *nomoi* support particular freedoms. In other words, without *nomoi* freedom cannot arise at all; yet only certain *nomoi* can preserve freedom by giving shape to a freedom that can sustain itself and the popular participation which provides its vital force. Different nomistic bases for freedom lead to better and worse freedoms; *nomoi* of equality best sustain the collective power that keeps freedom alive. This prefigures the "democratic entity" that James Lovelock identifies with Gaia.

Freedom does not, however, name Herodotus's highest good. Because of his concern with nonhuman as well as human things, Herodotus orients freedom toward a higher goal: earthly flourishing. Earthly flourishing names the condition of dynamic equilibrium where human and nonhuman flourish equally well. Nonhumans as well as humans participate in the broader conditions of earthly flourishing for which freedom is a necessary but not sufficient ingredient. Because *nomoi* are not just human-made things but rather arise in dynamic and responsive interaction with nonhuman things—what might go by the name of "environment" today but for Herodotus includes gods, fate, contingency, and cosmic principles such as reciprocity—the particular freedom realized by a people arises within a particular ecology of things. Earthly flourishing is not simply a human achievement, although human beings can do a great deal to advance it. Freedom provides only a condition for earthly flourishing, which in turn emerges from complex ecologies of dynamic things, human and nonhuman. The political ingredients of earthly flourishing include particular *nomoi* and a collective affirmation of these *nomoi*; its nonpolitical ingredients include many things beyond human influence and control.

This theory of earthly flourishing illuminates the political function of Herodotus's processual and situated inquiry described in chapters 2 and 4. Herodotus's inquiry elucidates the ecologies of human *nomoi* (and thus the potential freedom they might help to realize) in ways that allow people to understand the conditions of earthly flourishing. Such an understanding, Herodotus implies, is necessary to preserve flourishing as much as possible. Participants need guidance when deciding which *nomoi* to preserve and when to yield to powers outside their control. Good counsel in the *Histories* speaks with an eye toward earthly flourishing. Good counsel depends upon understanding the ecologies of *nomoi* and the freedom they may provide.

The *Histories* also underscores the importance of particular kinds of freedom that make such inquiries possible. This points to the underlying favoring of democracy as a political regime. Although the Persians embrace many other *nomoi*, their lack of a certain kind of public life—symbolized by Cyrus's mockery of the Greek agora—precludes open discussion of the conditions of freedom. The Persians have traditions of counsel that approximate this, yet they still exclude the vast majority of citizens. Herodotus would not have lasted long at the court of Xerxes, since the Persians lack the particular *nomoi* that support Herodotean inquiry. This lack suggests that Persian freedom cannot last, as its constitutive *nomoi* prevent self-critical evaluation. Without freedom, earthly flourishing becomes impossible.

Judged from the perspective of people's ability to sustain themselves, the *Histories* offers an implicit rank order of different forms of freedom. Anticipating Lovelock, Herodotus appears to favor democracy; Athens' *isêgoria* provides the strongest candidate for a *nomos* that sustains freedom and conduces to earthly flourishing. But Athens is not an ideal. Although Athens receives the most praise for its role in saving the Greek world, Herodotus criticizes the Athenians' dependence on certain leaders—Pericles in particular—as well as their tyrannical behavior around the Mediterranean. The Athenians seem not to understand the distinctive conditions that contribute to earthly flourishing; they instead begin to tyrannize others in the name of freedom. The Panhellenic alliance that saves the Greeks from the attacking Persians limns the possible conditions of earthly flourishing among different peoples while showing what more might be required. Panhellenic political freedom and the broader project of political solidarity across difference illuminate the path forward in the Anthropocene, lest human beings, like the Greek gods themselves, succumb to rivalry, quarrel, and hapless self-destruction.

The *Nomos* of Freedom

In ancient Greek thought, "freedom" arose in contrast to "slavery," yet this individual or personal understanding of freedom was soon transposed to social and communal conditions, marking a new form of political freedom achievable only at a collective level. Solon is the first Greek author who explicitly opposes "freedom" (*eleutheria*) and slavery (*douleia*).[12] In the wake of adverse economic developments that had affected the social and political status of many Athenians, Solon extended the boundaries of freedom, claiming to have "made free" the earth by removing the mortgage stones enslaving it. This marks the first use of "free" and "slave" in terms of a group. When Solon was elected magistrate (*archon*), Athens suffered from civil strife; in this context, liberation from debt bondage made an individual issue into a political one.[13] Martin Ostwald comments: "Freedom is thus infused with a political value for which we have no evidence in earlier thought."[14] Although Solon takes responsibility for initiating this freedom, he also warns people of a "slavery" into which they can fall by turning the management of the people's affairs over to one man; his legendary departure from Athens following the instantiation of these "Solonic" reforms reinforces the maxim. Slavery has also become a fully political term, used to describe the people's deprivation of effective power. Freedom, in contrast, indicates popular power—the people's "capacity to do things," in Josiah Ober's language.[15]

After Solon, Herodotus provides the next significant treatment of freedom and slavery in political terms. Although Solon anticipates it, Herodotus provides the main source for the decisive step giving freedom its political

dimension. Two different kinds of unfreedom appear in Herodotus as antino-
mies to freedom: first, the unfreedom of being under the control of an alien
power; and second, the unfreedom imposed by a single, arbitrary ruler. Each
of these conditions of unfreedom Herodotus likens to slavery. These forms of
bondage also have corresponding positive contrasts that Herodotus develops
across the *Histories*: freedom from domination and freedom to rule. Yet on my
reading of the *Histories* a third freedom emerges through *nomoi* of equality:
freedom as power, a power realized through collective and political action.

Spartan Freedom

The cynosure for most discussions of freedom in Herodotus is the exchanges
between Demaratus, the exiled Spartan king, and Xerxes (some of which I discussed earlier). Demaratus has sought refuge at the court of Darius, the first
king of Persia to invade Greece. Darius's son and successor, Xerxes, takes Demaratus to survey the vast army Xerxes has assembled to invade once again.
"So tell me," Xerxes asks Demaratus, "will the Hellenes stand their ground
against me? Will they resist?" (7.101). Demaratus replies that they will, dumb-
founding Xerxes. Xerxes laughs and asks: "How could a thousand men—or
ten thousand or fifty thousand, for that matter—when every man among
them is as free as the next man and they do not have a single leader, oppose
an army the size of ours?" Xerxes continues, elaborating his reasoning:

> If they had a single leader in the Persian mould, fear of him might make them
> excel themselves and, urged on by the whip, they might attack a numerically
> superior force, but all this is out of the question if they're allowed their free-
> dom. (7.103)

Demaratus responds, insisting that he tells the truth despite Xerxes's disbelief:

> That's how the Lacedaemonians are: they're as good as anyone in the world
> when it comes to fighting one on one, but they're best when they're fighting
> in groups. The point is that although they're free, they're not entirely free:
> their master is the law [*despotês nomos*], and they're far more afraid of this
> than your men are. At any rate, they do whatever the law commands, and its
> command never changes: it is that they should not turn tail in battle no matter
> how many men are ranged against them, but should maintain their positions
> and either win or die. (7.104)

This telling exchange illuminates one particular kind of freedom: freedom for
the Spartans consists not in license, as Xerxes imagines it, but rather in rule by
the laws. Yet the story is complicated by the language of *despotês*. Although this

freedom consists in collective power, it is power under the despotic constraint of *nomos*. The language of *despotês* suggests different modes of obedience: Demaratus describes *nomos* as akin to Xerxes's tyranny; it thus names the respect in which the Lacedaemonians are *not* free.[16] On the one hand, then, "*nomoi* are the guiding principle behind men's actions" such that all freedom depends upon *nomoi* as its basis and substance.[17] On the other hand, Demaratus's language raises a question about the degrees of freedom and unfreedom—the amount of fear and coercion—contained within the Spartan conception of freedom.

The exchange between Demaratus and Xerxes also highlights a contrast often missed in interpretations of Greek freedom. On the one hand, Kurt Raaflaub and Christian Meier have argued that freedom depends upon a separation from the "nomistic thinking" that preceded the development of freedom.[18] For example, Meier writes that "only when the nomistic basis of thought had been eroded by constitutional and legal organization could *nomos* come to designate a statute and so be transformed from a term expressing something given and preexistent . . . into one denoting a legal disposition."[19] The Spartan example shows, in contrast, that this "nomistic basis" can create the very conditions of freedom rather than being that which needs overcoming. This is more akin to Rousseau's vision of the "civic freedom" of the government formed through the Social Contract, one where citizens are "forced to be free" but without truly recognizing their coercion. The Spartans have traded natural freedom for this political form and sustain it through obedience to the ancestral laws of their people.

Another way of reading this episode could focus on how this exchange also suggests that Greek freedom is not so much made possible but rather *limited* by the despotism of *nomos*. As Demaratus describes the Spartans, "although they're free, they're not entirely free" (*eleutheroi gar eontes ou pantaeleutheroi eisi*). They are free but not free in every respect. Indeed, Ellen Millender has argued that Demaratus's description of the Lacedaemonians' despotic *nomos* creates a distorted portrait of the Spartans precisely to set off Athenian freedom as unconstrained, contrasting Spartan autocracy with Athenian democracy.[20] Herodotus, however, does not seem to judge this limited or mediated freedom as lesser. The battle of Thermopylae, where the Spartans lose but do so gloriously, explicitly alludes to the Spartans' obedience when Herodotus reports the Spartan inscription left at the memorial:

> Stranger, tell the people of Lacedaemon
> That we who lie here obeyed their commands [*rêmasi peithomenoi*]. (7.228)

If the implication is that compulsion motivated Spartan participation in the Persian Wars, as Millender argues, Herodotus does not cast aspersions. If anything, Xerxes's reaction comes most into question—for he underestimates the power of Spartan freedom, the basis of their triumph even in defeat.

Persian Freedom

Xerxes's disbelief at the Spartans' freedom also provides a striking contrast to the Persians' previous realization of freedom. The greatest concentration of freedom-related words in the *Histories* comes in book 1 and the stories around Cyrus's liberation of the Persians from the Medes. As Herodotus turns to this story, he notes that Cyrus's acts were not without precedent—he reenacts a liberation that the Medes had performed before:

> Assyrian dominance of inland Asia had lasted for 520 years when the Medes first rebelled against them. In fact, their war of independence against the Assyrians improved them; they cast off the yoke of slavery and became free men. Their example was later followed by all the rest of the peoples who made up the Assyrian empire. (1.95)

In this anticipation of Cyrus's liberation of the Persians, Herodotus also anticipates his description of the Athenians' improvement once liberated (5.78): all three involve collective acts—"they cast off the yoke of slavery and became free men"—that improve those who have liberated themselves. Refusing rule by the Medes, the Persians led by Cyrus also perform such an act. Cyrus says to them: "free yourselves from slavery." Herodotus continues:

> The Persians had hated Median rule for a long time, so now that they had found a leader, they enthusiastically went about gaining their independence. (1.128)

The success the Persians achieve in their conquests immediately following this liberation confirms their collective improvement.

Before noting the difference from Spartan freedom, it's worth remarking on their common basis. The substance of this freedom is collective power. The freedom of the Persians came not just from Cyrus but from their collective affirmation of this freedom. Cyrus does not force the Persians to be free. He persuades them. The Persian *nomoi* depend "on a moment in Persian political decision-making," in Carolyn Dewald's words.[21] When Cyrus replaces Astyages as the ruler of Asia, freedom comes not from his unilateral royal policies but rather from what Rosaria Munson describes as "the collectivity of the Persians and the choices by which they intend to preserve their status as 'rulers' (in the plural)."[22] The plural predominates in this passage: Zeus gives the land to "the Persians"; Artembares then declares, "let us move out of it" because "it is only reasonable for rulers" to act this way (literally, "men who rule": *andras . . . archontas*). All the Persians are, in effect, rulers; their affirmation of this power forms the substance of their freedom.[23]

Yet Persian freedom differs from the Spartan variety. Whereas the Spartans' freedom comes under the despotism of *nomos*, the Persians' freedom declines with the deterioration of the *nomoi* that first liberated them from bondage. Cyrus does not speak the language of the law so much as the Sophistic language of interest: do this and you will benefit, he promises in the episode involving the brambles and the feast recounted in chapter 3. The Medes' collective liberation ends when Deioces inveigles the people into granting him tyrannical power (1.96); you could read Cyrus as doing something similar, although the subsequent follies of Cambyses, Darius, and Xerxes make Cyrus look noble in comparison. When Cyrus receives Harpagos's message encouraging his rebellion against Astyages, his grandfather who had tried to have him killed, Herodotus describes Cyrus as beginning to "think up a subterfuge to persuade the Persians to rebel" (*ephorntize hoteôi tropôi sophôtatô Persas anateisei apistasthai*, 1.125). There's a trick at the root of this Persian freedom. It lacks the clarity of Spartan freedom. Neither has the Athenian commitment to ongoing political reflection and participation instantiated in *isêgoria*.

Scythian Freedom and Ionian Unfreedom

The Persians also have the ignoble role in the *Histories* of spreading unfreedom around the Mediterranean. The Ionians provide the most unfortunate example, but their unfree state does not come just through external domination.[24] Here again Herodotus's account suggests the intertwinement of so-called external and internal freedom, how resistance to tyranny and freedom from foreign control come together—and that when one of these two supports is missing, the other is likely to disappear as well. Recall the episode of the bridge Darius constructed to Scythia. When the Scythians come to the Ionians posted to guard the bridge, they offer the Ionians freedom if they only destroy it and prevent the Persians from escaping (4.133):

> "Previously it was fear that kept you here, but if you dismantle the bridge now, you can leave straight away without any worries, with the gods and the Scythians to thank for your freedom." (4.136)

The Ionians confer, and although leaders speak on both sides of the issue, Histiaeus of Miletus wins with his argument that only the power of Darius allows the Ionian leaders to preserve their tyrannies; all the cities would prefer democracy if given the chance. The Ionians tear down their end of the bridge and tell the Scythians that they have obeyed, but when the Persians return, the Ionians rebuild the bridge, allowing the Persians to escape. The Scythians seethe in response:

> The Scythian opinion of the Ionians is that they make the worst and most cowardly free people in the world, but that if they were to think of them as slaves, they would have to say that no master could hope to find more loyal and submissive captives. (4.142)

This passage underscores the complexity of the Ionian situation: the people ostensibly desire democracy, a fact attested both by Miltiades's proposal to destroy the bridge as well as by the subsequent Ionian revolt against the Persian-supported tyrants (6.5), but the rule exerted over Ionia is, almost without exception, tyrannical. These rulers practice a perverted form of democracy when they make arguments and vote to trick the Scythians (and not gain their freedom), and they do so, like the Persians debating forms of rule in the so-called Constitutional Debate, to preserve a nondemocracy. Herodotus's account intimates that the internal contradictions of the Ionian *nomoi* prevent the Ionians from becoming free: a contradictory desire to be free and a history of unfree practices.

A later story of the Ionians' involvement in the Persian Wars underscores how they lack the *nomoi* constitutive of collective power and freedom. Following the Ionian revolt and with the Persians advancing on Miletus, an important Ionian island, the Ionians call an assembly. The Phocaean commander Dionysius rises to speak, which Herodotus reports as follows:

> Men of Ionia, our affairs are balanced on a razor's edge. We can remain free or we can become slaves—and runaway slaves at that. If you are prepared to accept hardship, then in the short term there'll be work for you to do, but you will defeat the enemy and be free; if, on the other hand, you choose softness and lack of discipline, I am quite sure that you'll be punished for rebelling against the king. (6.11)

Persuaded by Dionysius's speech, the Ionians entrust their future to him. He begins to train the Ionians in naval combat, having the rowers practice the *diekplous* maneuver,[25] with the marines armed. For seven days the Ionians are obedient, but then they begin to flag. "Anything in the world is better than this misery," they say among themselves, "even so-called slavery in the future, since it's slavery we're enduring at the moment." Herodotus comments:

> This line of thought immediately made them ungovernable. They stayed on the island as if they were a land army; they pitched tents and kept to the shade, and refused to board their ships or practice their maneuvers. (6.12)

Unlike the Spartans, the Ionians cannot abide the discipline of *nomoi* that freedom requires. Herodotus's way of telling this is also notable: the Ionians' comparison of Dionysius to an enslaving tyrant draws their example closer to that of the Persians. Like the Persians and unlike the Spartans, the Ionians depend on the persuasion of a leader. Unlike the Persians and like the Spartans, they require continuing discipline. Yet neither of these conditions obtains for the Ionians for long.

The Ionian example also illuminates a specific difference between their potential freedom and the Scythians' freedom. The Scythians encourage the Ionians to embrace freedom by abandoning their post guarding the Persians' bridge. Yet this only accentuates the difference between Scythian freedom, which, according to Herodotus, requires no particular place of inhabitation, and Ionian freedom, which the Ionians consider dependent on their particular place. Early in the narrative, Herodotus remarks on the suggestion by Bias of Priene that the Ionians decamp from their land in the middle of the Greek and Persian conflict and sail to Sardo (today's Sardinia) and found a single city for all Ionians:

> This, he said, would enable them not just to avoid slavery, but to thrive, since they would inhabit the largest island in the world and exercise authority over all the rest. However, he added, if they stayed in Ionia, he could not foresee freedom for them. (1.170)

Bias offered this proposal after the Ionians' defeat at the hands of Harpagos; nothing comes of it, although its prediction bears out. Ionian freedom proved impossible in its particular place. Despite being the fairest region in the whole world according to Herodotus (1.142), freedom could not take root.

Athenian Freedom

The Ionians' story of freedom contrasts with the account Herodotus gives of Athens' becoming free of the tyrants, a story that also appears in the midst of the story of the Ionians' tribulations at the hands of the Persians. As I noted before, Herodotus's rendition rejects the conventional Athenian account that Aristogiton and Harmodius's slaying of Hipparchus ended the tyranny (5.55, 6.123). Indeed, Herodotus points out, four years after this act, the Athenians lived under an even harsher tyranny than before. Herodotus argues that the Alcmaeonidae, joined by King Cleomenes of Sparta, rid Athens of the Pisistratid tyranny. This series of crucial moments—the successive vanquishing of the tyrants—culminates with the affirmative joining of leaders and people. Following the departure of the Pisistratidae, two powerful men vie for power:

Cleisthenes, an Alcmaeonid, and Isagoras, a man from another distinguished house. Their competition for power ends when Cleisthenes enlists the common people into his association of supports. The Athenians were not passively freed; they wanted freedom (*boulomenoisi einai eleutheroisi*, 5.64). By joining Cleisthenes, the Athenians achieve their desire for freedom, and the Cleisthenic reforms of Athenian *nomoi*—dividing the tribes and solidifying the democratic identity that was already in the process of forming—create conditions to sustain this freedom for future Athenians (5.69).[26] Athenian freedom thus involves a crucial collective transformation of certain *nomoi*—reorganizing the institutions and thus the broader political culture in order to support continuing participation in the formation of practices of collective power.[27] This offers another intimation of what the *Histories* might say to the Anthropocene.

Unlike the Spartans, whose freedom depends upon the despotism of *nomoi*, the Athenians achieve freedom by reorganizing institutions, infusing them with the temper of equality to sustain collective power.[28] This transformation catalyzes further changes as the free Athenians become even more powerful.[29] At the end of his description of Athens' freedom, Herodotus emphasizes the connection between the affirmative political moment of employing collective agency to realize freedom and the transformation this affirmation wrought on the Athenians:

> While they were oppressed under tyrants, they had no better success in war than any of their neighbors, yet, once the yoke was flung off, they proved the finest fighters in the world. This clearly shows that, so long as they were held down by authority, they deliberately shirked their duty in the field, as slaves shirk working for their masters; but when freedom was won, then every man amongst them was interested in his own cause. (5.78)

Arlene Saxonhouse writes of this passage, "freedom of speech [*isêgoria*] was the tool of self-government, not a bulwark. Freedom of speech was the practice of men in public, not a protection for self-development."[30] Although the Spartans have a kind of equality in *isokratia*, this does not empower ongoing collective participation. It fosters equality but without the agora. The Spartans obey the laws set in place by Lycurgus; the Athenians participate in the transformation of their own laws in cooperation with Cleisthenes. Both of these are collective acts of self-rule: the Spartans change their constitution to *eunomia* (in the plural: 1.65.2), just as the Athenians desire and win their freedom collectively. Yet the crucial difference lies in the particular *nomoi* themselves.

Unlike the Spartans, the Athenians embrace a temper of equality, *isêgoria*, that lessens the burdens of the discipline of freedom. *Isêgoria*, as I described in chapter 3, enlists individual passions for the sake of the collective;

the Athenians, like the Ionians, not only want freedom but create a structure of *isêgoria* that fosters the common good through a kind of "self-interest well understood." The Ionians are given *isonomia* by Mardonius but this does not change the structure of society; it is a *nomos* without a practice, dead on the vine. Judging by the association in Herodotus's account, *isêgoria* involves a realignment of society, encouraging use of *isêgoria* from the level of the deme all the way to the *polis*.[31] In the *polis*, every citizen[32] had equal (*isê-*) access to the public space (agora); no distinctions of class could interfere with participation. Herodotus anticipates Aristotle's analogy of democracy as a "feast to which all guests contribute"; *isêgoria* encourages a diversity of dishes and thus a richer spread for all to enjoy.[33]

Unlike the Persians, the Athenians adjust their *nomoi* to foster and sustain collective power, the essential condition of freedom. The Athenians do not depend on the persistence of a fragile consensus between leader and people but rather distribute authority and invent institutions for practicing collective power. Although a leader like Themistocles can rise to a position of prominence, the institutionalized power of the Athenian people means he must compete for their attention. When faced with an alarming oracle that seemed to suggest they should abandon Attica in the face of the Persian invasion, the Athenians allow Themistocles to propose an alternative interpretation. Themistocles does not persuade them or demand their obedience. Note Herodotus's language when he describes how the Athenians respond to Themistocles's advice:

> So he advised [*sunebouleue*] them to get the fleet ready for a battle at sea, on the grounds that the "wall of wood" referred to the fleet. The Athenians decided [*Athênaioi . . . egnôsan*] that Themistocles' explanation of the oracle was preferable to that of the official interpreters who would rather they did not prepare for battle—whose advice, in fact, was that the Athenians should not resist at all, but should abandon Attica and find somewhere else to live. (7.143)

Themistocles offers an argument and advice; the Athenians are the ones to decide. Were this deliberation conducted within Persian *nomoi*, the ruler alone would decide and advisers would fear to disagree lest they displease him. Only under the leadership of Cyrus do the Persians have a leader who defers to others—namely, Croesus, who turns out to give bad advice. Athenian freedom depends on robust democratic power.[34]

Political Freedom across the *Histories*

Examining the nuances among Spartan, Persian, Scythian, Ionian, and Athenian freedoms, it becomes clear how the variety of *nomoi* within the *Histories* corresponds to a variety of concepts of freedom. Although ancient discussions of freedom began in the contrast of status between free man and slave, Herodotus focuses almost exclusively on collective, political freedom.[35] At the same time, political freedom is not reducible to a single form; freedom in the Mediterranean world, moreover, is not only Greek freedom.[36] Despite these differences, however, each of these peoples experiences freedom in similar ways at a general level. Freedom consists of collective power across two dimensions: not being subjected to internal domination by tyrants as well as not being under the control of an alien power.[37] But these two dimensions join in a *political* way for Herodotus: freedom is an achievement of the people themselves and one that creates and attempts to sustain "the political" as a moment of commonality and collective power.[38] Particular *nomoi* suit sustainable and robust freedom best. The Athenians appear to exemplify this most developed form of political freedom, in which *isêgoria* plays a crucial role.

This reconstruction of political freedom in the *Histories* supplants the often-drawn distinction between internal and external freedom.[39] "Internal freedom," or the freedom to rule oneself (and not just be free from external domination), proves inadequate to the story of political freedom that unfolds in the *Histories*. The description of the Athenians' improvement upon their liberation already suggests this: *isêgoria* involves not just resistance to tyrants but the ability to defend themselves against external threats; the corollary is that simply cultivating the private delights of domestic freedom will not forestall external challenges. Internal freedom cannot be maintained apart from external freedom; both are components of a political freedom involving a collective organization of powers around *nomoi* that also faces outward to radically different others.

The limits of the concept of internal freedom appear sharply in the story of Otanes. At first glance, Otanes's example appears to suggest an alternative to political freedom. Recall that as a member of the seven who liberate Persia from the usurping Magi, Otanes contributes to the so-called Constitutional Debate, advocating *isonomia* and a set of institutions much like those in democratic Athens. When the seven select Darius's proposal for a monarchy, however, Otanes requests to withdraw from the arrangements:

> My comrades, it is clear that one of us must become King, and whether he who will be entrusted with the administration of the kingdom is chosen by lot, by the majority of the Persians, or by some other method, I shall not compete with you, for I wish neither to rule nor to be ruled. So I now withdraw from this contest on the following condition: that neither I nor my descendants will be subject to you. (3.83)

Withdrawing from "ruling and being ruled" appears to deny the substance of political freedom: namely, the baseline of collective affirmation that creates and sustains the political. The other six agree to this condition and Herodotus comments: "Even now, Otanes' family is the only free one among the Persians; it submits to rule only as much as it wants to, although it does not transgress Persian laws" (3.83). But are Otanes's people really free?

Persian freedom, according to many interpreters, amounts to freedom from external domination, but Herodotus's broader account suggests that this is not the whole of freedom either. The Persians' freedom during Cyrus's regime depends on collective affirmation as well as nonhuman factors outside their control. Only subsequent to Cyrus's efforts at persuasion do the Persians lose sight of this concept of political freedom; Herodotus suggests that this lack of vision is to their detriment. The Ionians provide a contrasting example. The Ionians cannot defend themselves against external threats because they cannot rule themselves; they feel the constraints of the new *nomoi* Dionysius institutes as too abrasive and demanding. Unable to sustain internal freedom, neither can they preserve freedom from the outside. So, too, the Scythians: their reputation for being unconquerable rests on their nomadic power; they preserve this freedom by excluding connections to the outside world as much as possible and not building cities that can then be occupied. These are collective choices.

When Herodotus pointedly calls Otanes's descendants free, he appears to deny the basic tenet that one can be free only through the collective creation of "the political" that appears throughout the *Histories*. But Otanes's withdrawal is not really a withdrawal. As Herodotus notes, Otanes's descendants live by Persian *nomoi*—they choose only to what degree they wish to submit to the regnant ruler (3.83). Thus, while they appear to have opted out of political freedom, they really approximate a version of freedom different from the Persian convention, a freedom more Spartan than Persian: the *nomoi* become traditional and rulers are limited in their influence; *nomoi* limit freedom while also making it possible. Perhaps Otanes's comprehension of something like *isonomia* draws him closer to this Greek form of freedom.[40]

The examples of the Persians and the Ionians could prove misleading if they are taken to purport that freedom depends solely on the political moment of a given people; Herodotus, on the contrary, provides many examples of how deeply interrelated the distinct freedoms of the various peoples are. The politics of freedom is not, in other words, simply a national politics. It is an intercultural and international politics. As the case of the Ionians suggests, their inability to be free not just from tyrants but from the global webs of influence into which their struggles for freedom put them forces them to recognize their interdependence with the Greeks and Persians who surround them. The vacillating Spartan support for Athens both liberates Athens and allows their own self-liberation to stand. The Scythians once conquered the Medes and then withdrew, creating the vacuum that Croesus and then Cyrus filled. The collective affirmation of *nomoi* that Herodotus calls freedom cannot come through isolation or withdrawal; the world of things, human and nonhuman, is inextricably entangled across lines of apparent difference. Otanes's withdrawal is not, after all, a withdrawal but a complex negotiation of separation and connection, maintaining Persian *nomoi* even while greater Persia continues to change and to rule.[41]

Seen in its intercultural and international form, this concept of political freedom provides the best way of understanding the efforts of many of the Greeks to unite and defend themselves from the Persian invasion. For much of the *Histories* political freedom appears as a phenomenon limited to a particular people who secure their freedom through collective action; the threat of the Persian invasion, however, leads Greeks to articulate a political notion of freedom not just as resistance to tyranny but as something secured through their cooperative effort—that is, as a political achievement. Herodotus seems to plot this shift quite intentionally, reserving the vast majority of his uses of *eleutheria* in the final three books of the *Histories* to describe this Panhellenic concept.[42]

Because the freedom of the Greeks depends on their cooperative efforts to resist the Persians, it becomes clear that the conditions of political freedom apply. The Greek *poleis* must organize collective efforts to resist; they also must be open to persuading and being persuaded by one another to agree about this organization. The exchange between Gelon, the tyrant of Syracuse, and the Hellenic envoys offers an example of this in a negative light. With the Persians approaching, the envoys implore Gelon to join them in defense of Hellenic freedom, using the term *suneleutheros* to describe the collective freedom for which they fight.[43] Yet while Gelon responds using the term, he does not recognize its cooperative spirit. Rather than joining forces, Gelon agrees only to keep economic trade routes free and hangs back when the Hellenes sail to confront the Persians on Greek territory (7.165). Herodotus comments in a way that implies that Gelon's status as a tyrant prevents him from joining these efforts at liberation:

> The situation did cause Gelon some alarm, in case Greece might not have the resources to overcome Persia, but he could not stand the idea of going to the Peloponnese and having to take orders from Lacedaemonians, when he was the tyrant of Sicily; he found that prospect intolerable. (7.163)

You might object that Gelon plays the classic free rider, enjoying the benefits of Hellenic cooperation without paying its price—and you would be right. But Herodotus calls attention to this and implies that only Sicily's remote location kept it free for the time being. It would not withstand future contingencies.[44]

In contrast to Gelon, the Hellenes embrace a Panhellenic political freedom. The invocations of *eleutheria* in the final three books of the *Histories* come during scenes of deliberation and exhortation that signal its function as a unifying concept: Leotychidas's plea to the Ionians to join the Hellenes' efforts (9.98); Pausanias's speech before the great Greek victory at Plataea (9.60); the Athenians' refusal to choose their own freedom over the Greeks' (8.140–43); and Herodotus's long quotation of the oracle of Bacis, which concludes with the following lines:

> Weapon shall clash with weapon, and with blood shall Ares
> Crimson the sea. Then freedom will dawn for Greece,
> Brought on by far-seeing Zeus and noble Victory. (8.77)

Herodotus prefaces his quotation of this oracle with a striking qualification: "I cannot argue against the truth of oracles," he writes, "because when they speak clearly I do not want to try to discredit them." After the oracle, he repeats himself: "Faced with the clarity of this kind of statement (from Bacis, in this instance), I hesitate to challenge the validity of oracles myself, and I do not accept such challenges from others either." It would seem that the triumph of Panhellenic political freedom is destiny.

Earthly Flourishing

Political freedom may well be destiny for the Greeks, yet to what degree human beings can encourage or entice divine intervention remains unclear across the *Histories*. Herodotus identifies miraculous events that he attributes to the gods, and figures like Croesus who seek to manipulate the oracles do not succeed. Human beings cannot guarantee earthly flourishing; the Greeks' success, however brief, clearly depends on more than just their own efforts.

Herodotus frequently comments on unpredictable, miraculous events that either save or condemn figures and peoples across the *Histories*. The most striking examples, however, occur around the Hellenic victories at Mycale and Plataea. About the shrine of Demeter at Plataea, Herodotus writes:

> When the Persians were routed by the Lacedaemonians at Plataea, they fled in disorder back to their encampment and to the wooden stronghold they had built on Theban land. I find it surprising [*thôma de moi*] that although the battle took place by the grove of Demeter, not a single Persian, as it turned out,

either entered the precinct or died there; most of them fell around the outside
of the sanctuary on unconsecrated ground. In so far as one may speculate
about divine matters, I think the goddess herself kept them away because they
had burnt her temple in Eleusis. (9.65)

Here wonder returns as a response to the inexplicable that nonetheless leaves
its strangeness in place. Thomas Harrison points out that Herodotus shows
us the deductive reasoning that leads him to speculate about divine matters:
by reasonable standards, the bodies should not have fallen as they did; only
an unreasonable or divine explanation seems sufficient.[45] But from the perspective of earthly flourishing, this example also seems to suggest that the
gods favor the Greeks—that their star is on the rise. This narrative arc becomes more undeniable when Herodotus describes the coincidences between
the victories at Mycale and Plataea. The Persian defeat at Plataea happened
the same day as their defeat at Mycale. A herald's wand is seen lying on the
beach at Mycale, and a rumor spreads through the ranks of the Greek army
that the Greeks had defeated Mardonius and his army at Plataea in Boeotia,
a rumor that serves to boost Greek morale. Herodotus sees divine action behind the unlikely spreading of the rumor, not to mention behind the coincidence of the two victories: "There is plenty of convincing evidence that the
divine plays a role in human affairs" (9.100). Another coincidence was that
there were precincts of Demeter of Eleusis near both battle sites. Herodotus's
historical perspective allows him to recognize these striking occurrences.

Two things seem worth noting here. First, unlike Thucydides, Herodotus
is willing to acknowledge the importance of the divine. No impersonal necessity is at work here; rather, the gods intervene in concrete situations. Second,
these interventions are unpredictable. The gods affect and even transform
the conditions of earthly flourishing, but they do so without discernible reason. The miracle at Plataea appears to be divine retribution for the Persians'
hubris, but when the Cnidians are punished for trying to escape the Persian
invasion—and must ultimately submit—this does not bespeak any divine justice (1.174).

Herodotus's treatment of one natural miracle in particular, the storm at
Aphetae (8.13), gives a sense of how he fits these fluctuations of nonhuman
forces into the theory of earthly flourishing. Following the Greek naval victory at Artemesium, the Persians regrouped near Aphetae. After dark, a heavy
rainstorm broke and lasted all night. Violent peals of thunder sounded from
Mount Pelium, unseasonable in summer. Corpses and debris from wrecked
ships floated to the ships and became tangled with the blades of the oars. Ter-
ror descended on the troops. Herodotus continues:

> But if it was a bad night for this lot of Persians, it was far more cruel for those who had been detailed to sail around Euboea. It was not that the night-time conditions were any different, but they occurred while they were out on the open sea. The upshot was disastrous. The rainstorm struck when they were off a place in Euboea called Coela; they were driven off course by the wind, without any idea where they were heading, and were wrecked on the rocky coast. This all happened by divine will [*epoieeto te pan hupo tou theou*], to reduce the Persians' numerical advantage and bring their forces down to the level of the Greeks. (8.13)

Herodotus says no more about the divine; his remark comes at the end of a sequence of events for which "divine will" bore responsibility. Yet the logic has antecedents in Herodotus's opening comment about covering great cities as well as small because human happiness—*eudaimonia*, earthly flourishing—never rests in one place (1.5). And Artabanus anticipates it when he tells Xerxes that "the god blasts living things that are prominent and prevents their display of superiority, while small creatures don't irritate him at all" (7.10). Divine will does not smile on the great and mighty; it actually exerts a leveling force, an inclination toward equality. When it comes to earthly flourishing, small is beautiful.

Yet the storm at Aphetae also has another dimension. The storm does not determine the outcome of the subsequent conflict. Divine will evens the odds but it leaves to the Greeks and the Persians to struggle for victory. Herodotus, then, does not explain human events with divine intervention alone; these miracles play contributory roles alongside other human and nonhuman causes. The gods, rivers, storms, and camels (among many other actors) contribute to the course of events alongside their human counterparts. Earthly flourishing involves all these dynamic things, the things to which Herodotus directs his readers' attention.

The Counsel of the *Histories*

Although the *Histories* begins by promising to explain the *aitios*—the cause or responsibility—for the conflict between the Greeks and the barbarians, the *Histories* introduces another overarching purpose: to explain the *aitios* for the Greeks' earthly flourishing. Conflict and freedom come intertwined across the *Histories*. As Herodotus introduces Croesus at the beginning of book 1, he also notes that "before the reign of Croesus all the Hellenes had been free" (1.6). In effect, history begins with a struggle for freedom: this explains the early conflicts in Athens (1.62) as well as the situation of the Medes, who proved themselves truly courageous men by fighting the Assyrians for the cause of freedom (1.95). As I have shown in this chapter, a variety of free-doms appears across the *Histories*. Although one freedom story culminates in the final three books, freedom is present from the very beginning. Cyrus leads the Persians to greatness with the promise of freedom, a freedom that they—in the *plural*—win by liberating themselves from the Medes. Darius proposes a return to this freedom in the Constitutional Debate (3.82). The Scythians offer the Ionians the chance for freedom from the Persians but the Ionians refuse (4.133).

Attending to Herodotus's varied accounts of freedom across the *Histories* changes the significance of what appears like the culmination of a single story: namely, the Greeks' victory over the Persians. Throughout the *Histories*, Herodotus notes both the particular glories of those fighting and the general influence on events exerted by different parties, but in an oft-cited passage in support of his pro-Hellenic (if not pro-Athenian) sympathies, Herodotus seems emphatic about the importance of the Athenians for winning this freedom:

> They [the Athenians] chose that Hellas should survive in freedom; and after rousing to that cause all the other Hellenes who had not medized, they repelled the King with the help of the gods. (7.139)

Some readers have taken this statement as Herodotus's final word about the *aitios* of freedom in the *Histories*—that this is a story of *Athenian* victory and, if not an apologia for the Athenian Empire in his own day, at least a sign of Herodotus's ambivalence. But in the context of the sequence of victories and defeats that mark the second half of the *Histories*, the narrative of freedom appears more complicated. Herodotus interjects his own narrative comment in this passage in a way that should also arrest any quick conclusions. Before giving his reasons for the opinion about Athens' crucial choice, Herodotus writes:

> I have now reached a point at which I am compelled to declare an opinion that will cause offense to many people, but which nevertheless appears to me to be true, so I shall not restrain myself. (7.139)

He then proceeds to consider the counterfactual: if the Athenians had evac-uated their land or surrendered, no one would have tried to oppose the Per-sians at sea; without such opposition, the Peloponnesians would have lost all their allies not tied to the land, as these allies saw themselves conquered by sea; the Peloponnesians would have resisted nobly but ultimately lost. "Hellas would have been conquered by the Persians." Returning to the passage quoted earlier but in its context, Herodotus concludes this line of thought:

So anyone who said that the Athenians proved to be the saviors of Hellas would not have strayed from the truth. For whichever course they chose to follow was certain to tip the scales of war. They chose that Hellas should survive in freedom; and after rousing to that cause all the other Hellenes who had not medized, they repelled the King with the help of the gods. Indeed, not even the frightening oracles they received from Delphi threw them into a panic or persuaded them to abandon Hellas. Instead, they stood fast and had the courage to confront the invader of their land. (7.139)

Does this reveal a "profound pro-Athenian bias"?[46] Herodotus's careful language suggests something more nuanced. Herodotus declares an opinion that appears to be true but one for which he does not offer his usual evidence. He can point to no concrete facts or specific stories; no other inquirer has considered the *aitios* of the Greeks' flourishing. Herodotus has prepared his readers to doubt precisely such claims, to respond to unsubstantiated claims with inquiry. He proposes a counterfactual about how events might have gone if not for the Athenians' stand at sea (and abandonment of Athens); this kind of reasoning is quite rare in the *Histories*.

Naming the Athenians as the sole *aitios* would also strike a dissonant note given the dynamic complexity of the world of things that Herodotus considers throughout the *Histories*. Even in this passage, Herodotus notes "the help of the gods." The subsequent events also introduce the importance of other influences: the compelling interpretation of Themistocles; the Spartans' joining of the Athenians; and the Macedonian king Alexander's respect for the Greeks' freedom. The complexity of the *Histories* resists the reader's desire to attribute sole responsibility—be it to the Athenians or others. A more democratic form of cooperation seems at work.

But why would Herodotus offer an assertion so at odds with the deeper currents of the *Histories*? The *Histories* does not simply lead you to the edge of a sea of complexity to gaze on its boundless waves with speechless wonder. The form of the *Histories* elicits response and reflection from its readers. Even in the passages where Herodotus seems most explicit about a single cause— the Athenians' stand against the Persians—he reminds readers of his own role as a fallible narrator offering opinions. At the same time, in the absence of definitive evidence, Herodotus does not refuse to express an opinion. Putting his own process of inquiry to a reading and listening public for their own judgment, Herodotus invites deliberation.

That Herodotus would make the Athenians the subject of his most obvious and important unsubstantiated claim may not be an accident. Athens provided Herodotus's most obvious audience. It also held both the hope and the feared fate of earthly flourishing in the Mediterranean world. The counsel of the *Histories* elicits the judgment of readers and auditors in a way that might support the flourishing it chronicles. Although the pursuit of earthly flourishing requires much more than particular actions and choices, these do influence the course of events. Earthly flourishing requires continuing inquiry and judgment under conditions of dynamic complexity within a particular ecology. Athens needed to continue to do this work in democratic ways. To do so would involve confronting its own disavowed tendencies.

The *Histories* illuminates the challenge of seeing *nomoi* as political, as more than just natural inheritances or "the way of the world" but rather as ongoing outcomes of the political, outgrowths of the moment of cooperative commonality that forms the basis of earthly flourishing. Recall Herodotus's comments, in the context of describing Cambyses's crazed disregard of *nomoi*, that everyone would choose their own customs as best and only a madman would treat such things as a laughing matter (3.38). For Herodotus, each one of you favors your own customs, yet witnessing the dynamic interaction of cultures across the *Histories* may well prevent you from assuming that your own customs aren't always already in relationship with another's. The context of this passage itself underscores this reading: Cambyses's conquests have taken him to Egypt, where he disregards their customs; Egypt itself, as Herodotus has shown by this point in the *Histories*, is the origin of many of the Greek customs. The Athenians favor their own customs as well as the self-congratulatory story they tell themselves about their own predominance in the Mediterranean—and their role in the victory over the Persians. The counsel of the *Histories* directed at the Athenians denies Athenian autochthony, insists on the democratic power of the Cleisthenic reforms, and reopens the question of the meaning of earthly flourishing.

Only certain kinds of political regimes can sustain the type of inquiry that the *Histories* models and initiates. The *Histories*' concern with free regimes came at a time when the Panhellenic political freedom Herodotus celebrates had begun to disintegrate under pressure from the imperial ambitions of the Athenians. Seen in this context, the *Histories* appears written with the hope that inquiry might persist and call into question the dangerous direction Athens had taken. In the dynamic complexity of the world of things, earthly flourishing cannot be pursued unilaterally. Political freedom is a collective project that must go beyond the boundaries of the *polis*. The *Histories* shows how the Mediterranean world—which consisted of a multitude of peoples, not just Greeks and non-Greeks—constituted a single field of action. The Panhellenic democracy figures the kind of cooperation necessary for taking on the challenges of the Anthropocene. Human beings are "partner," in James Lovelock's words, to the "democratic entity" needed to self-govern the earth.[47] The Gelons of the twenty-first century can no longer rest on their pretense of isolation. Instead, Herodotus encourages human beings to fashion deliberative spaces that encourage participants to transcend their provisional boundaries and craft a middle ground for mutual invention of new common conventions. Whether or not the gods will favor the inhabitants of the Anthropocene remains another question.

"Why even bother with these relics of a savage time?" asks Roy Scranton in the context of the Anthropocene.[1] What can Herodotus's theory of politics and the inquiry that supports it say to people like the Syrian refugee Kemal Ali, the outlines of whose story I presented in the introduction? A Herodotean inquiry would complicate any simple explanation and thus might frustrate immediate political action. Because the dynamic complexity of the world of things exceeds social scientific grasp, grand strategies become feckless if not hubristic. Yet beginning with *nomoi* in a place marked by radically different practices in violent competition with one another—a description as apt for Syria as for the United States—can seem fruitless. What would Herodotus make of a "people"—Syrians, say—whose collective power appears so diffused, both concentrated in tyrannical leaders like Bashar al-Assad and challenged and countered from many other directions, by insurgent democrats, Islamic fundamentalists, Kurdish separatists, and so forth?

Only a broader inquiry into the conditions of the Anthropocene can begin to explain the causes of the massive movement of humanity which Kemal Ali's story bespeaks.[2] Just as the *Histories* starts with the recent war between the Greeks and the Persians as the still-shattering memory shared by Herodotus's contemporary audience, you might begin with the imperial wars of the nineteenth century (or perhaps even earlier, with the first days of imperialism). To examine the dynamic complexity of the world of things, a Herodotean inquiry might then pursue stories of buried sunshine, colonialism, industrialization, and the CIA.[3] Amid these stories Herodotus would also celebrate modern wonders like the internal combustion engine, air-conditioning, vaccination, and jet travel. And a Herodotean inquiry would also alight on representative individuals and groups who somehow encapsulate or speak for the era and its conflicts: Woodrow Wilson and Hafez al-Assad, Sulah al-Dia and George W. Bush, Aramco and Ataturk.[4]

The solution to the crisis of reason, as Sheldon Wolin reads Montesquieu, lies not in simplification but in complexity.[5] Anticipating Wolin, Herodotus treats complexity not as something you can achieve but rather as the beginning of a relational and iterative inquiry—the kind of processual and particular inquiry put on display in the *Histories*. Embracing complexity requires a transformation of politics; this inquiry illuminates the conditions that can encourage "diverse claims and life-forms" to flourish; inquiry is supported by and supports regimes marked by equality such that collectives can create and sustain *nomoi* for earthly flourishing.

Such an inquiry has not yet begun, but it might reveal quite a few *nomoi* that pursue equality and collective power to reach toward earthly flourishing.[6] Rather than reaching for entirely new practices, Herodotus would encourage attention to what is already taking place. How, to borrow from Josiah Ober's definition of democracy, are the people developing capacities to do things?[7] Today most communities suffer from a deficit of democratic practices that might empower collective action. "Politics is everything," David Wallace-Wells asserts toward the end of his book on climate change, yet politics both repels and excludes the very people most affected. Herodotus anticipates an alternative future. Recall that in crisis conditions similar to those that led Ali to Lesvos, the Athenians continue their collective practice. When the Persians invade Greece yet again and threaten the *polis* of Athens itself, the Athenians decide to abandon the city. Herodotus describes their sudden nomadism as akin to the Scythians': they detach themselves from their place, from the Acropolis and the walls of the city and all the elements that seemed integral to the Athenian community's existence, becoming a vagrant community; yet by doing so collectively, they repeat what began with their collective liberation with the help of Cleisthenes. They continue to practice transformed *nomoi* even while changing their conditions (8.41).

The Athenian example suggests the upshot of Herodotean politics for Lesvos and the increasing number of places like it: the most successful pursuits of earthly flourishing emerge from a particular history of cooperative effort—the repeated achievement of "the political" in Wolin's sense of a moment of commonality reached through collective power.[8] An organization such as Lesvos Solidarity illustrates what this might look like. Lesvos Solidarity operates PIKPA Camp, the open refugee camp in Mytilini, Lesvos, where Kemal Ali found himself after fleeing Syria.[9] Lesvos Solidarity provides humanitarian support to vulnerable refugees, offering on-site medical care, psychosocial assistance, legal support, food, clothing, and hygiene kits. It also runs children's activities, language classes, and social support services. Yet Lesvos Solidarity does not simply tend to the stateless and suffering in these immediate, urgent ways. It also fosters solidarity and public awareness through programs for refugees and the local community as well as upcycling projects where life jackets left on the shorelines are made into bags sold to the global market. These things too—nonhuman and considered waste—have political life.

Lesvos Solidarity appears even more Herodotean when considered in terms of a Greek history of collective efforts to empower communities through participation and self-provision.[10] In this example, Efi Latsoudi, one of the founders of Lesvos Solidarity, assumes the role of Cleisthenes by enlisting the people, many of them climate refugees like Ali, to re-create the *nomoi* of equality and participation begun thousands of years ago. Latsoudi had left Athens and moved to Lesvos in 2001 for a "quieter life," but when refugees began to appear, peaking at ten thousand a day in October 2015, Latsoudi joined with others to create PIKPA, the "village of all together," which became Lesvos Solidarity, in a former run-down holiday camp near the Mytilini airport. Before the camp opened in 2012, vulnerable refugees were held in police cells, preventing local support groups from accessing them. PIKPA allowed locals to come and help. They opened with a capacity of one hundred people; at their peak in 2015 they were hosting around six hundred.

What drove refugees to the shores of Lesvos remains a matter of controversy, but in response to actants both human and nonhuman, Lesvos Solidarity has refused the rigid practices of police and the state that prevented collective response. Instead of arrogating authority to experts, Lesvos Solidarity is open and self-organizing. In the light of the *Histories* these practices appear continuous with histories such as the Scythians' and the Athenians'. Lesvos Solidarity does not invent new *nomoi*; its members rather sustain a history of collective efforts in equalizing, political fashion. Moreover, they do not promise a solution to the "refugee crisis," not to mention the climate change that has played some role in producing it; instead, they exemplify the kind of clever response that Herodotus might have cherished: occupying a derelict holiday resort and repurposing life jackets to raise money for food, shelter, and textbooks.

Improvised responses to crisis like Lesvos Solidarity offer a repertoire of *nomoi* fitting for the displacements of the Anthropocene. These practices, moreover, echo the Panhellenic vision that informed Herodotus's own participation in the founding of Thurii. Located on the sole of the boot that forms today's Italy, Thurii was a Panhellenic colony begun with the leadership of Athens. No contemporary source exists, but Diodorus, writing generations later, places all the events around the year 446/45.[11] The Sybarites had located a settlement there after their original community had been destroyed by the neighboring Crotonites late in the sixth century and again in the middle of the fifth. Yet the Sybarites' resettlement failed and the Athenians organized another expedition in 444/43, which garnered supported from many other parts of Greece. This cooperation among *poleis* made the new community Panhellenic. The site was chosen according to instructions by the Delphic oracle, and the land was divided equally among the settlers regardless of their place of origin. A democratic constitution was established and the new Thurians were divided into ten tribes, organized into a Peloponnesian group, a Dorian group, and one consisting of Ionians, Athenians, Euboeans, and other islanders. (This method of division may seem like a highly Athenian model, but as Eric Robinson points out, democracy was a well-established phenomenon in Magna Graecia at this time.)[12] Charondas and Protagoras served as lawgivers and drafters of the constitution. Hippodamus of Miletus, the famous city planner, was also involved.

Early references to Herodotus often called him Herodotus of Thurii rather than Herodotus of Halicarnassus. Halicarnassus was Herodotus's birthplace; Thurii was most likely the site of his death. Yet the connection may be deeper: Ionia is the center of the canvas of the *Histories*; Thurii, although unmentioned in the chronicle itself, serves in effect as Ionia's utopian alter ego. Although questions about the influence of the Athenians on Thurii persist,[13] it seems clear that this settlement was intended to create a community founded on equality. This was also a settlement in uninhabited territory, an act of reconciliation and repair rather than one of aggression.[14]

What would a Thurii for the Anthropocene look like? Little territory is now uninhabited; Thurii's colonial model cannot be reproduced today. Yet the ideals of Thurii may infuse ongoing political projects like that of Lesvos Solidarity. Although no sources exist to say so, Thurii could have developed beyond a mere commitment to equality of law to create and sustain robust practices of equal participation (*isêgoriê*) and equal influence (*isokratia*). The lack of a Periclean leader and the attention to an architecture supportive of continuous practices of political equality could further develop these *nomoi* oriented toward equilibrium. I imagine a vibrant agora unshadowed by an Areopagus, one built to diffuse freedom by multiplying spaces of deliberation and debate. The collective cooperation that led to the settlement's founding was a moment of commonality, a figuring of the kind of political freedom necessary (although not sufficient) for earthly flourishing.

I imagine Herodotus offering his own inquiry for this new community: stories and observations about the dynamic complexity of things; collections of cultural narratives, customs, and laws—the *nomoi*—from the various

Greeks who were becoming Thuriians; and a committed defense of forms of equality, in particular *isêgoria*, as the best way to achieve and sustain political freedom. I imagine further Herodotus presenting his inquiry with diverting stories and implicit wisdom, entertaining while also provoking his audience into reflecting on the ecologies from which they had come and those that they might join in their new home. His characters would have a touch of Sophocles, and his political insights, a hint of Protagoras. There would be laughter around the campfire and quite a few unforgettable yarns.

Now imagine a Mediterranean Solidarity organized around equality, equilibrium, and the pursuit of earthly flourishing.[15] The derelict holiday resorts on the Ionian coast, emptied by tourists fearful of Turkey's political instability, are refashioned as twenty-first-century public forums (*agorai*) where people from the many groups that live along the shores of the Mediterranean Sea ("the Sea") can gather. Moroccans chat with Greeks, Albanians with Libyans, Algerians with Croatians. The Cypriots are split between two tables and the Sardinians throw the best parties. The Sea itself has many who speak on its behalf, some of whom consider themselves Adriatic while others are Aegean or Balearic. Sprat, shad, bonito, and other species of fish have voices. So, too, do shearwaters, shags, and other seabirds.

Mediterranean Solidarity would recognize that nonhumans must join humans to consider the possibilities and prospects for earthly flourishing. "Nature" and "culture" cannot be separated: people rely on the fish in the Sea but so do seabirds; the fish themselves rely on one another as well as many other nonhuman actants. Shared group knowledge—what political scientists have called "epistemic communities"[16]—exists among each of these groups; their *nomoi* reflect responsive interactions among different communities. Each would need to figure out how to listen to others and how to wonder at their differences. The human communities involved, from the leisured residents of the French Riviera to the denizens of far-flung Cycladic islands, would practice *nomoi* oriented toward equilibrium, recognizing that their power lies in convening all the actants of their community.

Although all earthly actants would find a place, human beings would initiate and sustain the *nomoi* of these parliaments. Human beings would convene the dialogic democracy, assembling those affected by the Sea's dynamic presence.[17] One basis for this solidarity would be contiguity, which also implies that this convention around the Sea would have porous borders—nothing on earth is sufficient to itself, and everything, all things, must find a voice in some parliament of things. Another basis for solidarity would be a desire for earthly flourishing along with the realization that such flourishing will come only with cooperative ventures uniting actants across conventional domains of species, nation, language, and beliefs.

Imagine further how these parliaments of things might hold their dialogues. So-called experts could speak on the basis of processual inquiries and the itineraries they traveled. Others might offer witness from their experience. Facts, testimonies, stories, and demonstrations would be placed *es meson*, into the common space for consideration and consultation. National governments, regional alliances, religious sects, and nongovernmental organizations could contribute here too. At times the conventional decision-making procedures would suffice; yet at others, these parliaments of things would have to invent new forms, such as the Greek alliance against the invading Persians. An alliance against those insistent on the primacy and priority of the status quo (to the detriment of earthly flourishing, present and future) may prove necessary.

The parliaments of Mediterranean Solidarity would have storytellers. These storytellers would invent stories with the amplitude to hold unpredictability and wonder toward the yet unknown.[18] Their stories would connect observations and evidence as well as tales about the past and what brought them to the forums of Mediterranean Solidarity. These stories would also evoke solidarity for the beloved yet beleaguered Sea that convenes them all, from the cedars of Lebanon to the hoopoes that roost on the rock of Gibraltar along their migrations.

The stories of Mediterranean Solidarity would also shift the mistaken beliefs of so many human beings living in the Anthropocene. While chronicling the possibilities of equality and equilibrium in an expansive political life, these stories would also point to how earthly flourishing is especially needful as an alternative to the destructive ideology of the neoliberal era, in which so many humans find themselves today.[19] A system sustained by unfulfillable hopes has shattered the earthly equilibrium that seemed so self-evident to Herodotus; this state of affairs does not, however, render the telos of earthly flourishing obsolete. Today's ideology of the good life entangles subjects in self-destructive *nomoi* and obscures their ability to change the collective conditions of existence. The stories of Mediterranean Solidarity would offer counters to the pathological desires for accumulation that undercut the very basis of collective power.[20] If this sounds familiar, you would do well to study Herodotus's story of the Persians. Storytellers of Mediterranean Solidarity would craft their narratives in a Herodotean vein.

Could this vision of Mediterranean Solidarity bespeak an Earthly Solidarity? Herodotus illustrates how stories are crucial, both for the complexity they can hold beyond information's explanatory function but also for the faith they can inspire in the possibility of miraculous human action. Recall that Herodotus begins the *Histories* with the wondrous deeds of human beings. His catalogs of wonders do not supplant the centrality of human freedom and thus human responsibility. Herodotus encourages his contemporaries to exalt greatness, including the greatness of the inquirer willing to pursue understanding to the point of exhaustion, to discover and elaborate an abundance of human practices, to celebrate human initiative and creativity. Unlike today's ascendant ecopessimism, Herodotus confronts readers with a wondrous spectacle of human and nonhuman, with stories of earthly flourishing meant to inspire miraculous action.

"Even—especially—in its twilight," writes Bill McKibben in the final sentence of his latest book on climate change, "the human game is graceful and compelling."[21] Herodotus celebrates this human game, from beautiful Persian marriage lotteries to cruel cycles of fate ignited by a golden ring. Herodotus also celebrates the human game of inquiry, the questioning and listening and pursuit of wonder. In the course of the *Histories*, Herodotus confronts again and again the miracle of human action: when Cyrus changes his mind and orders Croesus removed from the pyre; when Hippoclides shrugs off his rejection as the chief suitor for Cleisthenes's daughter; when the Athenians agree to abandon their city and retreat to Salamis—and then join together to overcome the Persian invasion one more time. Herodotus's *Histories* testifies to how what seems inevitable does not always come to fruition. As Arendt puts it: "Historical processes are created and constantly interrupted by human initiative." Herodotus anticipates Arendt's advice to "look for the unforeseeable and unpredictable, to prepare for miracles in the political realm."[22] He adds that this must take place together as collectives. Twilight takes place not just at dusk; the sun's half-light also glows at dawn. What will *we*, creatures of a day, do in this new dawning?

Acknowledgments

> She picks up the notebook that lies on the small table beside his bed. It is the book he brought with him through the fire—a copy of *The Histories* by Herodotus that he has added to, cutting and gluing in pages from other books or writing in his own observations—so they all are cradled within the text of Herodotus.
>
> MICHAEL ONDAATJE, *The English Patient*[1]

Herodotus's *Histories* stands at the center of Michael Ondaatje's 1992 novel *The English Patient*. Its eponymous hero, a nameless traveler under the care of an intrepid Canadian nurse in a villa outside Florence, has carried the *Histories* through desert crossings, abductions, airplane crashes, love and loss. The *Histories* has become a kind of commonplace book for the English patient. The nurse, Hana, discovers maps, diary entries, writings in many languages, paragraphs cut from other books, even a small fern glued into its pages.

Herodotus has accompanied the English patient but the relationship has not been one-sided. Some of these interlineations are corrections. The English patient respects his guidebook "of supposed lies" enough to improve it: bringing out his glue pot and pasting in maps or news clippings; adding sketches of men in skirts with curious and forgotten animals beside them. "The early oasis dwellers had not usually depicted cattle, though Herodotus claimed they had. They worshipped a pregnant goddess and their rock portraits were mostly of pregnant women."[2] Although updating this ancient book, the English patient nonetheless reveres it. The *Histories* does not simply travel with him; its author figures in the English patient's dialogues with himself. This means that the structures of the *Histories* begin to shape the structures of the English patient's reality, his interactions with others. "No more books. Just give me the Herodotus," he says. He reminisces about Herodotus as if he were a contemporary—not some gleaming, sculpted bust but a comrade, "one of those spare men of the desert who travel from oasis to oasis, trading legends as if it is the exchange of seeds, consuming everything without suspicion, piecing together a mirage." How else could "the cul-de-sacs within the sweep of history be discovered"?[3] When Hana falls in love with the English patient, she looks to Herodotus in search of the patient's identity, yet his character remains opaque. Herodotus's circuitous and digressive text evades comprehensive understanding.

I turn to Ondaatje's evocation of Herodotus because there's something in the present book that resembles the English patient's 1890 edition. Reflecting on my reading of Herodotus, I often find myself adding commentary—not a line-by-line exegesis populated with alternative translations, dates, and names so much as one step in an unending process of sense making, a discourse that, in Hans Ulrich Gumbrecht's words, "never reaches its end."[4] The task of understanding the present better "by means of antiquity" has no end. "What can't be exhausted," Nietzsche continues, "is the always-new adjustment every age makes to the classical world, measuring itself against it."[5] This book offers a reading of Herodotus in the Anthropocene. Just as the end of the *Histories* points back to its beginning, this book circles from head to tail with the *Histories* at its center. I begin and end in the present but between these points there's quite a lot of ancient history. This is not to apologize for the digressions but rather to call attention to how books like the *Histories* bring readers into conversations with themselves during the course of their ordinary lives.

I have often found myself, like the English patient, carrying around Herodotus. I turn to Herodotus both out of a tempered romanticism about the political as experienced in classical Greece—an inheritance from Hannah Arendt, among others—and out of a sense of disquiet about the narrowness of present political languages and political visions. My reading and rereading of Herodotus have also always taken place with others: translating the Croesus and Cyrus stories in a Greek intensive at UC Berkeley; reading aloud from a translation to my brother, Peter, in my Durham, North Carolina, apartment when prepping for my first experience teaching the *Histories*; and declaiming salient passages to students taking a course on ancient political thought at Penn. Herodotus is wonderful to read and even more so to read to an audience.

Many audiences have shaped this work: students at Carleton College and Deep Springs College, where I taught courses on the *Histories*; the Classical Studies Colloquium at Bryn Mawr College; the Western Political Science Association Annual Conference in Las Vegas; the University of Pennsylvania Graduate Student Political Theory Workshop; Kirkland House at Harvard University; Middlebury College; the University of Virginia Political Theory Workshop; the Northeastern Political Science Association Annual Conference in Boston; and the Center for Hellenic Studies Fall 2016 Symposium. I'm grateful to audience members, discussants, and interlocutors in all these places.

The research and writing of this book received support from Deep Springs College, Bryn Mawr College, the Bryn Mawr College Department of Political Science, the Bryn Mawr College Social Sciences Institute, the Isabel H. Benham Fund for Faculty Research at Bryn Mawr College, the American School of Classical Studies, and the Center for Hellenic Studies at Harvard University. I am honored by this support and I hope the resulting work is worthy of this generosity.

I'm indebted beyond measure to many people who discussed the ideas in this book and read parts of the manuscript. Clara Hardy, who joined my "Justice among Nations" seminar at Carleton College in 2010, deserves special mention, as does Larry Cooper, who invited me back to campus to teach the course in his absence. Akira Yatsuhashi never tired of discussing Herodotus (among other myriad topics) over lunch at Burton Dining Hall or runs in the Carleton College arboretum. At Deep Springs College, I found a formidable interlocutor with his own substantial opinions about Herodotus in David Neidorf. I'm also grateful to the student body for supporting an entire course devoted to the *Histories* as well as to John Tanner Horst, Kennan Lantz, Jackson Melnick, Pablo Uribe, and Nathan Wheeler, who made so much of it. I've often described this book as "my Deep Springs book," and while the conception predates Deep Springs, I hope its gestation in that wondrous, shimmering place is evident.

Before my first semester at Bryn Mawr, Radcliffe Edmonds invited me to join the Bryn Mawr College Classics Colloquium; I soon discovered what a delightful and generative community Bryn Mawr and Haverford faculty and students have created for the study of antiquity. Paulina Ochoa-Espejo and I have hoped to do the same for political theory with the Tri-Co Political Theory Workshop. These conversations have contributed directly and indirectly to my thinking across the last five years. We are both grateful for support from the Tri-Co Mellon Grant, shared by Bryn Mawr, Haverford, and Swarthmore, as well as our dedicated constituency of political theorists, including Ben Berger, Craig Borowiak, Tom Donahue, Jeremy Elkins, Molly Farneth, Steve Salkever, Ken Sharpe, Jill Stauffer, Jonny Thakkar, and many other locals from the Main Line, Philadelphia, and beyond.

Early key support for the underlying wager of this book—that Herodotus can speak to the present—came from the Center for Hellenic Studies at Harvard University. Many before me have gushed about the fertile atmosphere beside the burble of Rock Creek in Washington. I thank my fellow fellows as well as Greg Nagy, Kenny Morrell, Zoie Lafis, Lanah Koelle, and Alli Marbry for stewarding my stay at the center. I especially thank the library staff—Erika Bainbridge, Sophie Boisseau, Michael Strickland, and Temple Wright (as well as many others in Cambridge whom I never met)—for supporting my daily quest for obscure books and articles, many of which traveled on my hard drive to Kigali, Rwanda, and other far-flung places.

I found a rival to the Center for Hellenic Studies in the American School of Classical Studies in Athens. I'm grateful for the support from Bryn Mawr College that took me there and to all the staff and administration who assisted me in my work. I completed my first draft of this book with a view of the Acropolis.

With the support of the Tri-Co Political Theory Workshop as well as the Department of Political Science and the Provost's Office at Bryn Mawr College, I organized a manuscript workshop held at Bryn Mawr College for an earlier version of this book. I'm grateful to Alex Gottesman, Jeff Green, Melissa Lane, and Rosaria Munson for their deep and thorough engagement. I can only hope that I've learned from their questions and merited their commitment. I'm also grateful to the participants in the workshop, especially Rad Edmonds and Steve Salkever for chairing the two sessions, as well as to the chair of my department, Michael Allen, for his support.

Outside these formal environments, many friends and colleagues have supported my writing and thinking. These ideas grew from conversations at conferences, over meals, during walks, in offices and seminar rooms and coffee shops, and while summiting fourteeners with Danielle Allen, Libby Anker, Jed Atkins, Andreas Avgousti, Ryan Balot, David Belanich, Brother Kenneth Cardwell, Evan Carver, Jody Cohen, Rom Coles, Anne Dalke, Stefan Dolgert, Bob Dostal, Jeremy Elkins, Laura Ephraim, Sofia Fenner, Mark Fisher, Jill Frank, Marissa Golden, Carol Hager, Danielle Hanley, Kinch Hoekstra, Matthew Holbreich, Bonnie Honig, Seth Jaffe, Deme Kasimis, Alisa Kessel, Matt Landauer, Rebecca LeMoine, Thornton Lockwood, John Lombardini, Lindsay Mahon, Richard Mahon, Liz Markovits, Lida Maxwell, Chris Meckstroth, Charlie Nathan, David Neidorf, Seung-Youn Oh, Charles Petersen, Syd Roy, Steve Salkever, Arlene Saxonhouse, Dan Schillinger, Rachel Templer, Norma Thompson, and Alicia Walker. Bill English hosted me at Kirkland House and Keegan Callanan at Middlebury College. Xavier Marquez invited me to contribute an essay on Herodotus to his volume *Democratic Moments*. Murad Idris brought me to UVA and Jeff Green invited me to address multiple audiences at Penn. Jill Frank gave generous and profound responses many times across the life of this project. My two most frequent interlocutors—Ali Aslam and David McIvor—read the entire manuscript at a crucial juncture in its revision and development. The editors and anonymous reviewers at *Political Theory* also deserve mention, as do my anonymous reviewers and the staff of the University of Chicago Press, especially my editor, Chuck Myers.

My many families—Schlosser and Loveness, Trent and Huhn—have always supported my inquiries; I remain deeply grateful for all they've given me. Peter Schlosser laughed at the story of Hippoclides and later memorialized it with a T-shirt. Sarah Trent remains my greatest support and most playful interlocutor. She has led me to live and work in the many unlikely places where this manuscript grew beyond the comfortable groves of Carleton, Deep Springs, and Bryn Mawr. Above all else, she has joined me in welcoming Alden Jai Trent to the world, an occasion of greater and more joyful transformation for me (and us) than I could possibly have imagined.

Two great teachers and dear friends passed away while I completed this manuscript. Wes Robb was my great-uncle, mentor, and fount of encouragement.

My last conversation with Peter Euben, my teacher and dissertation supervisor, delved into my Herodotus project in its early days. Peter had more questions than I could answer then or now; I remain inspired by the example of his work and humbly hopeful that I can carry his great legacy forward.

Notes

Introduction

1. Wendle, "Ominous Story of Syria's Climate Refugees."

2. Wendle, "Ominous Story of Syria's Climate Refugees."

3. Kelley et al., "Climate Change in the Fertile Crescent." See also Gleick, "Water, Drought, Climate Change and Conflict in Syria."

4. Wendle, "When Climate Change Starts Wars."

5. http://www.unhcr.org/climate-change-and-disasters.html.

6. See the panel's Working Group II report "Impacts, Adaptation and Vulnerability," http://www.ipcc.ch/ipccreports/tar/wg2/index.php?idp=0.

7. See Selby, "Climate Change and the Syrian Civil War, Part II"; Selby et al., "Climate Change and the Syrian Civil War Revisited"; as well as Peter Gleick's response, "Climate, Water, and Conflict"; and Selby et al., "Climate Change and the Syrian Civil War: A Rejoinder."

8. Hasakah was not the first mover in the uprising; Derah and Homs were. Thanks to Sofia Fenner for this point.

9. Here I lean on Nicholas Hénin's *Jihad Academy*.

10. This is not to say that ISIS holds sole responsibility for the war in Syria—nor that the Western powers do either. The point here is that each contending explanation offers a partial, if important, explanation of the causes of the conflict.

11. See the illuminating contrast between California and Syria discussed by Pete Spotts in his "Tale of Two Droughts."

12. Lisa Wedeen anticipates her forthcoming work on liberal autocracy in the 2015 preface to her *Ambiguities of Domination*.

13. Wedeen, "Ideology and Humor in Dark Times."

14. United Nations Development Program, 2015 Human Development Report, cited in Wennersten and Robbins, *Rising Tides*, 4.

15. For a general overview of the consequences, both ongoing and potential, of climate change, see Wallace-Wells, *Uninhabitable Earth*. On food crises, see Palmer, *Hot, Hungry Planet*. On migrations, see Kingsley, *New Odyssey*.

16. See Chakrabarty, "Human Significance of the Anthropocene," for discussion of the difference between the *name* of the Anthropocene and the *concept* of the Anthropocene. In *A Billion Black Anthropocenes or None* Kathryn Yusoff highlights how this geologic concept is still fraught with politics.

17. Crutzen and Stoermer, "'Anthropocene.'" The exact starting point of the Anthropocene remains controversial. As Tim Flannery (*Weather Makers*) comments, Bill Ruddiman ("Anthropocene") has argued that human beings first began to influence methane emissions eight thousand years ago when wet agriculture, specifically flooded rice paddies, tipped the balance.

18. The concept of "the Anthropocene" risks confusing the issue of human responsibility by attributing the state of affairs to some generic human being, or *anthropos*. Understanding the Anthropocene, however, requires examining the various and particular human communities that bear differential responsibility and burden for this geologic shift. Echoing the approach I locate in Herodotus's *Histories*, Christophe Bonneuil and Jean-Baptiste Fressoz (*Shock of the Anthropocene*, 70) advance a differentiated history of the Anthropocene that seeks to shift focus "from the environments affected and the biogeochemical cycles disturbed onto the actors, institutions, and decisions that have produced these effects."

19. Purdy, *End of Nature*, 2. See also Morton, *Ecological Thought*, for the useful language of "the mesh" as an alternative to the human-nature divide.

20. Here I note Andreas Malm's (*Fossil Capital* and *Progress of This Storm*) searing criticisms of New Materialism and "hybrid" approaches to the nature/culture divide. I return to the importance of human responsibility and agency in chapter 3; Herodotus, on my argument, anticipates New Materialism while also emphasizing what human beings have done and must do to pursue earthly flourishing.

21. "Dr. Frankenstein failed not because he created a monster," Bonneuil and Fressoz (*Shock of the Anthropocene*, 83) comment, alluding to a discussion by Bruno Latour, "but because he fled in horror instead of repairing and improving him."

22. The term "actants" comes from the work of Bruno Latour (see, e.g., "On Actor-Network Theory"). See also Bennett, *Vibrant Matter*; Tsing, *Mushroom at the End of the World*; Massumi, *What Animals Teach Us about Politics*; Haraway, *Companion Species Manifesto*; and Kohn, *How Forests Think*.

23. Latour, "On Actor-Network Theory," 373. Quoted and discussed in Bennett, *Vibrant Matter*, 9.

24. Frost, *Biocultural Creatures*.

25. On "the force of things," see Bennett, *Vibrant Matter*. William Connolly describes the "fragility of things" in his book by that title. Noortje Marres invokes the language of the stage in "Front-Staging Non-humans."

26. I'm thinking here of Timothy Mitchell on mosquitoes (in *Rule of Experts*) and Romand Coles on grassroots organizing and climate change (in *Visionary Pragmatism*). I invoke these here in the spirit of hybridity explained and celebrated by Michel Callon, Pierre Lascoumes, and Yannick Barthe in *Acting in an Uncertain World*.

27. Scholars in science and technology studies have developed a powerful critique of scientific authority contemporaneous with the rising questions generated by the Anthropocene. Such interrogations have definite intersections with Herodotus, as will become clearer in what follows. On the politics of science, see Ephraim, *Who Speaks for Nature?*

28. Tsing et al., *Arts of Living on a Damaged Planet*, G11. Note here the easy invocation of "us," as if everyone were "modern" (in Latour's sense) and just realizing entanglement, complexity,

and shimmer. As Kohn points out in *How Forests Think*, this "us" does not include everyone affected by the Anthropocene.

29. The insightful work of James C. Scott (*Seeing like a State*) details how modern political institutions fail because of their limited epistemology. Like me, Scott turns to ancient forms of inquiry, specifically *mêtis*, as an alternative.

30. Dryzek, *Politics of the Earth*, 93. Compare this to Murray Bookchin's argument against centralization and hierarchy in *Ecology of Freedom*.

31. Lane, "Political Theory on Climate Change," offers a survey of recent work in this vein. See also Phillips, "The Solution Is Democracy," for a critique of "Climate Leviathan" tendencies occasioned by the Anthropocene.

32. Latour, *We Have Never Been Modern*, 142. Fien Veldman provides a useful overview of Latour's theory (see https://theparliamentofthings.org/into-latour/). Bennett connects Latour's theory to John Dewey and Jacques Rancière in *Vibrant Matter*. Recent discussion by Noortje Marres and Javier Lezaun in their "Materials and Devices of the Public" expands the parliament of things with a wider materialist approach. See also critical discussion of Latour in Whiteside, "A Representative Politics of Nature?"; and Simons, "The Parliament of Things and the Anthropocene."

33. Ober, *Athenian Legacies*.

34. Serres, "Science of Relations," 227.

35. For a concrete example of this in practice, see the vision of ecological democracy in Romand Coles, *Visionary Pragmatism*.

36. Political theorists seem to have come rather late to these questions of form, despite outstanding examples of the interweaving of matter and form—what I call the *what* and the *how*—from Plato onward.

37. Gibson, Rose, and Fincher, *Manifesto for Living in the Anthropocene*, ii.

38. Solnit, *Hope in the Dark*, xvi.

39. See Puchner, *Written World*; and Robert Coles, *Call of Stories*.

40. As Naomi Klein (*This Changes Everything*, 462) writes: "The task is to articulate not just an alternative set of policy proposals but an alternative worldview to rival the one at the heart of the ecological crisis—embedded in interdependence rather than hyperindividualism, reciprocity rather than dominance, and cooperation rather than hierarchy." This is the work of stories.

41. "Science describes accurately from the outside; poetry describes accurately from the inside. Science explicates; poetry implicates" (LeGuin, "Deep in Admiration," M16).

42. Ophuls, *Plato's Revenge*, 163. See also Melissa Lane's treatment of the imagination and metaphors in response to climate change in *Eco-republic*.

43. Here and in all that follows I will refer to the narrator of the *Histories* as "Herodotus." I do this while heeding Leslie Kurke's (*Coins, Bodies, Games, and Gold*, 28–32) warning about the difference between "Herodotus" the historical figure and "Herodotus" the narrator created by this historical figure.

44. M. Bookchin, *Ecology of Freedom*, 89.

45. To be fair, in *Down to Earth*, Latour does appear to shift more responsibility toward human beings for pursuing practices that can sustain life on earth. It only took the 2016 US presidential election.

46. Alasdair MacIntyre (most recently in *Ethics in the Conflicts of Modernity*) has influenced my understanding of flourishing, but here I note how his Aristotelian concept differs from Herodotus's in at least three ways: (1) Aristotle focuses only on human beings; (2) Herodotus puts

much more emphasis on *nomoi* as responsive interactions between humans and nonhumans; and (3) the gods (and divinity more generally) count as much more important for Herodotus. I thank Stephen Salkever for conversations about MacIntyre and Herodotus.

47. Sharon Krause ("Politics beyond Persons") writes in a review of recent articles on non-humans: "What we really need is to see ourselves as a part of the earth rather than as its masters, to wake up to our constitutive interdependence with the non-human."

48. Here I anticipate criticisms of New Materialism and its politics by Andreas Malm (in *The Progress of This Storm*). I expand on this in chapter 3.

49. Parry, "Thucydides' Historical Perspective," 48.

50. See the recent argument by Norma Thompson in *Herodotus and the Origins of the Political Community*.

51. Marincola, "History without Malice," 104.

52. Fehling, *Herodotus and His "Sources."*

53. See Latour, *Down to Earth*, 23.

54. Pritchett, *Liar School of Herodotos.*

55. Fowler, "Herodotus and His Contemporaries."

56. Evans, *Herodotus, Explorer of the Past*, 89–146.

57. I would argue that this expansive and self-reflective approach to theorizing politics is characteristic of ancient Greek political thought more generally, as J. Peter Euben (*Tragedy of Political Theory*) has argued about Greek tragedy and Plato, Jill Frank (*Democracy of Distinction* and *Poetic Justice*) about Aristotle and Plato, and Gerald Mara (*Civic Conversations*) about Thucydides and Plato.

58. Leslie, "In Praise of Anachronism."

59. Yusoff, *A Billion Black Anthropocenes or None.*

60. As this book goes to press, exciting collective actions such as the Extinction Rebellion in Europe as well as ongoing indigenous efforts across the Americas continue to provide models from which collective resistance could build.

61. See Norgaard, *Living in Denial.*

Chapter One

1. Chakrabarty, "Climate of History," 207.

2. Herodotus, *The Histories*, trans. Waterfield, 5. Unless otherwise indicated, I quote from this translation in the following pages. All Greek references come from Hude's Oxford Classical Texts edition.

3. Lateiner, *Historical Method of Herodotus*, 10. Lateiner does note that Thucydides's "precision" comes in tragic and rhetorical forms, which may in fact elicit a quality of concern for and tending to the world similar to what the *Histories* provokes.

4. Hans van Wees ("Herodotus and the Past," 323) usefully adds: "As is often pointed out, there is a great difference between ancient and modern standards of proof, plausibility, and acceptable invention, but this does not affect the essential point that Herodotus strove for accuracy by the standards of his time."

5. As J. A. S. Evans (*Herodotus, Explorer of the Past*, 24) puts it: "*Physis* was in no sense a technical word: it might refer to the appearance of the hippopotamus, the life cycle of the crocodile, or the physical stature of man—all qualities over which man (or the crocodile or hippopotamus, as the case may be) has no control."

6. According to Powell's lexicon (*Lexicon to Herodotus*, 9), the word *aitia* (in Herodotus's Ionian Greek, *aitie*) occurs fifty-one times in the *Histories*. According to Evans (*Herodotus, Explorer of the Past*, 29), twenty-two times the meaning is "fault," "blame," or "the sort of charge a plaintiff might launch in a court of law"; an equal number of times it can be translated simply as "cause." The remaining seven uses of *aitia* are puzzling, but Evans makes decent sense of them.

7. Scott, *Seeing like a State*, 2.

8. Martha Nussbaum's reading of Sophocles in *Fragility of Goodness* highlights a similar critique of tyranny and its projects of simplification. See also J. P. Euben, *Tragedy of Political Theory*, 96–129.

9. The path to what Kathryn Yusoff calls "a billion Black Anthropocenes" follows from this kind of attention to what lies beyond the salient and significant at the present moment.

10. Here I allude to James Tully's *Strange Multiplicity*. For its connections with the Herodotean approach I develop here, see my "Herodotean Realism."

11. I begin with the Proem while heeding Seth Benardete's trenchant argument (against Felix Jacoby) that the Proem should not determine the interpretation of the whole book. I follow Benardete's approach, moreover, of educing general insights from the welter of details that Herodotus provides. As Benardete (*Herodotean Inquiries*, 4) puts it: "The universal *logos* which Herodotus tries to uncover lies completely embedded in the particulars that he narrates." Henry Immerwahr's discussion of the Proem in "Aspects of Historical Causation in Herodotus" has influenced my own. I depart from him by showing Herodotus's concern for nonhuman factors as part of the *aitios* into which Herodotus inquires. Analysis of the Proem by Benedetto Bravo and Marek Węcowski, "The Hedgehog and the Fox," has been instructive, although I disagree with its "monistic" reading of the *Histories*.

12. Waterfield's translation breaks up the first, long sentence into two sentences and also obscures the prominence of the first words, *Hêrodotou halikarnêsseos*, which call attention to Herodotus's perspective at the very beginning of the work. Daniel Mendelsohn provides a useful comparison of recent translations of the Proem in "Arms and the Man."

13. I find Gregory Nagy's (*Pindar's Homer*) account of *aitios* in this sense entirely cogent yet also, as Leslie Kurke's *Aesopic Conversations* helped me to see, partial.

14. This describes what Daniel Kahneman (*Thinking, Fast and Slow*) calls the "WYSIATI rule": what you see is all there is. Herodotus, defying this rule, introduces his approach as a challenge to the conventional accounts of the conflicts between the Greeks and the barbarians.

15. You can garner this sense of *astus* especially in Hesiod's *Works and Days*.

16. My invocation of the nonhuman here aligns me with Harrison, *Divinity and History*, against arguments such as in Fornara, "Human History and the Constraint of Fate," that read Herodotus as a "secular" (29) thinker.

17. As one of the first and most striking characters in the *Histories*, Croesus has received a great deal of attention. I'm particularly indebted to Pelling, "Educating Croesus," and Segal, "Croesus on the Pyre," both of which articulated my own inchoate intuitions about the importance of Croesus for questions of learning, tragedy, and the fragility of human understanding. Harrison's treatment of Croesus in *Divinity and History* also speaks insightfully to these themes.

18. I owe a great deal of my understanding of focalization and narration in Herodotus to Irene J. F. de Jong's many insightful articles on the subject, especially the summative "Aspects narratologiques."

19. Thucydides, *Peloponnesian War* 1.23.

20. One may observe the influence of Thucydides on political thinking in particular among the so-called "realist" writers on politics, as treated with care and skepticism by many essays in Morley and Lee's edited volume *Handbook to the Reception of Thucydides*. See also my "'What Really Happened.'"

21. To be fair, Thucydides offers more than material explanations as well, although readers of Thucydides have often missed these, as S. N. Jaffe points out in *Thucydides on the Outbreak of War*.

22. Mark Fisher ("Heroic Democracy," 101) sees continuity between Herodotus's and Thucydides's use of *aitios*. Mario Vegetti ("Culpability, Responsibility, Cause," 276–77) describes the "embryonic transference from the domain of responsibility to that of causality" in Herodotus.

23. In "The Herodotean Solon" and "Solon's Poetry and Herodotus' Historiography" Charles Chiasson elucidates how Herodotus recasts themes in Solon's poetry to fit Herodotus's own concerns in the *Histories*. Although I depart from some of Chiasson's assertions about Herodotus, the general thematic contrast between Solon and Herodotus is instructive.

24. The word *elpis* appears repeatedly in the Croesus *logos* but then largely disappears in the remainder of the *Histories*. This may suggest that Herodotus is borrowing specific language from previous accounts of Croesus. In general, the sense of *elpis* feels consonant with its use in Sophocles as a delusional force that does not stem solely from the hopeful person but has a life of its own. *Elpis* has a cosmic shape much like *tisis* in Gould's ("Give and Take in Herodotus") account of Herodotus.

25. Emily Baragwanath's discussion in *Motivation and Narrative* illuminated for me the complex psychologies at work in Herodotus's *Histories*. Her rich analysis begins from an insightful reading of Plutarch, who criticizes Herodotus for ascribing unsavory motives to many of the Greeks he depicts. Baragwanath then shows the layers within these motives, extending while also countering Plutarch's reading.

26. As both a critical response to attempts to extricate Herodotus from his own religious sensibilities and a sensitive and persuasive reading of the *Histories* in its own right, Harrison's *Divinity and History* has deeply affected my own approach to Herodotus and political thinking in his age.

27. John Gould's *Herodotus* (esp. 63–85) and "Give and Take in Herodotus" have led me to recognize this "pervasive pattern of historical causation" ("Give and Take in Herodotus," 301) in the *Histories*.

28. Although I resist its conclusion that Herodotus places these events into a "master narrative," Harrison's "'Prophecy in Reverse'?" illuminates how the shaping of events by forces other than the actors' own volition takes place across the *Histories*.

29. Here Asheri (Asheri, Lloyd, and Corcella, *Commentary*, 134) notes that "the three causes of the war represent respectively rational and political factors, religious and irrational factors, and a personal element. One may add, without contradiction, the fear of Persian expansionism (46,1)."

30. So what causes historical change according to Herodotus? Many other commentators have attempted to answer this question; I have found the work of Emily Baragwanath, Jacqueline De Romilly, John Gould, Thomas Harrison, Henry Immerwahr, Donald Lateiner, Rosaria Vignolo Munson, and Hans van Wees useful for considering these many factors. But here I ask a different question: not what precisely causes historical change but rather how the dynamic complexity of the world must affect political understanding and political practice.

31. As Evans (*Herodotus, Explorer of the Past*, 21) notes, the explanations here do not include revenge. Evans persuasively shows that vengeance in the *Histories* is a matter of choice—"a simple axiom of statecraft"—rather than divine necessity. Given the expansive description of the causes Herodotus uses to begin this passage, Asheri (Asheri, Lloyd, and Corcella, *Commentary*, 214) seems not quite correct in asserting that Herodotus "only sees the personal reasons for the campaign."

32. Here I acknowledge the massive literature on tyranny in Herodotus, much of which has been instructive. Yet the essential question in much of that conversation—"does Herodotus think tyranny is bad?"—seems less important to me here than what in particular makes tyrannies ineffective and what, if anything, political leaders could have learned had they listened to Herodotus. Matthew Christ, in "Herodotean Kings and Historical Inquiry," comes closest to addressing these questions, showing how the kings who fare best in the *Histories* are those who, like Herodotus, concede the superiority of *nomoi* to their own ambitions and desires.

33. Compare this response to Herodotus's comment about the Egyptians following the death of their king. The grasping for a king by a people proves equally as destructive as the grasping for power by the monarch himself.

34. In "The Wise Adviser in Herodotus," Richmond Lattimore distinguishes between "wise advisers" like Solon and "practical advisers" like Themistocles. The distinction illuminates the degree to which the failure to listen by rulers is not simply a tragic theme; practical advice often goes unheeded too.

35. I depart here from Hans-Peter Stahl's ("Learning through Suffering?," 36) insistence that the "long and painful process of learning . . . does not provide the learner . . . with any clue to apply his recent learning appropriately." Stahl considers the wisdom of advisers in Herodotus meaningless, yet as Susan Shapiro ("Learning through Suffering") has argued, while wisdom is limited both by the power of divine intervention and by the tendency of human beings to learn only by direct experience, wisdom still provides a ballast against the changeability of fortune. Herodotus's emphasis on human agents equipped with choice locates a place for this wisdom to have consequences. Herodotean inquiry offers an alternative to "learning through suffering" even while maintaining, with the tragic poets, that the world eludes complete comprehension.

36. As Harrison ("Cause of Things," 157) puts it, Herodotus emphasizes a multitude of individual causes, many of them human, for significant historical action: "Herodotus' achievement then consists in stringing such individual (and collective) motives together into a chain, to reveal, from a starting point of primal isolation, the gradual thickening of such personal motivations, the accumulation of contact and of contingency, the broadening of the horizon of human ambition."

37. Sophocles, *Oedipus tyrannos*, lines 1329–35 (my translation).

38. As François Hartog (*Mirror of Herodotus*, 336) writes, the tragic schemas function as a model of intelligibility for despotic power. Charles Segal ("Croesus on the Pyre," 40), among others, notes the connection between Croesus and Sophoclean drama.

39. In this vein, Harrison ("Cause of Things," 160–61) writes that the result of history is "to understand much but to have no power," riffing on a story Herodotus recounts of an anonymous Persian's remark to Thersander at the Theban banquet (9.16). Herodotus tells this story immediately before his account of the Greek victory at Plataea, however, which suggests the possibility of reversing seemingly fateful occurrences: the Persians *should* have won yet the Greeks were victorious.

40. The connection between *archê* and *aitios* will have ramifications for the meaning of the *Histories* in its own time, in particular vis-à-vis Athens; I treat this more fully in chapter 4.

41. Here I draw on John G. Gammie's useful summation in "Herodotus on Kings and Tyrants," 172–75.

42. Dewald, "Form and Content," 32.

43. Dewald, "Form and Content," 33.

44. Dewald ("Form and Content," 35) comments: "Herodotus thinks the personal failures of despotism occur for structural reasons: the way despotism works leads it to overreach itself." See further discussion in Landauer, *Dangerous Counsel*.

45. Dewald, "Form and Content," 42.

46. Asheri (Asheri, Lloyd, and Corcella, *Commentary*, 129) asserts that Herodotus views the removal of Orestes's bones as the origin of Spartan superiority in the Peloponnese, which explains why Croesus sought an alliance with Sparta.

47. Here my reading is deeply influenced by Jonathan Lear's brilliant essay on *Oedipus tyrannos*, "Knowingness and Abandonment."

48. The use of *thôm-* composites is repeated in the next paragraph, as noted by Asheri (Asheri, Lloyd, and Corcella, *Commentary*, 130).

49. This is not to say that Croesus has learned a lesson he could apply more broadly, as the bad advice he later offers to Cyrus (about attacking the Massagetae) seems to suggest.

50. Plato and Aristotle name wonder as the starting point of philosophy, suggesting continuity between Herodotus's *historia* and the practice of philosophy.

51. Dewald, "Narrative Surface and Authorial Voice," 159. Here I draw on my discussion of wonder and politics in "Herodotean Realism."

52. Mary Dietz ("Between *Polis* and Empire") treats Aristotle as a thinker moving beyond the *polis*. Other ancient Greek thinkers such as Homer and Hesiod write prior to the prominence of the *polis* as well.

53. Heraclitus 36, in Kahn, *Art and Thought of Heraclitus*, 45.

54. Herodotus thus recalls earlier antecedents in the wisdom literature tradition, such as Hesiod. As Laura Slatkin ("Measuring Authority, Authoritative Measures," 28) points out, Hesiod lacks an abstract term for "nature" to represent the world: "What 'nature' is and how it operates emerges from accounts of its specific, concrete individual elements, and from their presence in a range of tropes, including metaphor, personification, riddle, fable, and proverb."

55. Scott's *Seeing like a State* offers a crucial example. The work of Bent Flyvbjerg (e.g., *Making Social Science Matter* and *Rationality and Power*) offers another. Both Scott and Flyvbjerg return to ancient sources: Scott on *mêtis* (as elaborated by Marcel Detienne and Jean-Pierre Vernant) and Flyvbjerg to Aristotle.

56. Mann and Wainwright, *Climate Leviathan*.

57. Quoted in Hamilton, *Defiant Earth*, 23.

Chapter Two

1. Yusoff, *A Billion Black Anthropocenes or None*, 2.

2. These first words instantly distinguish Herodotus from Homer: Herodotus speaks in his own voices and not as a channel of the Muses. I discuss the differences between Homer and Herodotus more fully in chapter 4.

3. Hartog, *Miroir d'Hérodote*. I cite the English translation by J. Lloyd in all that follows.

4. Seth Benardete has convinced me of the centrality of the Egypt narrative for understanding Herodotus's inquiry and, in particular, its discovery of the universal in the particular (as one

can see in Benardete, *Herodotean Inquiries*, 67). Here I try to bring this level of analysis to the question of Herodotus's presence in the *Histories*.

5. In the passage quoted in one of this chapter's epigraphs: Yusoff, *A Billion Black Anthropocenes or None*, 2.

6. Momigliano, "The Place of Herodotus in the History of Historiography," 3.

7. Robert Fowler's "Herodotus and His Contemporaries" convinced me of the distinctiveness of Herodotus's use of the first person, which is the key to understanding the inquirer's presence.

8. As noted by How and Wells in their *Commentary*, 237.

9. In his illuminating discussion of this episode, "Herodotus and an Egyptian Mirage," Ian Moyer shows how Egyptians constructed a "visual genealogy" consisting of statues with genealogical descriptions and relief sculptures representing generations of priests succeeding to their fathers' office in order to cultivate links with the historical past in the Late Period of Egyptian history. This interpretation amplifies my own by emphasizing the agency of the Egyptian priests as well as other non-Greek "informants" in Herodotus; their self-representations were not merely mirrors of Herodotus's position. As Moyer puts it: "Analyses of the Herodotean 'other' fail to grasp this contribution of Egyptian culture to Herodotus' attempt at formulating a new Greek historical consciousness because their approach to understanding the cultural representations at play is decidedly Hellenocentric" (75).

10. Here Robert Fowler ("Herodotus and His Prose Predecessors," 32) adds: "As a matter of rhetoric too, simple pronouncements ex cathedra, in the manner of a Hecataeus, no longer persuade an audience. One must give evidence of how one arrived at one's conclusions, weighing pros and cons." A number of interpreters of Herodotus have helped me to grasp the nuances of his self-presentation in the *Histories*, and I incorporate many of their insights in the following pages. I am especially indebted to Bakker, "Making of History"; Boedeker, "Herodotus's Genre(s)"; Dewald, "Narrative Surface and Authorial Voice"; Luraghi, "Meta-*historiê*" and "Importance of Being λόγιος"; and Marincola, "Herodotean Narrative."

11. Christ, "Herodotean Kings and Historical Inquiry," 185.

12. Matthew Christ ("Herodotean Kings and Historical Inquiry," 172) notes that there is a "striking affinity" despite these criticisms, one that appears in how Herodotus uses the same phrase (*es diapeiran . . . apichesthai*) that here describes Psammetichus's experiment when he later characterizes his own inquiries.

13. This anticipates an approach Aristotle develops, as Jonathan Lear (*Aristotle*) elaborates. Thank you to Jill Frank for this point.

14. This resembles Thucydides's approach in the first book of his *History*; however, as I have argued elsewhere ("Herodotean Realism"), Herodotus foregrounds his process of inquiry more explicitly than Thucydides.

15. Hartog is not alone in making this criticism, and I have cut my teeth against similar arguments in Cartledge, "Herodotus and 'the Other'"; Gray, "Herodotus and the Rhetoric of Otherness"; Redfield, "Herodotus the Tourist"; and Vasunia, *Gift of the Nile*. As will become clear in what follows, I find these approaches inadequate for comprehending the tensions within Herodotus's work, tensions that draw the readers and auditors into self-conscious and relational inquiry. The writings of Carolyn Dewald, Ian Moyer, Rosaria Munson, Christopher Pelling, Tim Rood, and Rosalind Thomas discussed below have contributed to my reading that pulls away from Hartog's approach.

16. Hartog, *Mirror of Herodotus*, 368.

17. Hartog, *Mirror of Herodotus*, 370.

18. It seems worth noting that Herodotus *could* have described Egypt and Scythia in solely strategic terms given that the story turns to Egypt and Scythia because of invasions by the Persians. And yet he doesn't—he's instead quite expansive about both places.

19. Hartog, *Memories of Odysseus*, 92.

20. Hartog, *Memories of Odysseus*, 91.

21. The writings of Kostas Vlassopoulos led me to understand the networks and interactions that formed the world in which Herodotus wrote; his *Greeks and Barbarians* offers the most approachable and general introduction, while his *Unthinking the Greek Polis* provides a more focused account. In *A Small Greek World*, Irad Malkin cogently applies a network analysis to the formation of Hellenism, showing how physical divergence created the conditions for cultural convergence.

22. Hartog and critics in this vein tend to underplay (if not ignore) the *metahistorical* aspect of Herodotus's *Histories*, an aspect that is not simply unique to Herodotus but appears in the inquiries of his contemporary Hippocratic writers (with their emphasis on situated empirical knowledge) as well as many pre-Socratics (given the importance of the *practice* of philosophy to their speculative inquiries).

23. Dewald, review of *Mirror of Herodotus*, 220.

24. Dewald, review of *Mirror of Herodotus*, 220.

25. Hartog, *Mirror of Herodotus*, 348.

26. This highlights the limits of Phiroze Vasunia's reading of the *Histories* in *Gift of the Nile*, which treats the trope of inversion as determinative for everything that follows while ignoring the particular examples of cooperation and mixture that I have adduced.

27. The story of the Scythians anticipates the argument of James C. Scott's *Against the Grain*. Certain *nomoi*—such as grain cultivation—serve the projects of legibility and control characteristic of modern states as well as ancient tyrants. Herodotus's admiration for the Scythians anticipates Scott's (which is explicit: *Against the Grain*, 235–39).

28. This phrase appears three times in Hartog, *Mirror of Herodotus*, 55, 200, and 221.

29. Purves, *Space and Time in Ancient Greek Narrative*, 126.

30. Purves, *Space and Time in Ancient Greek Narrative*, 127.

31. For illuminating the dimensions of Herodotus's inquiry into Egypt, I'm especially grateful to John Marincola's "Herodotean Narrative."

32. The implicit presupposition of this is that "local knowledge" counts for a great deal. As Nino Luraghi ("Local Knowledge in Herodotus' *Histories*," 144) helpfully puts it: "One may expect any human group, people or polis, to have a version of its own past which puts that group into a favorable light."

33. This contrasts with James Romm's (*Herodotus*) account of Herodotus's mapping. I owe Romm for bringing the importance of *oikeomenê* in the *Histories* to my attention; I depart from Romm, however, with my emphasis on its construction through the travels and relationships that the inquirer undertakes.

34. Brooke Holmes educes such a reading of the Hippocratic writers in her persuasive *The Symptom and the Subject*. Her work builds on the foundational writings of G. E. R. Lloyd, in particular *Magic, Reason, and Experience* and *Revolutions of Wisdom*, from which I have learned a great deal.

35. Dewald, review of *Mirror of Herodotus*, 221.

36. Kapuściński (*Travels with Herodotus*, 177) writes: "I was quite consciously trying to learn the art of reportage and Herodotus struck me as a valuable teacher. I was intrigued by

his encounters, precisely because so much of what we write about derives from our relation to other people—I-he, I-they. That relation's quality and temperature, as it were, have their direct bearing on the final text. We depend on others; reportage is perhaps the form of writing most reliant on the collective."

37. Quoting Redfield, "Herodotus the Tourist," 98. He translates *Odyssey* 1.1–5.

38. Nightingale, "On Wandering and Wondering," 32.

39. Another reading of this story could concern the kind of political community hospitable to inquiry and the implicit contrast between Scythia and Herodotus's adopted Athens.

40. These last few paragraphs should clarify my differences from Roxanne Euben (*Journeys to the Other Shore*) and Susan McWilliams (e.g., *Traveling Back*), both of whom take Herodotus as a practitioner of *theoria*. I agree that the *Histories* offers rich accounts of *theoria*, but I aim to show here that these accounts elicit a contrast with the practice of relational inquiry. (Arlene Saxonhouse also invokes *theoria* to describe Herodotus, likening him to Solon, but she does not rely on this description for her own sensitive reading of the *Histories* in *Athenian Democracy*, 31–57.) The point of my argument here is that Herodotus did not simply export Greek values and cultures; rather, the conversations he recounts and the travels he reports imprint the narrative as a whole. The known world is not what Herodotus's preconceptions tell him it is; rather, it is the product of the historian's interactive itinerary through this world, an itinerary that often undermines or destabilizes the ideas with which the historian begins. James Redfield ("Herodotus the Tourist," 102) is thus wrong to assert that Herodotus "did not so much derive his interpretations from his inquiries; rather he brought to his inquiries value [*sic*] and categories wherewith to interpret them." This interpretation echoes Hartog's assertion about the predetermined grids and polarities that shaped Herodotus's accounts of non-Greeks. Granted, Herodotus does often begin with such conventional approaches. The trajectory of the narrative, however, is toward complexity and complication of these assumptions.

41. Thompson's *Herodotus and the Origins of the Political Community* teems with suggestive observations, many of which have excited my own thinking about passages within the *Histories* as well as questions that it raises.

42. I treat the contrast between Herodotus's and Thucydides's inquiries more in my "Herodotean Realism."

43. R. Euben, *Journeys to the Other Shore*, 55.

Chapter Three

1. Latour, *Facing Gaia*, 235.

2. Here I depart from Lauren Apfel's argument in *Advent of Pluralism*, which connects Herodotus and Protagoras on the basis of their pluralism. Apfel does not discuss the political forms of equality that Herodotus introduces and how these distinctions separate Herodotus from Protagoras.

3. Chakrabarty, "Climate of History," 207.

4. Hamilton, *Defiant Earth*, 63.

5. Malm, *Progress of This Storm*, 60.

6. I write "so-called" because the debate concerns, not "*politeiai*" in the sense of holistic political regimes, but rather forms of rule that will be imposed regardless of the inhabitants' desires. Arlene Saxonhouse (*Athenian Democracy*, 53) rightly argues that debate is not the first theoretical defense of democracy; rather, the debate presents individuals having to decide where

to allocate authority, on the basis of an assessment of which institutional arrangements will promote the values of most importance to the debaters. Along these lines, Christopher Pelling ("Speech and Action," 139) describes this as a debate "not so much on 'the constitutions,' [and] more on tyranny." While Darius's proposal carries the day, the debaters' abstraction from the Persians' wishes anticipates the decline of freedom that follows. An early version of my reading of the Constitutional Debate appears in my "Herodotus' Political Ecologies."

7. Saxonhouse's argument in *Athenian Democracy* inclines me not to read all of Herodotus's political thinking through the lens of this particular episode, which has been the tendency of many approaches; here I offer the previous two chapters as broader contexts that facilitate my own reading.

8. Danielle Allen ("Origins of Political Philosophy," 78) describes the "birth" of political philosophy in Herodotus's *Histories*. Her account suggests in particular how Herodotus's treatment of different regimes opens a rich vein that later ancient political thinkers continued to mine.

9. Contrary to many of these readings (and as Gerry Mara has reminded me), it's important to note in advance that this comparative political assessment takes place through particular characters depicted with their own desires, orientations, and relative power. In other words, the presentation of an incipient "comparative politics" approach is not disinterested.

10. The writings of Kurt Raaflaub and Sarah Forsdyke do impressive work to show how Herodotus's concerns reflect certain Athenian preoccupations in his own day (ca. 440 BCE). I discuss these more in chapter 5.

11. As Martin Ostwald in *Nomos and the Beginnings of Athenian Democracy* persuasively shows. My discussion has also benefited a great deal from John Lombardini's analysis of *isonomia* in his "Isonomia and the Public Sphere."

12. Waterfield translates *isonomia* here as "equality before the law." As I describe in what follows, I prefer "equality of law" as a translation.

13. Sarah Forsdyke illuminates the particular details of this correspondence in her "Athenian Democratic Ideology."

14. I owe a great deal of my understanding of the workings of Athenian democracy to the writings of Josiah Ober. "What the Ancient Greeks Can Tell Us about Democracy," his general overview of research on ancient Athenian democracy and its relevance for thinking about contemporary politics, remains sterling.

15. In addition to Ober's work, I have found the following writings helpful: Rhodes, *Athenian Boule*, on the council; Gagarin and Cohen, *Cambridge Companion to Ancient Greek Law*, and Todd, *Shape of Athenian Law*, on law in ancient Greece; and Lanni, *Law and Justice in the Courts of Classical Athens*, on the scope of jury discretion.

16. I discuss accountability in chapter 2, "Beyond Socratic Citizenship," of *What Would Socrates Do?* This includes references to much of the excellent research that informs my view, including Roberts, *Accountability in Athenian Government*; and Hansen, *Athenian Democracy in the Age of Demosthenes*. Since my book's publication, Matthew Landauer's work has given me a great deal more understanding of the democratic politics of accountability, past and present, especially his "Democratic Theory and the Athenian Public Sphere."

17. I expand on this point in my "Herodotean Democracies."

18. Here using the translation by George Rawlinson.

19. David Asheri's magnificent (and sadly unfinished) commentary pointed me to the Theognis reference (Asheri, Lloyd, and Corcella, *Commentary*, 475).

20. The richest treatment of these contexts comes in R. Thomas, *Herodotus in Context*, from which I have learned immensely, in particular about the deep entanglements between Herodotean

inquiry and nascent scientific inquiry around the Mediterranean. Other instructive discussions come in Apfel, *Advent of Pluralism*, on Sophists and the tragedians; Fornara, *Herodotus*, on Athenian politics; Fowler, "Herodotus and His Contemporaries," on historiography; Harrison, *Divinity and History*, on religious beliefs and practices; Gould, *Herodotus*, on Ionian science; and Nagy, *Pindar's Homer*, on poetic inheritances. These are some of the most influential general treatments of the context of the *Histories* relevant to considering *nomoi*.

21. As Sally Humphreys ("Law, Custom, and Culture in Herodotus," 211) writes: "More specifically, by Herodotus' time *nomos* could mean a law formally enacted at a known date and recorded in writing; it could refer to aspects of human behavior observed to vary from one culture to another, in opposition to *physis*; and it had also been used by Presocratics to denote regularities in the working of the cosmos—what we might call 'laws of nature.'"

22. Ostwald, *Nomos and the Beginnings of Athenian Democracy*, 86.

23. *Thesmos*, as Rosalind Thomas ("Writing, Law, and Written Law," 51) notes, was the general term for "law" typically used outside the Peloponnese. Institutional development led to the introduction of the term *nomos*, although this still remained vague and thus adaptable.

24. Sally Humphreys ("Law, Custom, and Culture in Herodotus," 214), for instance, accuses Ostwald of offering "flimsy" evidence for his account of the development of *nomos* toward law. Here I am less interested in adjudicating sweeping claims about Greek history than in educing an implicit theory of *nomos* within Herodotus.

25. As Ostwald notes in *Nomos and the Beginnings of Athenian Democracy*, 5.

26. Ostwald (*Nomos and the Beginnings of Athenian Democracy*, 46) points out that we lack evidence that Solon's laws were written down, which he regards as a crucial aspect of the formalization of *nomos* into law.

27. Ostwald, *Nomos and the Beginnings of Athenian Democracy*, 75.

28. This reliance on formalized law as achieving good order comes under criticism in Plato's *Nomoi*, usually translated *Laws* but perhaps best left in the ambiguous original. Thank you to Jill Frank for this point.

29. Lateiner, *Historical Method of Herodotus*, 103.

30. Apfel, *Advent of Pluralism*, 161, 132.

31. My reading here is informed by Seth Benardete's rich reading in *Herodotean Inquiries*, esp. 68–97.

32. Lateiner, *Historical Method of Herodotus*, 51. Cornelia Roy ("Political Relativism," 16) led me to this quotation. Benardete offers a similar observation in *Herodotean Inquiries*, 80.

33. In addition to the examples I adduced earlier, Herodotus offers similar suggestions about this relationship between custom and place at 1.71, 1.142, 2.35, 4.29, 7.102, and 9.122. I discuss many of these passages in what follows.

34. R. Thomas, *Herodotus in Context*, 102.

35. Dihle, "Herodot und die Sophistik."

36. R. Thomas, *Herodotus in Context*, 111.

37. This language mirrors what Jill Frank ("On *Logos* and Politics in Aristotle") uses to describe *logos* as speech in Aristotle's political thought.

38. As described in Humphreys, "Law, Custom, and Culture in Herodotus," 217.

39. The "practice theory" approach to cultural anthropology provides a useful analogy to Herodotus's description of *nomoi*. Synthesizing the work of Bourdieu, Giddens, Sahlins, and others, Sherry Ortner describes this approach in terms of its dialectical rather than oppositional account of the relation between the structural constraints of culture and the practices of social

actors. "History makes people," writes Ortner, "but people make history" (*Anthropology and Social Theory*, 2).

40. Immerwahr, *Form and Thought in Herodotus*, 319.

41. William Sewell enriched my understanding of synchrony and diachrony as approaches to the study of history in his "Geertz, Cultural Systems, and History." Josiah Ober first called my attention to Sewell's work.

42. As Rosalind Thomas notes in "Written in Stone?," *nomoi* may well have been sung prior to their being inscribed. This gives a concrete example of the dependence of *nomoi* on practice: if nobody sang the *nomoi*, the words would be forgotten.

43. Translation by de Sélincourt.

44. J. Peter Euben ("Political Equality and the Greek Polis") helped me recognize this logic.

45. I use the word "temper" to capture how these *iso-* words refer not solely to "principles" or to "practices" but to ways in which political organization—which includes both principles and practices—is *tuned* or *trued*. In these terms, Herodotus would call Athens following the Cleisthenean revolution or Corinth after the overthrow of the Cypselid tyrants "well tempered."

46. Ober, "Original Meaning of 'Democracy.'"

47. Vlastos's two articles on *isonomia* ("Isonomia" and "Isonomia Politike") have been foundational to my own understanding. Ostwald's discussion in *Nomos and the Beginnings of Athenian Democracy*, esp. 96–136, has also proven immensely useful.

48. Vlastos, "Equality and Justice in Early Greek Cosmologies." MacKinney, "Concept of Isonomia in Greek Medicine," also provides instructive context.

49. Vlastos, "Equality and Justice in Early Greek Cosmologies," 156.

50. Vlastos, "Equality and Justice in Early Greek Cosmologies," 172.

51. The description of *isonomia* as a buzzword comes from Cartledge, "Democracy, Origins of," quoting Vlastos. Cartledge immediately assimilates *isonomia* and *isêgoria* (referring to *Histories* 5.78, which I discuss further below), attributing to *isonomia* the success the Athenians experienced. Herodotus is more precise than this.

52. Thucydides has a similar mention of *isonomia* when describing the factions on Corcyra (3.82). Here *isonomia* is invoked but not connected to concrete practices. Paul Cartledge (Comparatively Equal," 177) comments: "For the disabused Athenian historian, this was but a specious slogan, a cloak for the selfish ambitions of a power-mad clique. The speciousness was due, however, not only to the alleged motives of its propagators but also partly to the slogan's inherent radical ambiguity, or vapidity."

53. Herodotus's refusal to identify Athens and *isonomia* despite the history of such an association is important. I discuss this more below.

54. Hansen, "Anniversary of Cleisthenes' Reforms," 27.

55. Nakategawa, "Isegoria in Herodotus," is the one exception; I have profited from close reading of this piece. Saxonhouse, *Athenian Democracy*, and Ober, "Original Meaning of 'Democracy,'" have some discussion.

56. As Ostwald, among others, reminds me in *Nomos and the Beginnings of Athenian Democracy*, 109n2.

57. Nakategawa, "Isegoria in Herodotus," 270.

58. Very few commentators have examined the concept of *isokratia*. Ostwald's "Isokratia as a Political Concept" is a notable and useful exception.

59. Ostwald, "Isokratia as a Political Concept," brought this reading to my attention.

60. That Socleas could liken the Athenians' *isokratia* to the Spartans' suggests that the innovations of Cleisthenes had a deeper effect on political culture than many scholars recognize. These innovations did not just create effective institutions for devolving power but rather transformed the *dêmos* into a political unit capable of sustaining equality—and thus realizing this collective power through the ongoing practice of their *nomoi*.

61. This captures the characterization of democracy—described in terms of *isonomia*—that Socrates raises in book 8 of Plato's *Republic*.

62. Ostwald, "Isokratia as a Political Concept."

63. In "Comparatively Equal," Cartledge elucidates how Spartan "equality" might have appeared as such to an external observer (such as Socleas), but the existence of the Helots made Sparta into a military society such that no genuine equality could exist.

64. How and Wells (*Commentary*, 312) note that "the reference here is probably not to a system of primitive matriarchy, but to the fact that, in a low state of civilization, men and women alike have to hunt." While narrow, this interpretation also supports my deeper point: namely, that *isokratia* describes the organization of society into equal parts that cooperate.

65. Dewald, "Women and Culture in Herodotus' *Histories*," 109. This article has an exhaustive appendix of all the moments when women appear in the *Histories*, counting 128 "Passive" appearances and 212 "Active" ones.

66. Dewald, "Women and Culture in Herodotus' *Histories*," 107.

67. Among others, I have benefited from the insights proffered in Immerwahr, "Aspects of Historical Causation in Herodotus"; A. Lloyd, "Account of Egypt"; Gould, *Herodotus*; and R. Thomas, *Herodotus in Context*.

68. Gould, *Herodotus*, 10.

69. Hussey, *Presocratics*, 7.

70. R. Thomas, "Intellectual Milieu of Herodotus," 64.

71. This also highlights how Herodotus anticipates later Greek thinkers like Aristotle, who, while drawing geographical distinctions, seeks to distinguish ethnicities capable and not capable of self-rule in *Politics* 7.1327b23–31. Rosalind Thomas first called my attention to these connections in her *Herodotus in Context*, 93.

72. Frost, *Biocultural Creatures*, 4.

73. Here I draw on the very helpful and insightful article by Charles Chiasson, "Scythian Androgyny and Environmental Determinism," esp. 46–47.

74. Kaplan, "Ethnicity and Geography," 304 (my italics).

75. The history of Mount Athos shows how this engineering could take place. When the Persians returned to the site of the disaster, Xerxes, the new king, anticipated the problem suffered by his father, Darius. Xerxes ordered a canal cut through the isthmus connecting Mount Athos to the mainland. Herodotus describes the digging in close detail (7.23): the trench; the carrying of excavated soil up via a scaffold; and the Phoenicians' suggestion to double the width at the top of the canal to prevent the banks from caving in. When the canal is completed, the laborers clear the mounds of earth they had heaped at the entrances to the canal to prevent the water from rushing in while construction was under way (7.37).

76. *Hippocratic Writings*, 160.

77. *Hippocratic Writings*, 167.

78. R. Thomas, *Herodotus in Context*, 92.

79. Saxonhouse (*Athenian Democracy*, 43) comments: "There is no attempt by the law to erase natural inequalities in beauty. Instead, custom works to perpetuate those inequalities and

is thus judged the ugliest of customs." I would resist, however, the inclination to *naturalize* these differences. Beauty, too, is cultural and the product of *nomoi*.

80. Antiphon, frag. A. Translation by J. S. Morrison in Sprague, *Older Sophists*, 289.

81. Michael Gagarin's *Antiphon the Athenian* offers a close reading of Antiphon's "Truth" to this end.

82. Herodotus defers to the wisdom of people for creating *nomoi*; however, Herodotus's inquiry implies the usefulness of an outsider's perspective and insight concerning these *nomoi*. Herodotus does not spell out how *historia* can contribute to well-functioning *nomoi* except to praise those customs that allow for open discussion of ideas, such as the Babylonian medical practices.

83. Farrar, *Origins of Democratic Thinking*, 44–98.

84. "Protagoras," in Plato, *Theaetetus*. Translation by Michael J. O'Brien in Sprague, *Older Sophists*, 15.

85. Here I depart from James Romm (*Herodotus*, 220), who notes that there are "hints" of a "Montesquieu-like pattern." I am grateful for conversations with Keegan Callanan about Montesquieu as a latter-day Herodotean.

86. The full title of Schmitt's work is *The Nomos of the Earth in the International Law of the Jus Publicum Europaeum*. Bruno Latour's insightful discussion in *Facing Gaia*, 228–54, led me back to Schmitt.

87. Schmitt, *The Nomos of the Earth*, 42. Quoted in Latour, *Facing Gaia*, 234.

88. Adorno, *Minima Moralia*, 151. Quoted in Wolin, "From Vocation to Invocation," 4.

89. Tully, *Strange Multiplicity*.

90. Morton, *Ecological Thought*.

Chapter Four

1. Wallace-Wells, *Uninhabitable Earth*, 30.

2. I mentioned the influence of Homer earlier and I treat it more below. Two important differences seem worth underscoring: Herodotus speaks with his own authority and not the authority of the Muses; Herodotus thus presents this as *his* work and not a product of divine inspiration. These differences both mark striking departures from the literary tradition.

3. These treatments of stories are useful for their illumination of how the stories function within networks of other stories in the *Histories*.

4. I am indebted to the perspicuous research of Charles Fornara, Sarah Forsdyke, John Moles, Kurt Raaflaub, Philip Stadter, and Hermann Strasburger on this topic. I discuss my differences with many of the details of these scholars' writings more below.

5. Benjamin (*Illuminations*, 89) writes: "Every morning brings us the news of the globe, and yet we are poor in noteworthy stories. This is because no event any longer comes to us without already being shot through with explanation. In other words, by now almost nothing that happens benefits storytelling; almost everything benefits information. Actually, it is half the art of storytelling to keep a story free from explanation as one reproduces it. . . . The most extraordinary things, marvelous things, are related with the greatest accuracy, but the psychological connection of the events is not forced on the reader. It is left up to him to interpret things the way he understands them, and thus the narrative achieves an amplitude that information lacks."

6. Wallace-Wells, *Uninhabitable Earth*, 30.

7. In the words of Alan Griffiths, "Stories and Storytelling in the *Histories*," 137. I draw on this helpful essay in this paragraph. Aly's 1921 work, *Volksmärchen, Sage und Novelle bei Herodot und seinen Zeitgenossen*, remains a classic.

8. To offer two examples: the story of Adrastus uses the trope of the triumph of the disregarded youngest brother, and the Hippoclides story—"For Hippoclides, no problem!" (which I retell below)—is a version of the "princess escapes marriage to a monster at the last minute" story.

9. Griffiths, "Stories and Storytelling in the *Histories*," 135.

10. Here I lean on the insightful account of Griffiths, "Stories and Storytelling in the *Histories*," 135–36.

11. The drawing of "lessons" is more consonant with subsequent so-called "moral history." For my critique of the reading of Herodotus through the lens of moral history, see Schlosser, review of *Moral History from Herodotus to Diodorus Siculus*.

12. Griffiths, "Stories and Storytelling in the *Histories*," 140.

13. In "Tragedy of Law," Michael Davis artfully brings together the Gyges stories from Herodotus and Plato around the question of the limits of political life (and the law in particular). This illustrates the polyvocality of Herodotus's stories—not to mention Plato's.

14. Rosalind Thomas (introduction to *The Landmark Herodotus*, xvii) explains: "We thus have an explanation within another explanation, a description hanging from another description, all of which are in fact important to our understanding of the train of events. In the form of a 'ring composition,' Herodotus returns neatly at the end of this main narrative and clearly signals the end of the section on Athens."

15. Seth Benardete's *Herodotean Inquiries* proceeds from this basic intuition about the *Histories*.

16. There is more to say about the Egypt narrative, in particular how its size and density provide a kind of counterweight to the faster tempo of the more contemporary sections later in the *Histories*. The slowing down this effects is both constitutive and a consequence of *historia*.

17. J. P. Euben, *Tragedy of Political Theory*. Euben has helped me to listen for this polyvocality in a range of ancient Greek texts, especially Greek tragedy, Thucydides, and Plato.

18. Too often academic commentators miss how the artfulness of Herodotus's storytelling motivates interest in the broader themes he discusses. In other words, you cannot separate the "lesson" of the story from the experience of the story itself. As Vivienne Gray ("Short Stories in Herodotus' *Histories*," 298) puts it: "The advice of Bias/Pittacus looks vivid because it is set into an annalistic account of Croesus's rise devoid of such features (1.26–8), and even within the story of Solon's advice, his philosophical lecture on the computation of a man's life is dull by comparison with his clear, vivid, simple and economical story of Cleobis and Biton."

19. Fornara, *Herodotus*, 23. Lisa Irene Hau's *Moral History from Herodotus to Diodorus Siculus* offers an instructive treatment of moral history from the classical through the Hellenistic periods.

20. This is not to say that the lessons are always straightforward and epigrammatic. For example, Harrison ("Moral of History," 355) writes: "The ultimate moral of history then, according to Herodotus—the right response to difference as it is to historical change—is not so much a practical one as a recommended mindset: a humility, infused by mindfulness of the gods."

21. This is the thrust of Plutarch's treatment of Herodotus in *On the Malice of Herodotus*, but as Christopher Pelling shows in his "De Malignitate Plutarchi," Plutarch's other works evince more positive treatments of his sometime adversary.

22. As John Marincola ("History without Malice," 103) points out, Plutarch's biographies "have a strong didactic character and were meant to indicate to his readers Plutarch's own notions of appropriate ethical behavior." Marincola helpfully demonstrates how Plutarch satisfies

his own criteria of a moral biographer even if his arguments and evidence adduced against Herodotus seem weak and biased.

23. This suggests that moral history isn't always moral; if the conditions of life have radically altered, the moral teachings of a text written in another era may no longer appear to be moral. The histories may be "evergreen," as Paul Cartledge's introduction to Tom Holland's translations of the *Histories* suggests, but not uniformly so.

24. Baragwanath, *Motivation and Narrative*, 10.

25. Plutarch, *Malice of Herodotus* 860E.

26. You might remember that this comes on the heels of Cleomenes's refusal of the offer of Aristagoras, when the latter tried to entice Cleomenes into joining the Ionians against the Persians. Cleomenes refuses because he obeys his daughter, Gorgo.

27. Marincola offers this reason in his thoughtful "Plutarch's Refutation of Herodotus," 203.

28. Bowen, introduction to *Malice of Herodotus*, 3.

29. Plutarch, *Malice of Herodotus* 874B.

30. Nagy, *Pindar's Homer*, 228.

31. Plutarch, *Malice of Herodotus* 862f–863a.

32. Baragwanath, *Motivation and Narrative*, 18.

33. As Baragwanath (*Motivation and Narrative*, 19) comments: "The possibility arises that Herodotus introduced this agonistic framework specifically so as to promote an especially *committed, active* sort of reader response (indeed, a response akin to that of Plutarch), and—so far from 'dancing away from the truth'—to underscore the *seriousness* of the responsibility he passes on to the readers."

34. I prefer a pithier translation of Hippoclides's response: "For Hippoclides, no problem!" The Greek is best: *ou phrontis Hippokleidêi*.

35. In her twenty-first-century interpretation of the *Histories* Debra Hamel (*Reading Herodotus*, 202–3) offers another iteration of the same sin Plutarch commits. Retelling the story, Hamel refers to the contests as "the ancient equivalent of *The Bachelorette*" and, on Hippoclides's dancing, comments that "he looked, in other words, like an idiot."

36. Fornara, *Herodotus*, 53–54.

37. Strasburger, "Herodot und das perikleische Athens."

38. Here Fowler ("Herodotos and Athens," 314) helpfully comments on these passages: "These things reveal serious anxiety about leadership in a democratic society."

39. Kurke, *Aesopic Conversations*, 412–26. I draw on Kurke extensively in this paragraph.

40. Kurke relies on the detailed analysis in R. W. Macan's 1895 commentary on Herodotus, which seems to be the only source to have recognized this parallel.

41. Kurke, *Aesopic Conversations*, 419.

42. Kurke, *Aesopic Conversations*, 421.

43. Fowler ("Herodotus and Athens," 313–14) comments along these lines: "It is Hippokleides, not Megakles, who wins the bride, is the true hero of the story; the man who beats all those would-be tyrants at their own game, and then shows he doesn't give a fig for the prize. He is the buffoon with whom the audience identifies; positively Aristophanic he is, much like old Philokleon, who even quotes a similar proverb, as he dances merrily and his creditors go begging. The story is a knowing nudge and wink at the expense of the Alkmaionids, in particular Perikles, who was descended from boring old Megakles."

44. Fowler, "Herodotos and Athens," 313.

45. Kurke, *Aesopic Conversations*, 426. To take one example, Rosalind Thomas (*Oral Tradition and Written Record*, 269) offers that "there may even be a hint of anti-tyrant sentiment" in the story. A hint?!

46. Steiner, *Tyrant's Writ*, esp. 186–241.

47. Kurke, *Aesopic Conversations*, 426.

48. I owe a great deal of my understanding of the relationship between Herodotus and the Sophists to Gould, *Herodotus*; Lateiner, "Empirical Element"; Raaflaub, "Philosophy, Science, Politics"; and R. Thomas, "Intellectual Milieu of Herodotus."

49. Nagy, "Herodotus the *Logios*." It's worth noting that Herodotus does not call himself a *logios*. Nagy rests his argument on a reading of this role as within the repertoire of poetic practices from which Herodotus draws.

50. Luraghi, "Meta-*historiê*."

51. Branscome, *Textual Rivals*.

52. David Branscome's *Textual Rivals* first drew my attention to this important episode and I acknowledge his guidance in my reading.

53. Discussing the same exchange, Branscome (*Textual Rivals*, 156) points out that "the democratic Athenians stress the cooperative action of a plural 'alone' that was evident even in Athens' distant past."

54. Dewald, "Narrative Surface and Authorial Voice," 155.

55. Benjamin, *Illuminations*, 90.

56. Lombardini, "Isonomia and the Public Sphere," 412.

57. Detienne, *Masters of Truth*, 95.

58. Quoting Saxonhouse, "Democratic Deliberation," 85.

59. John Moles ("Herodotus Warns the Athenians," 269) suggests that the warning Herodotus gives the Athenians is "fundamentally parrhesiastic"—fearless and frank speech that puts the issues of the day in the middle of the public sphere. Yet it's important to note that this practice of inquiry is not limited to the Athenians, as Herodotus's mentions of *es to meson* practices in places such as Babylon and even Persia suggest.

60. Kurke, *Coins, Bodies, Games, and Gold*, 333.

61. Detienne, *Masters of Truth*, 97.

62. *Suppliant Women* 438–39. Lombardini's ("Isonomia and the Public Sphere" 412) discussion illuminated this passage for me.

Chapter Five

1. Lovelock, *Gaia*, 137.

2. Lane, *Birth of Politics*, 7.

3. In "Die griechische ELEUTHERIA bei Herodot," Kurt von Fritz suggests a threefold definition of *eleutheria* in Herodotus; I expand on his arguments in the penultimate section of this chapter.

4. I follow Martin Ostwald's ("Freedom and the Greeks") argument that the distinctive turn in Greek thought is toward a politicization of the historic basis of freedom as the freedom of the master in contrast to the servitude of the slave. I discuss Herodotus's treatment of slavery in what follows. Orlando Patterson's provocative argument in *Freedom* (vol. 1) misses, in my opinion, how this politicization comes about in opposition not to personal slavery but rather to

enslavement by a tyrant or a foreign power. Patterson's discussion remains useful, however, for emphasizing how the personal dimension never fully disappears from the politicized version I discuss here.

5. Raaflaub, *Discovery of Freedom*, 72.

6. Raaflaub, *Discovery of Freedom*, 86.

7. As insightfully treated in J. P. Euben, *Corrupting Youth*, esp. 70–71.

8. Martin Ostwald ("Freedom and the Greeks") introduces this important distinction, which is missing from Meier and Raaflaub.

9. Meier, *Greek Discovery of Politics*, 170.

10. Meier, *Greek Discovery of Politics*, 165.

11. Meier, *Greek Discovery of Politics*, 165.

12. Here I draw on Ostwald, "Freedom and the Greeks."

13. As Raaflaub details in *Discovery of Freedom*, 45–57.

14. Ostwald, "Freedom and the Greeks," 40.

15. Ober, "Original Meaning of 'Democracy,' " 3.

16. Thank you to Jill Frank for leading me to this point.

17. Evans ("*Despotes Nomos*," 149) continues by asserting that *nomoi* "determine what men will do in a given situation." "Determine" seems right for the Spartans but goes too far, as I will show in what follows, for other kinds of freedom.

18. Meier, *Greek Discovery of Politics*, 173–76; and Raaflaub, *Discovery of Freedom*, 57.

19. Meier, *Greek Discovery of Politics*, 176.

20. Millender, "Nomos Despotes."

21. Dewald, "Wanton Kings, Pickled Heroes, and Gnomic Founding Fathers," 68.

22. Munson, "Who Are Herodotus' Persians?," 335.

23. I don't mean here to conflate ruling with concerted action as Arendt distinguishes them. When collective power "rules," it is not ruling in Arendt's sense; it is action in concert.

24. In the middle of the *Histories*, Herodotus creates a ring composition that emphasizes the contrast between the Scythians' love of freedom and the Ionians' slavish tendencies. As Asheri (Asheri, Lloyd, and Corcella, *Commentary*, 664) puts it: "the Scythians initially appeal to the Ionians in outrage at the mere mention of slavery (128,1); their last words, placed as an epigraph to the episode of the war, amount to an accusation against the servile disposition of the Ionians (ch. 142)."

25. This tactic, a "sailing through and out," involved the assembled ships sailing through the enemy's lines and then turning to attack the unguarded rear of the enemy fleet. I owe this explanation to Lazenby, "Diekplous."

26. I agree with Sheldon Wolin ("Norm and Form") that this marks the crucial beginning of Athenian democracy: "Democracy began as a demand for a 'share' of power in the institutions for making and interpreting the laws and deciding questions of diplomacy and warfare. It culminated in popular control over most of the main political institutions at Athens" (36).

27. My reading follows Ober, "Athenian Revolution of 508/7 B.C.E.," here, although I don't wish to pick a side on the controversial question of when Athens actually became democratic by today's metrics. I acknowledge many of Raaflaub's points in response to Ober, as well as those in Ober's response to Raaflaub's response in Morris and Raaflaub, *Democracy 2500?*

28. The Athenians resemble the Babylonians in developing *nomoi* that support equality and thus freedom. As Saxonhouse (*Athenian Democracy*, 42) writes, "Custom (*nomos*) has the capacity to equalize."

29. As Jill Frank ("Constitution") puts it, the *politeia* is "underwritten, in the texts of the philosophers, by a dynamic and reciprocal relationship between the habits, character, and practices that sustain the way of life of a city's citizens, on the one hand, and, on the other, the collective orders and institutions that structure the city's governing body." Herodotus adds the *diachronic* dimension to "the texts of the philosophers," emphasizing how this dynamic and reciprocal relationship takes place across time through iterated responsive interactions.

30. Saxonhouse, *Free Speech and Democracy in Ancient Athens*, 30.

31. Here Raaflaub ("Equalities and Inequalities," 147) comments that "under Cleisthenes' *isonomia* [*sic*] . . . Athens essentially was a 'republic' of hoplites and farmers." Active participation by large segments of the citizen body was encouraged and institutionalized. These same citizens were enabled to make use of *isêgoria*—primarily at the local level of demes but also beyond.

32. Lest I appear to glorify the Athenian *polis*, I note that "citizen" as a political category excluded a large part of the population.

33. Aristotle's particular use of this analogy is more complicated than this may indicate. As Daniela Cammack points out in her "Aristotle on the Virtue of the Multitude," the aggregate of voices is less important than the aggregate of virtues. This may be an implicit Aristotelian critique of *isêgoria* itself, one that accords with his general skepticism toward the arithmetic equality claimed by democrats.

34. Here Robert Fowler also points out a hint of foreboding in Herodotus's language. Herodotus begins by describing Themistocles as one who was aspiring to join the ranks of leaders. Fowler ("Herodotos and Athens," 314–15) comments: "Whatever the factual truth of the timing as Herodotos reports it, he has got the symbolic truth right: subsequent events showed that this was a man to watch very, very closely."

35. Of the eighty uses of *eleutheria* and its variations in the *Histories*, only eighteen are paired with slavery; only a handful of these—four by my count—deal with individual slaves. Liberation does mean not being a slave, but this is merely a necessary, not a sufficient, condition. The Medes fight the Assyrians for their freedom and cast off slavery (1.95); they win their freedom collectively and then fail to preserve it when they succumb to the Persians. So, too, the Egyptians free themselves from Ethiopian rule (2.147)—but they sustain this freedom (at least for a time) by maintenance of their political power.

36. Saxonhouse (*Athenian Democracy*, 39) writes: "Freedom is a much wider concept: it means not being ruled by an individual who is (or sees himself as) superior, or by a nation that is stronger." Saxonhouse's analysis helped me see that freedom is not reducible to democratic governance, nor is it merely a matter of either internal or external senses (which I discuss in what follows). But here I depart from her by emphasizing the *political* nature of freedom as not merely protective from tyranny and external influence.

37. "Rule" here is complicated, and I mean it not in the sense criticized in chapter 1 but rather in something more like Arendt's notion of *archein* in her "What Is Freedom?" Arendt also rejects the kind of rule Herodotus shows as both impossible and undesirable; freedom, for Arendt (following Herodotus), is "no-rule" (*On Revolution*, 30). What Arendt criticizes, as Patchen Markell points out (in "Rule of the People"), is not political power so much as diminished responsiveness, the routinization or calcification that can come about through regimes of rule.

38. Here I use "the political" in Sheldon Wolin's ("Fugitive Democracy," 31) sense: "an expression of the idea that a free society composed of diversities can nonetheless enjoy moments of commonality when, through public deliberations, collective power is used to promote or protect

the well-being of the collectivity." In Herodotus's *Histories* these "diversities" mostly refer to class differences; however, the freedom of the Greeks, which also depends on a realization of political freedom, does unite different peoples and ethnicities.

39. Although I have greatly benefited from the discussions of freedom by Kurt von Fritz ("Die griechische ELEUTHERIA bei Herodot"), Martin Ostwald ("Freedom and the Greeks"), and Rosaria Munson ("Freedom and Culture in Herodotus"), I depart from them on this point.

40. Herodotus's language here is interesting and distinguishes Otanes's people from the Spartans. Whereas the Spartans obey the laws as despot, Otanes's descendants simply "do not overstep the laws" (*nomous ouk huperbainousa tous Perseôn*). Might Herodotus be suggesting that this is the real meaning of *isonomia*?

41. In Herodotus's world (and unlike today's), a measure of isolation might still have been possible, as the example of the Satrae suggests. Of them, Herodotus comments that they "have never been subject to anyone, as far as we know; they are the only tribe in Thrace to have retained their independence all the way up to my day" (7.111). But I still wonder: doesn't this exception prove the rule of interculturalism?

42. *Eleutheria* is used in 7.3 to describe Cyrus's liberation of the Persians and then becomes the subject of the very important debate between Xerxes and Demaratus in 7.103–4 and the illustrative episode involving the Spartan messengers at 7.111 and 7.135. Herodotus announces the Athenians' integral role in protecting Hellenic freedom at 7.135, and after this moment, only once more out of the subsequent fifteen usages does it not apply to Hellenic freedom.

43. This term also appears at 5.46 and 7.51 to describe others joining in the liberation of place. Both of these examples concern external parties—"alien powers," in the language of interpretation in terms of internal freedom—participating in a political act that involves different peoples.

44. Gelon's story is also a slightly different version of that of Deioces. Both falsely see a separation between "their own affairs" and the affairs of the city at large. Both are or become tyrants. Herodotus does not give reason to admire either, apart from the cunning Deioces displays in his ascent to power. He lives and dies alone.

45. Harrison, *Divinity and History*, 66.

46. In the language of Andrea Purvis, translator of Strassler's *Landmark Herodotus*, 553.

47. In the passage quoted as one of this chapter's epigraphs: Lovelock, *Gaia*, 137.

Conclusion

1. Scranton, *Learning to Die in the Anthropocene*, 97.

2. As Latour (*Down to Earth*, 12) has recently recognized.

3. "Buried sunshine" comes from Timothy Mitchell's *Carbon Democracy*. His work on Egypt exemplifies a Herodotean approach to contemporary political history.

4. Herodotus should thus warn against the temptation of "great-man history," which certain accounts of the failed responses to climate change could well heed. See, e.g., Nathaniel Rich's *Losing Earth* and the critical response by Alyssa Battistoni, "How Not to Talk about Climate Change."

5. In the passage featured as one of this book's epigraphs: Wolin, "Montesquieu and *Publius*," 119.

6. Another example might be the Kurdistan Workers' Party (PKK), which Debbie Bookchin, daughter of Murray, argues carries forward the principles of *Ecology of Freedom*. See Bookchin, "How My Father's Ideas Helped the Kurds Create a New Democracy."

7. Ober, "Original Meaning of 'Democracy.'"

8. In Wolin's ("Norm and Form," 31) own words: "the political" names "an expression of the idea that a free society composed of diversities can nonetheless enjoy moments of commonality when, through public deliberations, collective power is used to promote or protect the well-being of the collectivity."

9. In this paragraph I draw on the descriptions from the Lesvos Solidarity web page, available at https://lesvossolidarity.org/en/home/about-us.

10. See Sarah Boseley, "Efi Latsoudi." I draw extensively from Boseley's article in this paragraph.

11. As pointed out in Kagan, *Outbreak of the Peloponnesian War*, 156. On Thurii in general, I have consulted with benefit writings by Donald Kagan (*Outbreak of the Peloponnesian War*, 154–69), Victor Ehrenberg ("Foundation of Thurii"), Rosaria Munson ("Alternate World"), Martin Ostwald ("Herodotus and Athens"), and Eric Robinson (*First Democracies*, 119–23).

12. Robinson, *First Democracies*, 120.

13. I do not have an opinion on this, although I'm aware of the dispute between, for example, Victor Ehrenberg ("Foundation of Thurii") and Donald Kagan (*Outbreak of the Peloponnesian War*).

14. As shown to me by Ostwald, "Herodotus and Athens."

15. Here I'm inspired by the political imagination of Donna Haraway and her "Camille Stories" (in *Staying with the Trouble*, 134–68). I propose a more immediate political response than her postapocalyptic one. Mohsin Hamid's stirring and brilliant *Exit West* creates a story similar to mine yet rooted in the particular experiences of two refugees from an unnamed yet war-wracked Middle Eastern country. Consider this a counter to Claire Vaye Watkins's harrowing *Gold Fame Citrus*.

16. See Haas, "Do Regimes Matter?"

17. See Callon, Lascoumes, and Barthe, *Acting in an Uncertain World*, on the differences between delegative and dialogic democracy.

18. Here Hannah Arendt (*Human Condition*, 192) reminds me: "Action reveals itself fully only to the storyteller, that is, to the backward glance of the historian, who indeed always knows better what it was all about than the participants."

19. As Lisa Wedeen ("Ideology and Humor in Dark Times," 841, 843) has argued, magazines like *Happynings*, "the most prestigious lifestyle and luxury magazine in Syria," mediate and manage the contradictions within neoliberal autocracy between "cultivating an aspirational consciousness for freedom, upward mobility, and consumer pleasure," on the one hand, and tethering all advancement to "citizen obedience and coercive control," on the other.

20. On the pathologies of desire in the late twenty-first century, see Honneth, *Freedom's Right*.

21. McKibben, *Falter*, 256.

22. In the passage featured as one of this book's epigraphs: Arendt, "What Is Freedom?," 169.

Acknowledgments

1. Ondaatje, *English Patient*, 14.

2. Ondaatje, *English Patient*, 244.

3. Ondaatje, *English Patient*, 116.

4. Gumbrecht, *Powers of Philology*, 42.

5. Nietzsche, "We Classicists," cited in duBois, *Trojan Horses*, 1.

Bibliography

Translations of Herodotus

Herodotus. *The History*. Translated by David Grene. Chicago: University of Chicago Press, 1987.

Herodotus. *The Histories*. Translated by Walter Blanco. Norton Critical Editions. New York: Norton, 1992.

Herodotus. *The Histories*. Translated by Robin Waterfield. Oxford World's Classics. Oxford: Oxford University Press, 1998.

Herodotus. *The Histories*. Translated by Aubrey de Sélincourt. Revised by John Marincola. New York: Penguin, 2003.

Herodotus. *The Landmark Herodotus: The Histories*. Edited by Robert B. Strassler. Translated by Andrea L. Purvis. New York: Pantheon, 2007.

Herodotus. *The Histories*. Translated by Tom Holland. Introduction and notes by Paul Cartledge. New York: Viking, 2013.

Herodotus. *The History of Herodotus*. Translated by George Rawlinson. Revised by Rosalind Thomas. New York: Random House, 2015.

Commentaries on Herodotus

Asheri, David, A. B. Lloyd, and A. Corcella. *A Commentary on Herodotus I–IV*. Edited by Oswyn Murray and Alfonso Moreno. Oxford: Oxford University Press, 2007.

Bowie, Angus M. *Herodotus: Histories Book VIII*. Cambridge: Cambridge University Press, 2007.

Flower, Michael A., and John Marincola. *Herodotus: Histories Book IX*. Cambridge: Cambridge University Press, 2002.

How, W. W., and J. Wells. *A Commentary on Herodotus*. 3rd ed. 2 vols. Oxford: Clarendon, 1936.

Lloyd, A. B. *Herodotus Book II: Introduction and Commentary*. 3 vols. Leiden: Brill, 1975–88.

Newmyer, S. T. *Herodotus, Book III*. Bryn Mawr, PA: Thomas Library, Bryn Mawr College, 1986.

Scott, Lionel. *Historical Commentary on Herodotus Book 6*. Leiden: Brill, 2005.

Sheets, George A. *Herodotus, Book I*. Bryn Mawr, PA: Department of Greek, Bryn Mawr College, 1993.

Secondary References

Adorno, Theodore. *Minima Moralia: Reflections from Damaged Life*. Translated by E. Jephcott. New York: Verso, 2005.

Allen, Danielle. "The Origins of Political Philosophy." In *Oxford Handbook of the History of Political Philosophy*, edited by G. Klosko, 75–95. Oxford: Oxford University Press, 2011.

Aly, Wolfgang. *Volksmärchen, Sage und Novelle bei Herodot und seinen Zeitgenossen: Eine Untersuchung über die volkstümlichen Elemente der altgriechischen Prosaerzählung*. Göttingen: Vandenhoeck und Ruprecht, 1921.

Angus, Ian. *Facing the Anthropocene: Fossil Capitalism and the Crisis of the Earth System*. New York: Monthly Review Press, 2016.

Apfel, Lauren. *The Advent of Pluralism*. Oxford: Oxford University Press, 2011.

Arendt, Hannah. *The Human Condition*. 2nd ed. Chicago: University of Chicago Press, 1998.

Arendt, Hannah. *On Revolution*. New York: Penguin, 1990.

Arendt, Hannah. "What Is Freedom?" In *Between Past and Future*, edited by J. Kohn, 142–69. New York: Penguin, 2006.

Bakker, E. J. "The Making of History: Herodotus' *Historiês Apodexis*." In *Brill's Companion to Herodotus*, edited by E. J. Bakker, I. J. F. De Jong, and H. van Wees, 3–32. Leiden: Brill, 2002.

Balot, Ryan. *Greek Political Thought*. Malden, MA: Blackwell, 2006.

Baragwanath, Emily. *Motivation and Narrative in Herodotus*. Oxford: Oxford University Press, 2008.

Barker, Ernst. *Greek Political Theory: Plato and His Predecessors*. London: Methuen, 1947.

Battistoni, Alyssa. "How Not to Talk about Climate Change." *Jacobin*. Accessed May 22, 2019. https://jacobinmag.com/2018/08/new-york-times-losing-earth-response-climate-change.

Benardete, Seth. *Herodotean Inquiries*. 1969. Reprint, South Bend, IN: St. Augustine's Press, 2009.

Benjamin, Walter. *Illuminations*. Translated by Hannah Arendt. New York: Schocken Books, 2006.

Bennett, Jane. *Vibrant Matter: A Political Ecology of Things*. Durham, NC: Duke University Press, 2010.

Best, Stephen, and Sharon Marcus. "Surface Reading: An Introduction." *Representations* 108, no. 1 (Fall 2009): 1–21.

Boedeker, Deborah D. "Herodotus's Genres." In *Matrices of Genre: Authors, Canons, and Society*, edited by Mary Depew and Dirk Obbink, 97–114. Cambridge, MA: Harvard University Press, 2000.

Bonneuil, Christophe, and Jean-Baptiste Fressoz. *The Shock of the Anthropocene*. Translated by David Fernbach. New York: Verso, 2017.

Bookchin, Debbie. "How My Father's Ideas Helped the Kurds Create a New Democracy." *New York Review of Books*, June 15, 2018. https://www.nybooks.com/daily/2018/06/15/how-my-fathers-ideas-helped-the-kurds-create-a-new-democracy.

Bookchin, Murray. *The Ecology of Freedom: The Emergence and Dissolution of Hierarchy*. Updated ed. Chico, CA: AK Press, 2005.

Bordes, J. *Politeia dans la pensée grecque jusqu'à Aristote*. Paris: Société d'édition "Les Belles Lettres," 1982.

Boseley, Sarah. "Efi Latsoudi: In Solidarity with Refugees." *Lancet* 389, issue 10074 (March 2017): 18–24.

Bowen, A. J. Introduction to *The Malice of Herodotus*, by Plutarch. Translated by A. J. Bowen. Warminster, UK: Aris and Phillips, 1992.

Brand, Stewart. *The Whole Earth Catalog.* Fall 1968. Self-published. http://www.wholeearth.com /issue/1010/.

Branscome, David. *Textual Rivals: Self-Presentation in Herodotus' Histories.* Ann Arbor: University of Michigan Press, 2013.

Bravo, Benedetto, and Marek Węcowski. "The Hedgehog and the Fox: Form and Meaning in the Prologue of Herodotus." *Journal of Hellenic Studies* 124 (2004): 143–64.

Callon, Michel, Pierre Lascoumes, and Yannick Barthe. *Acting in an Uncertain World: An Essay on Technical Democracy.* Translated by Graham Burchell. Cambridge, MA: MIT Press, 2009.

Cammack, Daniela. "Aristotle on the Virtue of the Multitude." *Political Theory* 41 (2013): 175–202.

Carson, Rachel. *Silent Spring.* 1962. 40th anniversary ed. e-book. New York: Houghton Mifflin, 2002.

Cartledge, Paul. *Ancient Greek Political Thought in Practice.* Cambridge: Cambridge University Press, 2009.

Cartledge, Paul. "Comparatively Equal." In *Demokratia: A Conversation on Democracies, Ancient and Modern,* edited by Josiah Ober and Charles Hedrick, 175–85. Princeton: Princeton University Press, 1996.

Cartledge, Paul. "Democracy, Origins of: Contribution to a Debate." In *Origins of Democracy in Ancient Greece,* edited by Kurt A. Raaflaub, Josiah Ober, and Robert Wallace, 155–69. Berkeley: University of California Press, 2007.

Cartledge, Paul. "Herodotus and 'the Other.'" *Echos du monde classique* 34, no. 9 (1990): 27–40.

Cartledge, Paul. "Introduction: Herodotus; Historian, Ethnographer, Pluralist, Contemporary." In *The Histories* by Herodotus, translated by Tom Holland, introduction and notes by Paul Cartledge, xv–xxxii. New York: Viking, 2013.

Chakrabarty, Dipesh. "The Climate of History: Four Theses." *Critical Inquiry* 35, no. 2 (Winter 2009): 197–222.

Chakrabarty, Dipesh. "The Human Significance of the Anthropocene." In *Reset Modernity!,* edited by B. Latour, 189–99. Cambridge, MA: MIT Press.

Chakrabarty, Dipesh. "The Politics of Climate Change Is More than the Politics of Capitalism." *Theory, Culture and Society* 34, nos. 2–3 (2017): 25–37.

Chiasson, Charles C. "The Herodotean Solon." *Greek, Roman, and Byzantine Studies* 27 (1986): 249–62.

Chiasson, Charles. "Scythian Androgyny and Environmental Determinism in Herodotus and the Hippocratic περὶ ἀέρων ὑδάτων τόπων." *Syllecta Classica* 12 (2001): 33–73.

Chiasson, Charles C. "Solon's Poetry and Herodotus' Historiography." *American Journal of Philology* 137, no. 1 (Spring 2016): 25–60.

Christ, Matthew R. "Herodotean Kings and Historical Inquiry." *Classical Antiquity* 13 (1994): 167–202.

Coles, Robert. *The Call of Stories: Teaching and the Moral Imagination.* Boston: Houghton Mifflin, 1989.

Coles, Romand. *Visionary Pragmatism: Radical and Ecological Democracy in Neoliberal Times.* Durham, NC: Duke University Press, 2016.

Connolly, William. *Aspirational Fascism: The Struggle for Multifaceted Democracy under Trumpism.* Minneapolis: University of Minnesota Press, 2018.

Connolly, William. *Facing the Planetary: Entangled Humanism and the Politics of Swarming.* Durham, NC: Duke University Press, 2017.

Connolly, William E. *The Fragility of Things: Self-Organizing Processes, Neoliberal Fantasies, and Democratic Activism.* Durham, NC: Duke University Press, 2013.

Crutzen, Paul, and Eugene Stoermer. "The 'Anthropocene.'" *Global Change Newsletter* 41 (2000): 17–18.

Davis, Michael. *The Soul of the Greeks*. Chicago: University of Chicago Press, 2011.

Davis, Michael. "The Tragedy of Law: Gyges in Herodotus and Plato." *Review of Metaphysics* 53, no. 3 (March 2000): 635–55.

de Jong, Irene J. F. "Aspects narratologiques des *Histoires* d'Hérodote." *Lalies: Actes des sessions de linguistique et de littérature* 19 (1999): 217–75.

De Romilly, Jacqueline. "La vengeance comme explication historique dans l'oeuvre d'Hérodote." *Revue des études grecques* 84 (1971): 314–37.

Detienne, Marcel. *The Masters of Truth in Archaic Greece*. New York: Zone Books, 1999.

Dewald, Carolyn. "Form and Content: The Question of Tyranny in Herodotus." In *Popular Tyranny: Sovereignty and Its Discontents in Ancient Greece*, edited by Kathryn A. Morgan, 25–58. Austin: University of Texas Press, 2003.

Dewald, Carolyn. "'I Didn't Give My Own Genealogy': Herodotus and the Authorial Persona." In *Brill's Companion to Herodotus*, edited by E. J. Bakker, I. J. F. De Jong, and H. van Wees, 267–89. Leiden: Brill, 2002.

Dewald, Carolyn. "Narrative Surface and Authorial Voice in Herodotus' *Histories*." *Arethusa* 20, nos. 1–2 (1987): 147–70.

Dewald, Carolyn. Review of *The Mirror of Herodotus: The Representation of the Other in the Writing of History*, by François Hartog. *Classical Philology* 85, no. 3 (July 1990): 217–24.

Dewald, Carolyn. "Wanton Kings, Pickled Heroes, and Gnomic Founding Fathers: Strategies of Meaning at the End of Herodotus' *Histories*." In *Classical Closure: Reading the End in Greek and Latin Literature*, edited by D. H. Roberts, F. M. Dunn, and D. Fowler, 62–82. Princeton: Princeton University Press, 1997.

Dewald, Carolyn. "Women and Culture in Herodotus' *Histories*." In *Reflections of Women in Antiquity*, edited by Helene P. Foley, 91–125. New York: Gordon and Breach Science, 1986.

Dietz, Mary. "Between *Polis* and Empire: Aristotle's *Politics*." *American Political Science Review* 106, no. 2 (May 2012): 275–93.

Dihle, Albrecht. "Herodot und die Sophistik." *Philologus: Zeitschift für das klassische Altertum* 106 (1962): 207–20.

Dryzek, John S. *The Politics of the Earth: Environmental Discourses*. 3rd ed. Oxford: Oxford University Press, 2013.

duBois, Page. *Trojan Horses: Saving the Classics from Conservatives*. New York: New York University Press, 2001.

Ehrenberg, Victor. "The Foundation of Thurii." *American Journal of Philology* 69, no. 2 (1948): 149–70.

Ehrenberg, Victor. "Origins of Democracy." *Historia: Zeitschrift für alte Geschichte* 1 (1950): 515–48.

Ephraim, Laura. *Who Speaks for Nature? On the Politics of Science*. Philadelphia: University of Pennsylvania Press, 2018.

Euben, J. Peter. *Corrupting Youth: Political Education, Democratic Culture, and Political Theory*. Princeton: Princeton University Press, 1997.

Euben, J. Peter. *Platonic Noise*. Princeton: Princeton University Press, 2003.

Euben, J. Peter. "Political Equality and the Greek Polis." In *Liberalism and the Modern Polity*, edited by M. J. Gargas McGrath, 207–29. New York: Marcel Dekker, 1978.

Euben, J. Peter. *The Tragedy of Political Theory: The Road Not Taken*. Princeton: Princeton University Press, 1990.

Euben, Roxanne. *Journeys to the Other Shore: Muslim and Western Travelers in Search of Knowledge*. Princeton: Princeton University Press, 2006.

Evans, J. A. S. "Despotes *Nomos*." *Athenaeum*, n.s., 43 (1965): 142–53.

Evans, J. A. S. *Herodotus, Explorer of the Past: Three Essays*. Princeton: Princeton University Press, 2014.

Farrar, Cynthia. *The Origins of Democratic Thinking: The Invention of Politics in Classical Athens*. Cambridge: Cambridge University Press, 1989.

Fehling, Detlev. *Herodotus and His "Sources": Citation, Invention and Narrative Art*. Leeds, UK: Francis Cairns, 1990.

Fisher, Mark Douglas. "Heroic Democracy: Thucydides, Pericles, and the Tragic Science of Athenian Greatness." PhD diss., University of California, Berkeley, 2017.

Flannery, Tim. *The Weather Makers*. New York: Atlantic Monthly Press, 2005.

Flyvbjerg, Bent. *Making Social Science Matter: Why Social Inquiry Fails and How It Can Succeed Again*. Translated by S. Sampson. Cambridge: Cambridge University Press, 2001.

Flyvbjerg, Bent. *Rationality and Power: Democracy in Practice*. Translated by S. Sampson. Chicago: University of Chicago Press, 1998.

Fornara, Charles. *Herodotus: An Interpretive Essay*. Oxford: Oxford University Press, 1971.

Fornara, Charles. "Human History and the Constraint of Fate in Herodotus." In *Conflict, Antithesis, and the Ancient Historian*, edited by June W. Allison, 25–45. Columbus: Ohio State University Press, 1990.

Forsdyke, Sarah. "Athenian Democratic Ideology and Herodotus' 'Histories.'" *American Journal of Philology* 122, no. 3 (Autumn 2001): 329–58.

Forsdyke, Sarah. "Herodotus, Political History and Political Thought." In *The Cambridge Companion to Herodotus*, edited by Carolyn Dewald and John Marincola, 224–41. Cambridge: Cambridge University Press, 2006.

Fowler, R. L. "Herodotos and Athens." In *Herodotus and His World: Essays from a Conference in Memory of George Forrest*, edited by P. Derow and R. Parker, 305–18. Oxford: Oxford University Press, 2003.

Fowler, R. L. "Herodotus and His Contemporaries." *Journal of Hellenic Studies* 116 (1996): 62–87.

Fowler, R. L. "Herodotus and His Prose Predecessors." In *The Cambridge Companion to Herodotus*, edited by Carolyn Dewald and John Marincola, 29–45. Cambridge: Cambridge University Press, 2006.

Frank, Jill. "Constitution." In *Cultural History of Law in Antiquity*, edited by J. Etxabe, 41–57. London: Bloomsbury, 2019.

Frank, Jill. *A Democracy of Distinction: Aristotle and the Work of Politics*. Chicago: University of Chicago Press, 2005.

Frank, Jill. "On *Logos* and Politics in Aristotle." In *Aristotle's "Politics": A Critical Guide*, edited by Thornton Lockwood and Thanassis Samaras, 9–26. Cambridge: Cambridge University Press, 2015.

Frank, Jill. *Poetic Justice: Rereading Plato's "Republic."* Chicago: University of Chicago Press, 2018.

Fritz, Kurt von. "Die griechische ELEUTHERIA bei Herodot." *Wiener Studien: Zeitschrift für klassische Philologie* 78 (1965): 5–31.

Frost, Samantha. *Biocultural Creatures: Toward a New Theory of the Human*. Durham, NC: Duke University Press, 2016.

Gagarin, Michael. *Antiphon the Athenian: Oratory, Law, and Justice in the Age of the Sophists*. Austin: University of Texas Press, 2002.

Gagarin, Michael, and David Cohen, eds. *The Cambridge Companion to Ancient Greek Law.* Cambridge: Cambridge University Press, 2005.

Gammie, John G. "Herodotus on Kings and Tyrants: Objective Historiography or Conventional Portraiture?" *Journal of Near Eastern Studies* 45, no. 3 (July 1986): 171–95.

Ghosh, Amitav. *The Great Derangement: Climate Change and the Unthinkable.* Chicago: University of Chicago Press, 2016.

Gibson, Katherine, Deborah Bird Rose, and Ruth Fincher, eds. *Manifesto for Living in the Anthropocene.* Brooklyn, NY: Punctum Books, 2015.

Gleick, Peter H. "Climate, Water, and Conflict: Commentary on Selby et al. 2017." *Political Geography* 60 (September 2017): 248–50.

Gleick, Peter H. "Water, Drought, Climate Change and Conflict in Syria." *Weather, Climate, and Society* 3, no. 3 (2014): 331–40.

Gould, John. "Give and Take in Herodotus." In *Myth, Ritual, Memory, and Exchange: Essays in Greek Literature and Culture,* 283–303. Oxford: Oxford University Press, 2001.

Gould, John. *Herodotus.* London: Weidenfeld and Nicolson, 1989.

Gray, Vivienne. "Herodotus and the Rhetoric of Otherness." *American Journal of Philology* 116 (1995): 185–211.

Gray, Vivienne. "Short Stories in Herodotus' *Histories.*" In *Brill's Companion to Herodotus,* edited by E. J. Bakker, I. J. F. De Jong, and H. van Wees, 291–317. Leiden: Brill, 2002.

Griffiths, Alan. "Stories and Storytelling in the *Histories.*" In *The Cambridge Companion to Herodotus,* edited by Carolyn Dewald and John Marincola, 130–44. Cambridge: Cambridge University Press, 2006.

Gumbrecht, Hans Ulrich. *The Powers of Philology: Dynamics of Textual Scholarship.* Urbana: University of Illinois Press, 2003.

Haas, Peter M. "Do Regimes Matter? Epistemic Communities and Mediterranean Pollution Control." *International Organization* 43, no. 3 (Summer 1989): 377–403.

Hamel, Debra. *Reading Herodotus: A Guided Tour through the Wild Boars, Dancing Suitors, and Crazy Tyrants of "The History."* Baltimore: Johns Hopkins University Press, 2012.

Hamid, Mohsin. *Exit West.* New York: Riverhead, 2017.

Hamilton, Clive. *Defiant Earth: The Fate of Humans in the Anthropocene.* Cambridge: Polity, 2017.

Hansen, Mogens Herman. *The Athenian Democracy in the Age of Demosthenes.* Translated by J. A. Crook. Norman: University of Oklahoma Press, 1999.

Hansen, Mogens Herman. "The 2500th Anniversary of Cleisthenes' Reforms and the Tradition of Athenian Democracy." In *Ritual, Finance, Politics: Athenian Democratic Accounts Presented to David Lewis,* edited by Robin Osborne and Simon Hornblower, 25–37. Oxford: Oxford University Press, 1994.

Haraway, Donna. *The Companion Species Manifesto: Dogs, People, and Significant Otherness.* Chicago: Prickly Paradigm Press, 2003.

Haraway, Donna. *Staying with the Trouble: Making Kin in the Chthulucene.* Durham, NC: Duke University Press, 2016.

Harrison, Thomas. "The Cause of Things: Envy and the Emotions in Herodotus' *Histories.*" In *Envy, Spite and Jealousy: The Rivalrous Emotions in Ancient Greece,* edited by David Konstan and K. Rutter, 143–63. Edinburgh: Edinburgh University Press, 2003.

Harrison, Thomas. *Divinity and History: The Religion of Herodotus.* Oxford: Oxford University Press, 2000.

Harrison, Thomas. "The Moral of History." In *Interpreting Herodotus,* edited by Thomas Harrison and Elizabeth Irwin, 335–55. Oxford: Oxford University Press, 2018.

Harrison, Thomas. "'Prophecy in Reverse'? Herodotus and the Origins of History." In *Herodotus and His World: Essays from a Conference in Memory of George Forrest*, edited by P. Derow and R. Parker, 237–55. Oxford: Oxford University Press, 2003.

Harte, Verity, and Melissa Lane. Politeia *in Greek and Roman Philosophy*. Cambridge: Cambridge University Press, 2013.

Hartigan, John, Jr. *Aesop's Anthropology: A Multispecies Approach*. Minneapolis: University of Minnesota Press, 2014.

Hartog, François. *Memoir d'Ulysse*. Paris: Gallimard, 1996. Translated as *Memories of Odysseus* by J. Lloyd. Chicago: University of Chicago Press, 2001.

Hartog, François. *Le miroir d'Hérodote: Essai sur la représentation de l'autre*. Paris: Gallimard, 1980. Translated as *The Mirror of Herodotus* by J. Lloyd. Berkeley: University of California Press, 1988.

Hau, Lisa Irene. *Moral History from Herodotus to Diodorus Siculus*. Edinburgh: University of Edinburgh Press, 2016.

Hénin, Nicholas. *Jihad Academy: The Rise of the Islamic State*. Translated by M. Makinson. New York: Bloomsbury, 2015.

Herodotus. *Historiae*. Edited by K. Hude. 3rd ed. 2 vols. Oxford Classical Texts. Oxford: Clarendon, 1927.

Hippocratic Writings. Edited by G. E. R. Lloyd. New York: Penguin, 1983.

Holmes, Brooke. *The Symptom and the Subject: The Emergence of the Physical Body in Ancient Greece*. Princeton: Princeton University Press, 2010.

Honig, Bonnie, and Marc Stears. "The New Realism: From *Modus Vivendi* to Justice." In *Political Philosophy versus History?*, edited by J. Floyd and M. Stears, 177–205. Cambridge: Cambridge University Press, 2011.

Honneth, Axel. *Freedom's Right: The Social Foundations of Democratic Life*. Translated by Joseph Ganahl. New York: Columbia University Press, 2014.

Hornblower, Simon. "Herodotus and His Sources of Information." In *Brill's Companion to Herodotus*, edited by E. J. Bakker, I. J. F. De Jong, and H. van Wees, 373–86. Leiden: Brill, 2002.

Humphreys, Sally. "Law, Custom, and Culture in Herodotus." *Arethusa* 20 (1987): 211–20.

Hussey, Edward. *The Presocratics*. London: Duckworth, 1972.

Immerwahr, Henry R. "Aspects of Historical Causation in Herodotus." *Transactions of the American Philological Association* 87 (1956): 241–80.

Immerwahr, Henry R. *Form and Thought in Herodotus*. Ann Arbor: University of Michigan Press, 1981.

Jaffe, S. N. *Thucydides on the Outbreak of War: Character and Contest*. New York: Oxford University Press, 2017.

Kagan, Donald. *The Outbreak of the Peloponnesian War*. Ithaca, NY: Cornell University Press, 1989.

Kahn, Charles. *The Art and Thought of Heraclitus*. Cambridge: Cambridge University Press, 1979.

Kahneman, Daniel. *Thinking, Fast and Slow*. New York: Farrar, Straus and Giroux, 2011.

Kaplan, Philip. "Ethnicity and Geography." In *A Companion to Ethnicity in the Ancient Mediterranean*, edited by J. McInerney, 298–311. London: John Wiley and Sons, 2014.

Kapuściński, Ryszard. *Travels with Herodotus*. Translated by K. Glowczewska. New York: Knopf, 2007.

Kelley, Collin P., Shahrzad Mohtadi, Mark A. Cane, Richard Seager, and Yochanan Kushnir. "Climate Change in the Fertile Crescent and Implications of the Recent Syrian Drought." *Proceedings of the National Academy of Sciences* 112, no. 11 (2015): 3241–46.

Kingsley, Patrick. *The New Odyssey: The Story of the Twenty-First-Century Refugee Crisis.* New York: Liveright, 2017.

Klein, Naomi. *This Changes Everything: Capitalism vs. the Climate.* New York: Simon and Schuster, 2014.

Kohn, Eduardo. *How Forests Think: Toward an Anthropology beyond the Human.* Berkeley: University of California Press, 2013.

Krause, Sharon. "Politics beyond Persons: Political Theory and the Non-human." *Political Theory,* June 5, 2016. http://journals.sagepub.com/doi/full/10.1177/0090591716651516.

Kurke, Leslie. *Aesopic Conversations: Popular Tradition, Cultural Dialogue, and the Invention of Greek Prose.* Princeton: Princeton University Press, 2011.

Kurke, Leslie. *Coins, Bodies, Games, and Gold: The Politics of Meaning in Archaic Greece.* Princeton: Princeton University Press, 1999.

Landauer, Matthew. *Dangerous Counsel: Accountability and Advice in Ancient Greece.* Chicago: University of Chicago Press, 2019.

Landauer, Matthew. "Democratic Theory and the Athenian Public Sphere." *Polis: The Journal for Ancient Greek Political Thought* 33 (2016): 31–51.

Lane, Melissa. *The Birth of Politics: Eight Greek and Roman Political Ideas and Why They Matter.* Princeton: Princeton University Press, 2014.

Lane, Melissa. *Eco-republic: What the Ancients Can Teach Us about Ethics, Virtue, and Sustainable Living.* Princeton: Princeton University Press, 2012.

Lane, Melissa. "Political Theory on Climate Change." *Annual Review of Political Science* 19 (2016): 107–23.

Lanni, Adrien. *Law and Justice in the Courts of Classical Athens.* Cambridge: Cambridge University Press, 2006.

Lateiner, Donald. "The Empirical Element in the Methods of Early Greek Medical Writers and Herodotus: A Shared Epistemological Response." *Antichthon* 20 (1986): 1–20.

Lateiner, Donald. *The Historical Method of Herodotus.* Toronto: University of Toronto Press, 1989.

Latour, Bruno. *Down to Earth: Politics in the New Climatic Regime.* Translated by C. Porter. Cambridge: Polity, 2018.

Latour, Bruno. *Facing Gaia: Eight Lectures on the New Climatic Regime.* Translated by C. Porter. Cambridge: Polity, 2017.

Latour, Bruno. *An Inquiry into Modes of Existence: An Anthropology of the Moderns.* Translated by C. Porter. Cambridge, MA: Harvard University Press, 2013.

Latour, Bruno. "On Actor-Network Theory: A Few Clarifications." *Soziale Welt* 47, no. 4 (1996): 369–81.

Latour, Bruno. *Politics of Nature: How to Bring the Sciences into Democracy.* Translated by C. Porter. Cambridge, MA: Harvard University Press, 2004.

Latour, Bruno. *We Have Never Been Modern.* Translated by C. Porter. Cambridge, MA: Harvard University Press, 1993.

Lattimore, Richmond. "The Wise Adviser in Herodotus." *Classical Philology* 34 (1939): 24–35.

Lazenby, J. F. "The Diekplous." *Greece and Rome* 34, no. 2 (October 1987): 169–77.

Lear, Jonathan. *Aristotle: The Desire to Understand.* Cambridge: Cambridge University Press, 1988.

Lear, Jonathan. "Knowingness and Abandonment: An Oedipus for Our Time." In *Open Minded: Working Out the Logic of the Soul,* 33–55. Cambridge, MA: Harvard University Press, 1998.

LeGuin, Ursula K. "Deep in Admiration." In *Arts of Living on a Damaged Planet: Ghosts and*

Monsters of the Anthropocene, edited by Anna Lowenhaupt Tsing, Heather Anne Swanson, Elaine Gan, and Nils Bubandt, M15–M21. Minneapolis: University of Minnesota Press, 2017.

Lepore, Jill. "The Right Way to Remember Rachel Carson." *New Yorker*, March 26, 2018. https://www.newyorker.com/magazine/2018/03/26/the-right-way-to-remember-rachel-carson.

Leslie, Margaret. "In Praise of Anachronism." *Political Studies* 18, no. 4 (1970): 433–47.

Levett, M. J., trans. *Plato: Theaetetus*. Revised by M. Burnyeat. Indianapolis: Hackett, 1990.

Liddell, H. G., and R. Scott. *A Greek-English Lexicon*. 9th ed. Oxford: Oxford University Press, 1995.

Lloyd, Alan. "The Account of Egypt: Herodotus Right and Wrong." In *The Landmark Herodotus*, edited by R. Strassler, 737–43. New York: Pantheon, 2007.

Lloyd, G. E. R. *Magic, Reason, and Experience*. Cambridge: Cambridge University Press, 1979.

Lloyd, G. E. R. *The Revolutions of Wisdom: Studies in the Claims and Practice of Ancient Greek Science*. Berkeley: University of California Press, 1987.

Lombardini, John. "Isonomia and the Public Sphere in Democratic Athens." *History of Political Thought* 34, no. 3 (Autumn 2013): 393–420.

Lovelock, James. *Gaia: A New Look at Life on Earth*. Oxford: Oxford University Press, 2016.

Luraghi, Nino. "The Importance of Being λόγιος." *Classical World* 102, no. 4 (Summer 2009): 439–56.

Luraghi, Nino. "Local Knowledge in Herodotus' *Histories*." In *The Historian's Craft in the Age of Herodotus*, 138–60. Oxford: Oxford University Press, 2001.

Luraghi, Nino. "Meta-*historiê*: Method and Genre." In *The Cambridge Companion to Herodotus*, edited by Carolyn Dewald and John Marincola, 76–91. Cambridge: Cambridge University Press, 2006.

MacIntyre, Alasdair. *Ethics in the Conflicts of Modernity: An Essay on Desire, Practical Reasoning, and Narrative*. Cambridge: Cambridge University Press, 2016.

MacKinney, L. "The Concept of Isonomia in Greek Medicine." In *Isonomia: Studien zur Gleichheitsvorstellung im griechischen Denken*, edited by Jürgen Mau and Ernst Günther Schmidt, 79–88. Berlin: Akademie-Verlag, 1964.

Main, George. "The Waterhole Project." In *Manifesto for Living in the Anthropocene*, edited by Katherine Gibson, Deborah Bird Rose, and Ruth Fincher, 62–69. Brooklyn, NY: Punctum Books, 2015.

Malkin, Irad. *A Small Greek World: Networks in the Ancient Mediterranean*. Oxford: Oxford University Press, 2011.

Malm, Andreas. *Fossil Capital: The Rise of Steam Power and the Roots of Global Warming*. New York: Verso, 2016.

Malm, Andreas. *The Progress of This Storm: Nature and Society in a Warming World*. New York: Verso, 2017.

Mann, Geoff, and Joel Wainwright. *Climate Leviathan: A Political Theory of Our Planetary Future*. New York: Verso, 2018.

Mara, Gerald. *The Civic Conversations of Thucydides and Plato: Classical Political Philosophy and the Limits of Democracy*. Albany: State University of New York Press, 2008.

Marincola, John. "Herodotean Narrative and the Narrator's Presence." In "Herodotus and the Invention of History," edited by D. Boedeker and J. Peradotto. Special issue, *Arethusa* 20 (1987): 121–37.

Marincola, John. "History without Malice: Plutarch Rewrites the Battle of Plataea." In *Brill's Companion to the Reception of Herodotus in Antiquity and Beyond*, edited by Jessica Priestley and Vasiliki Zali, 101–19. Leiden: Brill, 2016.

Marincola, John. "Plutarch's Refutation of Herodotus." *Ancient World* 25 (1994): 191–203.

Markell, Patchen. "The Rule of the People: Arendt, Archê, and Democracy." *American Political Science Review* 100, no. 1 (February 2006): 1–14.

Marres, Noortje. "Front-Staging Non-humans." In *Political Matter: Technoscience, Democracy, and Public Life*, edited by Bruce Braun and Sarah J. Whatmore, 177–209. Minneapolis: University of Minnesota Press, 2010.

Marres, Noortje, and Javier Lezaun. "Materials and Devices of the Public: An Introduction." *Economy and Society* 40, no. 4 (2011): 489–509.

Massumi, Brian. *What Animals Teach Us about Politics*. Durham, NC: Duke University Press, 2014.

Maxwell, Lida. "Queer/Love/Bird Extinction: Rachel Carson's *Silent Spring* as a Work of Love." *Political Theory* 45, no. 5 (2017): 682–704.

McGee, Kyle. *Heathen Earth: Trumpism and Political Ecology*. Brooklyn, NY: Punctum Books, 2017.

McKibben, Bill. *Falter: Has the Human Game Begun to Play Itself Out?* New York: Henry Holt, 2019.

McWilliams, Susan. "Hybridity in Herodotus." *Political Research Quarterly* 66, no. 4 (2013): 745–55.

McWilliams, Susan. *Traveling Back: Toward a Global Political Theory*. Oxford: Oxford University Press, 2013.

Meier, Christian. *The Greek Discovery of Politics*. Translated by D. McLintock. Cambridge, MA: Harvard University Press, 1990.

Mendelsohn, Daniel. "Arms and the Man." *New Yorker*, April 28, 2008.

Millender, Ellen. "Nomos Despotes: Spartan Obedience and Athenian Lawfulness in Fifth-Century Thought." In *Oikistes: Studies in Constitutions, Colonies, and Military Power in the Ancient World, Offered in Honor of A. J. Graham*, edited by Vanessa B. Gorman and Eric W. Robinson, 33–59. Mnemosyne Supplement 234. Leiden: Brill, 2002.

Mitchell, Timothy. *Carbon Democracy: Political Power in the Age of Oil*. New York: Verso, 2011.

Mitchell, Timothy. *Rule of Experts: Egypt, Techno-politics, Modernity*. Berkeley: University of California Press, 2002.

Moles, John. "Herodotus Warns the Athenians." In *Papers of the Leeds International Latin Seminar 9*, edited by F. Cairns and M. Heath, 259–84. Leeds, UK: Francis Cairns, 1996.

Momigliano, Arnaldo. "The Place of Herodotus in the History of Historiography." *History* 43, no. 147 (1958): 1–13.

Morley, Neville, and Christine Lee, eds. *The Handbook to the Reception of Thucydides*. New York: Wiley-Blackwell, 2014.

Morris, Ian, and Kurt Raaflaub, eds. *Democracy 2500? Questions and Challenges*. Archaeological Institute of America Colloquia and Conference Papers, no. 2. Dubuque, IA: Kendall/Hunt, 1997.

Morton, Timothy. *The Ecological Thought*. Cambridge, MA: Harvard University Press, 2010.

Moyer, Ian S. "Herodotus and an Egyptian Mirage: The Genealogies of the Theban Priests." *Journal of Hellenic Studies* 122 (2002): 70–90.

Mulgan, R. 1984. "Liberty in Ancient Greece." In *Conceptions of Liberty in Political Philosophy*, edited by Z. Pelcyznski and J. Gray, 7–26. London: Athlone Press.

Munson, Rosaria Vignolo. "An Alternate World: Herodotus and Italy." In *The Cambridge Companion to Herodotus*, edited by Carolyn Dewald and John Marincola, 257–73. Cambridge: Cambridge University Press, 2006.

Munson, Rosaria Vignolo. "*ANANKE* in Herodotus." *Journal of Hellenic Studies* 121 (2001): 30–50.

Munson, Rosaria Vignolo. *Black Doves Speak: Herodotus and the Languages of Barbarians.* Cambridge, MA: Center for Hellenic Studies and Harvard University Press, 2005.

Munson, Rosaria Vignolo. "Freedom and Culture in Herodotus." Unpublished manuscript, 2016.

Munson, Rosaria Vignolo. *Telling Wonders: Ethnographic and Political Discourse in the Work of Herodotus.* Ann Arbor: University of Michigan Press, 2001.

Munson, Rosaria Vignolo. "Who Are Herodotus' Persians?" In *Herodotus*, vol. 2, *Herodotus and the World*, edited by R. V. Munson, 320–35. Oxford Readings in Classical Studies. Oxford: Oxford University Press, 2013.

Murray, Oswyn. "Herodotus and Oral History." In *The Greek Sources: Proceedings of the Groningen 1984 Achaemenid History Workshop*, edited by Heleen Sancisi-Weerdenburg and Amélie Kuhrt, 93–115. Leiden: Brill, 1987.

Nagy, Gregory. "Herodotus the *Logios.*" In "Herodotus and the Invention of History," edited by Deborah D. Boedeker and J. Peradotto. Special issue, *Arethusa* 20 (1987): 175–84.

Nagy, Gregory. *Pindar's Homer: The Lyric Possession of an Epic Past.* Baltimore: Johns Hopkins University Press, 1990.

Nakategawa, Yoshio. "Isegoria in Herodotus." *Historia: Zeitschrift für alte Geschichte* 37 (1988): 257–75.

Nightingale, Andrea Wilson. "On Wandering and Wondering: 'Theôria' in Greek Philosophy and Culture." *Arion: A Journal of Humanities and the Classics*, 3rd ser., 9, no. 2 (Fall 2001): 23–58.

Norgaard, Kari Mari. *Living in Denial: Climate Change, Emotions, and Everyday Life.* Cambridge, MA: MIT Press, 2011.

Nussbaum, Martha C. *The Fragility of Goodness: Luck and Ethics in Greek Tragedy and Philosophy.* Updated ed. Cambridge: Cambridge University Press, 2001.

Ober, Josiah. *Athenian Legacies: Essays on the Politics of Going on Together.* Princeton: Princeton University Press, 2005.

Ober, Josiah. "The Athenian Revolution of 508/7 B.C.E.: Violence, Authority, and the Origins of Democracy." In *Cultural Poetics in Archaic Greece: Cult, Performance, Politics*, edited by C. Dougherty and L. Kurke, 215–32. Cambridge: Cambridge University Press, 1993.

Ober, Josiah. "The Original Meaning of 'Democracy': Capacity to Do Things, Not Majority Rule." *Constellations* 15, no. 1 (2008): 3–9.

Ober, Josiah. "What the Ancient Greeks Can Tell Us about Democracy." *Annual Review of Political Science* 11 (2008): 67–91.

Ondaatje, Michael. *The English Patient.* New York: Vintage, 1993.

Ophuls, William. *Plato's Revenge: Politics in the Age of Ecology.* Cambridge, MA: MIT Press, 2011.

Ortner, Sherry. *Anthropology and Social Theory: Culture, Power, and the Acting Subject.* Durham, NC: Duke University Press, 2006.

Ostwald, Martin. "Freedom and the Greeks." In *The Origins of Modern Freedom in the West*, edited by R. W. Davis, 2–63. Stanford, CA: Stanford University Press, 1995.

Ostwald, Martin. "Herodotus and Athens." *Illinois Classical Studies* 16 (1991): 137–48.

Ostwald, Martin. "Isokratia as a Political Concept (Herodotus, 5.92a1)." In *Islamic Philosophy and the Classical Tradition*, edited by S. M. Stern, A. Hourani, and V. Brown, 277–91. Columbia: University of South Carolina Press, 1972.

Ostwald, Martin. *Nomos and the Beginnings of Athenian Democracy.* Oxford: Clarendon Press, 1969.

Palmer, Lisa. *Hot, Hungry Planet: The Fight to Stop a Global Food Crisis in the Face of Climate Change*. New York: St. Martin's, 2017.

Parry, Adam. "Thucydides' Historical Perspective." *Yale Classical Studies* 22 (1972): 47–61.

Patterson, Orlando. *Freedom: Freedom in the Making of Western Culture*. Vol. 1. New York: Basic Books, 1991.

Pelling, C. B. R. "De Malignitate Plutarchi: Plutarch, Herodotus, and the Persian Wars." In *Cultural Responses to the Persian Wars: Antiquity to the Third Millennium*, edited by Emma Bridges, Edith Hall, and P. J. Rhodes, 145–66. Oxford: Oxford University Press, 2007.

Pelling, C. B. R. "Educating Croesus: Talking and Learning in Herodotus' Lydian Logos." *Classical Antiquity* 25 (2006): 141–77.

Pelling, C. B. R. *Herodotus and the Question Why*. Austin: University of Texas Press, 2019.

Pelling, C. B. R. "Speech and Action: Herodotus' Debate on the Constitutions." *Proceedings of the Cambridge Philological Society* 48 (2002): 123–58.

Phillips, Leigh. "The Solution Is Democracy." *Jacobin*. Accessed May 21, 2019. https://www.jacobinmag.com/2014/11/the-solution-is-democracy/.

Plumwood, Val. "Shadow Places and the Politics of Dwelling." *Australian Humanities Review* 44 (2008): 139–50.

Plutarch. *The Malice of Herodotus*. Translated by A. J. Bowen. Warminster, UK: Aris and Phillips, 1992.

Powell, J. Enoch. *A Lexicon to Herodotus*. Cambridge: Cambridge University Press, 1938.

Powers, Richard. *The Overstory*. New York: W. W. Norton, 2018.

Priestley, Jessica, and Vasiliki Zali, eds. *Brill's Companion to the Reception of Herodotus in Antiquity and Beyond*. Leiden: Brill, 2016.

Pritchett, William Kendrick. *The Liar School of Herodotos*. Amsterdam: Gieben, 1993.

Puchner, Martin. *The Written World: The Power of Stories to Shape People, History, Civilization*. New York: Random House, 2017.

Purdy, Jedediah. *The End of Nature: A Politics for the Anthropocene*. Cambridge, MA: Harvard University Press, 2015.

Purves, Alex C. *Space and Time in Ancient Greek Narrative*. Cambridge: Cambridge University Press, 2010.

Raaflaub, Kurt. *The Discovery of Freedom in Ancient Greece*. 1st English ed.; rev. and updated from the German. Chicago: University of Chicago Press, 2004.

Raaflaub, Kurt. "Equalities and Inequalities in Athenian Democracy." In *Demokratia: A Conversation on Democracies, Ancient and Modern*, edited by Josiah Ober and Charles Hedrick, 139–74. Princeton: Princeton University Press, 1996.

Raaflaub, Kurt. "Herodotus, Political Thought, and the Meaning of History." *Arethusa* 20, nos. 1–2 (1987): 221–48.

Raaflaub, Kurt. "Philosophy, Science, Politics: Herodotus and the Intellectual Trends of His Time." In *Brill's Companion to Herodotus*, edited by E. J. Bakker, I. J. F. De Jong, and H. van Wees, 199–224. Leiden: Brill, 2002.

Redfield, James. "Herodotus the Tourist." *Classical Philology* 80 (1985): 97–118.

Rhodes, P. J. *The Athenian Boule*. Oxford: Clarendon, 1985.

Rich, Nathaniel. *Losing Earth: A Recent History*. New York: Farrar, Straus and Giroux, 2019.

Roberts, Jennifer T. *Accountability in Athenian Government*. Madison: University of Wisconsin Press, 1982.

Robinson, Eric W. *The First Democracies: Early Popular Government outside Athens*. Stuttgart: F. Steiner, 1997.

Rockström, Johan, et al. "Planetary Boundaries: Exploring the Safe Operating Space for Humanity." *Ecology and Society* 14, no. 2 (2009). http://www.ecologyandsociety.org/vol14/iss2/art32/.

Romm, James S. *Herodotus*. New Haven, CT: Yale University Press, 1998.

Rood, Timothy C. B. "Herodotus and Foreign Lands." In *The Cambridge Companion to Herodotus*, edited by Carolyn Dewald and John Marincola, 290–305. Cambridge: Cambridge University Press, 2006.

Roy, Cornelia Sydnor. "The Constitutional Debate in Herodotus' *Histories*: An Exploration of Good Government." *Histos* 6 (2012): 298–320.

Roy, Cornelia Sydnor. "Political Relativism: Implicit Political Theory in Herodotus' *Histories*." PhD diss., University of North Carolina, Chapel Hill, 2010.

Ruddiman, William. "The Anthropocene." *Annual Review of Earth and Planetary Sciences* 41 (2013): 45–68.

Salkever, Stephen. Introduction to *The Cambridge Companion to Ancient Greek Political Thought*, edited by Stephen Salkever, 1–14. Cambridge: Cambridge University Press, 2009.

Saxonhouse, Arlene W. *Athenian Democracy: Modern Mythmakers and Ancient Theorists*. South Bend, IN: Notre Dame University Press, 1996.

Saxonhouse, Arlene W. "Democratic Deliberation and the Historian's Trade: The Case of Thucydides." In *Talking Democracy: Historical Perspectives on Rhetoric and Democracy*, edited by G. Remer and C. Nederman, 57–85. University Park: Pennsylvania State University Press, 2004.

Saxonhouse, Arlene W. *Free Speech and Democracy in Ancient Athens*. Cambridge: Cambridge University Press, 2006.

Schlosser, Joel Alden. "Herodotean Democracies." *CHS Research Bulletin* 5, no. 1 (2016). Accessed July 24, 2019. http://nrs.harvard.edu/urn-3:hlnc.essay:SchlosserJ.Herodotean_Democracies.2016.

Schlosser, Joel Alden. "Herodotean Realism." *Political Theory* 42 (2014): 239–61.

Schlosser, Joel Alden. "Herodotus's Political Ecologies." In *Democratic Moments*, edited by X. Marquez, 9–16. London: Bloomsbury Academic, 2018.

Schlosser, Joel Alden. Review of *Moral History from Herodotus to Diodorus Siculus*, by Lisa Irene Hau. *Polis: The Journal for Ancient Greek Political Thought* 35 (2018): 298–302.

Schlosser, Joel Alden. " 'What Really Happened': Varieties of Thucydides' Realism." In *The Cambridge Companion to Thucydides*, edited by P. Low. Cambridge: Cambridge University Press, forthcoming.

Schlosser, Joel Alden. *What Would Socrates Do? Self-Examination, Civic Engagement, and the Politics of Philosophy*. Cambridge: Cambridge University Press, 2014.

Schmitt, Carl. *The* Nomos *of the Earth in the International Law of the* Jus Publicum Europaeum. Translated by G. L. Ulmen. Candor, NY: Telos Press, 2003.

Scott, James C. *Against the Grain: A Deep History of the Earliest States*. New Haven, CT: Yale University Press, 2017.

Scott, James C. *Seeing like a State: How Certain Schemes to Improve the Human Condition Have Failed*. New Haven, CT: Yale University Press, 1998.

Scranton, Roy. *Learning to Die in the Anthropocene: Reflections on the End of a Civilization*. San Francisco: City Lights Books, 2015.

Segal, Charles. "Croesus on the Pyre: Herodotus and the Bacchylides." *Wiener Studien* 84 (1971): 39–51.

Selby, Jan. "Climate Change and the Syrian Civil War, Part II: The Jazira's Agrarian Crisis." *Geoforum*. Forthcoming.

Selby, Jan, Omar S. Dahi, Christiane Forlich, and Mike Hulme. "Climate Change and the Syrian Civil War: A Rejoinder." *Political Geography* 60 (2017): 253–55.

Selby, Jan, Omar S. Dahi, Christiane Forlich, and Mike Hulme. "Climate Change and the Syrian Civil War Revisited." *Political Geography* 60 (2017): 251–52.

Serres, Michel. "The Science of Relations: An Interview." *Angelaki: Journal of the Theoretical Humanities* 8, no. 2 (2003): 227–38.

Sewell, William. "Geertz, Cultural Systems, and History: From Synchrony to Transformation." *Representations* 59 (Summer 1997): 35–55.

Shapiro, Susan O. "Learning through Suffering: Human Wisdom in Herodotus." *Classical Journal* 89, no. 4 (April–May 1994): 349–55.

Simons, Massimiliano. "The Parliament of Things and the Anthropocene: How to Listen to 'Quasi-Objects.'" *Techné: Research in Philosophy and Technology* 21, nos. 2–3 (2017): 1–25.

Sinclair, T. A. *A History of Greek Political Thought.* London: Routledge and Kegan Paul, 1952.

Slatkin, Laura. "Measuring Authority, Authoritative Measures: Hesiod's *Works and Days.*" In *The Moral Authority of Nature,* edited by Lorraine Daston and Fernando Vidal, 25–49. Chicago: University of Chicago Press, 2003.

Solnit, Rebecca. *Hope in the Dark: Untold Histories, Wild Possibilities.* Updated ed. Chicago: Haymarket Books, 2016.

Spotts, Pete. "Tale of Two Droughts: What California, Syria Can Teach about Adaptation Gap." *Christian Science Monitor,* March 3, 2015. https://www.csmonitor.com/Environment/2015 /0303/Tale-of-two-droughts-What-California-Syria-can-teach-about-adaptation-gap.

Sprague, Rosamond Kent, ed. *The Older Sophists.* Indianapolis: Hackett.

Stadter, Philip. "Herodotus and the Athenian *Arche.*" *Annali della Scuola normale superiore di Pisa,* 3rd ser., 22 (1992): 781–809.

Stahl, Hans-Peter. "Learning through Suffering? Croesus' Conversations in the *History* of Herodotus." *Yale Classical Studies* 24 (1975): 1–36.

Steiner, Deborah. *The Tyrant's Writ: Myths and Images of Writing in Ancient Greece.* Princeton: Princeton University Press, 2004.

Stengers, Isabelle. *In Catastrophic Times.* Open Humanities Press, 2015. Accessed April 3, 2018. http://openhumanitiespress.org/books/titles/in-catastrophic-times.

Strasburger, Hermann. "Herodot und das perikleische Athen." *Historia* 4 (1955): 1–25.

Strauss, Leo. *The Rebirth of Classical Political Rationalism: An Introduction to the Thought of Leo Strauss.* Edited by T. Pangle. Chicago: University of Chicago Press, 1989.

Taleb, Nassim Nicholas. *The Black Swan: The Impact of the Highly Improbable.* 2nd ed. New York: Random House, 2010.

Thomas, Julia Adeney. "History and Biology in the Anthropocene: Problems of Scale, Problems of Value." *American Historical Review* 119, no. 5 (December 2014): 1587–1607.

Thomas, Rosalind. "Ethnicity, Genealogy, and Hellenism in Herodotus." In *Ancient Perceptions of Greek Ethnicity,* edited by Irad Malkin, 213–33. Cambridge, MA: Harvard University Press, 2001.

Thomas, Rosalind. *Herodotus in Context: Ethnography, Science and the Art of Persuasion.* Cambridge: Cambridge University Press, 2000.

Thomas, Rosalind. "The Intellectual Milieu of Herodotus." In *The Cambridge Companion to Herodotus,* edited by Carolyn Dewald and John Marincola, 60–75. Cambridge: Cambridge University Press, 2006.

Thomas, Rosalind. Introduction to *The Landmark Herodotus,* edited by R. Strassler, ix–xxxvi. New York: Pantheon, 2007.

Thomas, Rosalind. *Oral Tradition and Written Record in Classical Athens*. Cambridge: Cambridge University Press, 1989.

Thomas, Rosalind. "Writing, Law, and Written Law." In *The Cambridge Companion to Ancient Greek Law*, edited by David Cohen and Michael Gagarin, 41–60. Cambridge: Cambridge University Press, 2005.

Thomas, Rosalind. "Written in Stone? Liberty, Equality, Orality, and the Codification of Law." *Bulletin of the Institute of Classical Studies* 40 (1995): 59–74.

Thompson, Norma. *Herodotus and the Origins of the Political Community: Arion's Leap*. New Haven, CT: Yale University Press, 1996.

Todd, S. C. *The Shape of Athenian Law*. Oxford: Clarendon, 1993.

Tsing, Anna Lowenhaupt. *The Mushroom at the End of the World: On the Possibility of Life in Capitalist Ruins*. Princeton: Princeton University Press, 2015.

Tsing, Anna Lowenhaupt, Heather Anne Swanson, Elaine Gan, and Nils Bubandt, eds. *Arts of Living on a Damaged Planet: Ghosts and Monsters of the Anthropocene*. Minneapolis: University of Minnesota Press, 2017.

Tully, James. *Strange Multiplicity: Constitutionalism in an Age of Diversity*. Cambridge: Cambridge University Press, 1995.

van Wees, Hans. "Herodotus and the Past." In *Brill's Companion to Herodotus*, edited by E. J. Bakker, I. J. F. De Jong, and H. van Wees, 321–49. Leiden: Brill, 2010.

Vasunia, Phiroze. *The Gift of the Nile: Hellenizing Egypt from Aeschylus to Alexander*. Berkeley: University of California Press, 2001.

Vegetti, Mario. "Culpability, Responsibility, Cause: Philosophy, Historiography, and Medicine in the Fifth Century." In *The Cambridge Companion to Early Greek Philosophy*, edited by A. A. Long, 271–89. Cambridge: Cambridge University Press, 1999.

Vlassopoulos, Kostas. *Greeks and Barbarians*. Cambridge: Cambridge University Press, 2013.

Vlassopoulos, Kostas. *Unthinking the Greek Polis: Ancient Greek History beyond Eurocentrism*. Cambridge: Cambridge University Press, 2007.

Vlastos, Gregory. "Equality and Justice in Early Greek Cosmologies." *Classical Philology* 42, no. 3 (July 1947): 156–78.

Vlastos, Gregory. "Isonomia." *American Journal of Philology* 74, no. 4 (1953): 337–66.

Vlastos, Gregory. "Isonomia Politike." In *Isonomia: Studien zur Gleichheitsvorstellung im griechischen Denken*, edited by Jürgen Mau and Ernst Günther Schmidt, 1–36. Berlin: Akademie-Verlag, 1964.

Wallace-Wells, David. *The Uninhabitable Earth*. New York: Tim Duggan Books, 2019.

Watkins, Claire Vaye. *Gold Fame Citrus*. New York: Riverhead, 2015.

Wedeen, Lisa. *Ambiguities of Domination: Politics, Rhetoric, and Symbols in Contemporary Syria*. With a new preface. Chicago: University of Chicago Press, 2015.

Wedeen, Lisa. "Ideology and Humor in Dark Times: Notes from Syria." *Critical Inquiry* 39 (Summer 2013): 841–73.

Welzer, Harald. *Climate Wars: Why People Will Be Killed in the 21st Century*. Cambridge: Polity, 2012.

Wendle, John. "The Ominous Story of Syria's Climate Refugees." *Scientific American*, December 17, 2015. https://.scientificamerican.com/article/ominous-story-of-syria-climate-refugees.

Wendle, John. "When Climate Change Starts Wars." *Nautilus*, August 9, 2018. http://nautil.us/issue/63/horizons/when-climate-change-starts-wars-rp.

Wennersten, John R., and Denise Robbins. *Rising Tides: Climate Refugees in the Twenty-First Century*. Bloomington: Indiana University Press, 2017.

White, Hayden. *The Content of the Form: Narrative Discourse and Historical Representation.* Baltimore: Johns Hopkins University Press, 1987.

White, Richard. *The Middle Ground: Indians, Empires, and the Republics in the Great Lakes Region,* 1650–1815. 20th anniversary ed. Cambridge: Cambridge University Press, 2011.

Whiteside, Kerry H. "A Representative Politics of Nature? Bruno Latour on Collectives and Constitutions." *Contemporary Political Theory* 12, no. 3 (2016): 185–205.

Williams, Bernard. *Shame and Necessity.* Sather Classical Lectures. Berkeley: University of California Press, 1993.

Wolin, Sheldon S. "Democracy, Difference, and Re-cognition." *Political Theory* 21, no. 3 (August 1993): 464–83.

Wolin, Sheldon S. "From Vocation to Invocation." In *Vocations of Political Theory,* edited by Jason Frank and John Tamborino, 3–22. Minneapolis: University of Minnesota Press, 2000.

Wolin, Sheldon S. "Fugitive Democracy." In *Democracy and Difference: Contesting the Boundaries of the Political.* Seyla Benhabib, ed. Princeton: Princeton University Press, 1996: 31–45.

Wolin, Sheldon S. "Montesquieu and *Publius*: The Crisis of Reason and the Federalist Papers." In *The Presence of the Past: Essays on the State and the Constitution,* 100–119. Baltimore: Johns Hopkins University Press, 1996.

Wolin, Sheldon S. "Norm and Form: The Constitutionalizing of Democracy." In *Athenian Political Thought and the Reconstruction of American Democracy,* edited by J. P. Euben, J. Wallach, and J. Ober, 29–58. Princeton: Princeton University Press, 1994.

Wolin, Sheldon S. *Politics and Vision: Continuity and Innovation in Western Political Thought.* Expanded ed. Princeton: Princeton University Press, 2016.

Yusoff, Kathryn. *A Billion Black Anthropocenes or None.* Minneapolis: University of Minnesota Press, 2018.

Zylinska, Joanna. *The End of Man: A Feminist Counterapocalypse.* Minneapolis: University of Minnesota Press, 2018.

Index

accuracy, 19–20
Achilles, 94
Acropolis, 78
actants, 3–5, 37, 136, 138, 148; definition, 3; and *nomos*, 81–82; and the *polis*, 19
Adorno, Theodor, 87
Aeschylus, 113
Aesop, 94, 104–5
Agamemnon, 95
Agariste, 101, 103
agrarian crisis, 2
Airs, Waters, Places (Hippocratic author), 55, 84–85
aitia (plural of *aitios*). See *aitios*
aitios (responsibility), 20, 22–23, 30, 36, 100, 129–31; and stories, 89–90, 100, 105, 106–7
akouê (listening), 41, 53, 56, 72
Alcmaeon, 76, 81, 103
Alcmaeonidae, 90, 98–99, 100–101, 103–4, 121
Alexandros, 22, 57
Ali, Kemal, 1–3, 134–36
Aly, Wolf, 93
Amazons, 107
amplitude, 91, 105, 110
Anacharsis, 58–59
Anaximander, 76
ancient political thought, 89, 112
Anthropocene, 37, 38, 110, 132–34, 136–39, 148nn16–18; and collective power, 62; definition, 3–5; and the divine, 82; and freedom, 115, 122; and Herodotus, 6, 8, 9–10; and the *Histories*, 10, 91; and inquiry, 40, 89, 110; in the narratology of the *Histories*, 91, 110; and *nomos*, 62–63, 87–88; and the *polis*, 19–20; and wonder, 37–38, 110
anthropos (human being), 38, 40, 54. *See also* humans
anticipation, 16–18
Antiphon, 86–87

antiquity, 6, 89
Apfel, Lauren, 68, 157n2
Aphetae, 128
apodeixis (display), 8, 105, 111
Apsis, 69
Arcadians, 106
archê (rule), 30, 167n37
Arendt, Hannah, vi, 140, 142, 166n23, 167n37
aretê (excellence), 70–71, 112; as virtue, 71
Arion, 95
Aristagoras, 65, 77
Aristogiton, 121
Aristotle, 123, 149n46, 154n52, 159n37, 161n71, 167n33; and wonder, 154n50
Artabanus, 50, 83, 129
Artembares, 72, 75, 118
Asiatics, 84
astea (human settlements), 23
Astyages, 27
Athenians, 98–99, 106, 130; freedom of, 103, 121–23, 125–26; and Marathon, 106–8; as readers of stories, 90–91
Athens: democracy of, 64–65, 77–79, 90, 103, 104; and Herodotus, 101; *nomoi* of, 68, 74
autocrats. *See* tyrants
autopsis (self-observation), 42, 56
Awful Dilemma, 95

Babylon, 6, 35, 96
Babylonians, 28, 35; customs of, 86–87, 162n82, 165n59, 168n28
Baragwanath, Emily, 98, 100, 152n25
barbarians, 38–39
Benardete, Seth, 151n11, 154n4
Benjamin, Walter, 91, 102, 109–10
Bias of Priene, 121